University of
H....

The Women's Movement and Local Politics

The influence on councillors in London

JIM BARRY

Polytechnic of East London

Avebury

Aldershot · Brookfield USA · Hong Kong · Singapore · Sydney

©   Jim Barry 1991

Published by
Avebury
Academic Publishing Group
Gower House
Croft Road
Aldershot
Hants
GU11 3HR

Gower Publishing Company
Old Post Road
Brookfield
Vermont 05036
USA

A CIP catalogue record for this book is available from the British Library and the US Library of Congress

ISBN 1 85628 285 6

Printed and Bound in Great Britain by
Athenaeum Press Ltd., Newcastle upon Tyne.

Contents

Acknowledgements   viii
List of Tables   x

CHAPTER 1: INTRODUCTION   1

CHAPTER 2: METHODOLOGICAL CONSIDERATIONS   6
- (a) Theory and Method   6
- (b) The Choice of London   9
- (c) The Survey of London Councillors   11
- (d) The Interviews   17
    - (i) Selecting the Councillors   17
    - (ii) The Questions Asked   21
    - (iii) Arranging the Interviews   25
- (e) Concluding Remarks   27

CHAPTER 3: WOMEN AND LOCAL POLITICS   30
- (a) Introductory Remarks   31
- (b) Traditional Pre-Occupations and Current Concerns   31
- (c) The Political Tradition   33

v

(d)	Official Inquiries and Investigations		40
	(i)	The Maud Report (1967)	42
	(ii)	The Robinson Report (1977)	45
	(iii)	The Widdicombe Report (1986)	50
(e)	The State, Social Policy and Local Democracy		57
(f)	Concluding Remarks: Values, Hierarchies and Silences		60

CHAPTER 4: COUNCILLORS IN LONDON: REPRESENTATION AND SOCIAL BACKGROUND 66

(a)	Gender of Councillors	66
(b)	Political Representation	71
(c)	Length of Service: Party Membership/Office of Councillor	71
(d)	Reasons for Standing as a Councillor	75
(e)	Regular Reading: Newspapers and Journals	81
(f)	Councillors and 'Political Families'	83
(g)	Councillors by Age and Gender	85
(h)	Marital Status	88
(i)	Place of Birth and Time Lived in London	90
(j)	Perceptions of Ethnicity	92
(k)	Housing Tenure	96
(l)	Dependents Living in Same Household	98
(m)	Education	101
(n)	Employment and Social Class	109
(o)	Where Next?	128

CHAPTER 5: EXPERIENCE AND PARTICIPATION 133

(a)	The New Women's Movement in Britain	133
(b)	Local Government Women's Committees	138
(c)	Priority for Issues Specifically Affecting Women	141
(d)	Is it Now Easier for Women to Become Councillors?	146
(e)	Involvement in Organisations, Groups and Campaigns as a Route to Participation	156
(f)	Concluding Remarks	165

CHAPTER 6: WOMEN AND LOCAL POLITICS, AND SOCIAL MOVEMENTS AND POLITICAL PARTIES 169

(a)	Introductory Remarks	169
(b)	Women and Local Politics	171

	(i)	The 'Atypical Lot'	171
	(ii)	A Constellation of Constraints	172
	(iii)	Men as Frustrators and Facilitators	175
	(iv)	A Question of Priorities	177
	(v)	Civic Pride: the Local as a Major Political Aspiration	180
(c)	Social Movements and Political Parties		182
	(i)	Opportunities and Resistances	182
	(ii)	There is Nothing New About the New Women's Movement in Britain	184
	(iii)	The Women's Movement, Social Democratic Parties and the Media	187
	(iv)	Social Movements and Political Parties: the Potential for Change	190
	(v)	The Languages of Gender and the Vocabularies of Local Politics	192
(d)	Concluding Remarks		195

CHAPTER 7: CONCLUSION 198
(a) The Limits of Conventional Wisdom 198
(b) Women and Local Politics 199
(c) Social Movements and Political Parties 201
(d) Final Remarks 202

Appendix I: **Expert Informants Consulted** 203
Appendix II: **Organisations Consulted** 205
Appendix III: **The London Councillor Survey Questionnaire** 207

Bibliography 211

Index 229

Acknowledgements

This book is dedicated to my mother and my late father for believing in me.

I have learnt one thing above all else in the preparation of this research: that intellectual work depends on others. I am accordingly grateful to a great many people for help with this book which derives from research undertaken for a Ph.D. in the Department of Politics and Sociology at Birkbeck College, University of London.

First and foremost I would like to thank my supervisor, Susanne MacGregor, for her encouragement, patience, driving intellect and sense of humour, but above all else for that indefinable human quality which has for so long facilitated the realisation of intellectual potential in others. I would also like to thank Vicky Randall and Sami Zubaida for an enjoyable if gruelling *viva* and their encouragement to publish.

I would also like to thank Jo Gooderham and Suzanne Evins at Gower for their encouragement and support.

Generous financial help came from two sources: initially a three year grant from the Economic and Social Research Council and latterly from the Polytechnic of East London (formerly N.E.L.P.) who helped with fees.

I would also like to thank the expert informants and organisations I consulted, named in Appendices I and II, and the Library staff at Senate

House, the British Library and, particularly, Birkbeck College.

I used automated equipment as an authorised user of Birkbeck College's VAX-11/750 (registered with the University of London's Central Computing Services) to process my survey data and would like to thank the ever-tolerant and understanding Colin Chalmers who corrected my confused attempts at programming, and the helpful Data Processors. Ray Mezen from P.E.L. came to my rescue with statistical verification of some of the wilder assertions in Chapters 4 and 5.

Encouragement of others has always, for me, been crucial. To Harriet Lodge I owe a debt of thanks for not only competently typing the book but also for providing helpful critical commentary and encouraging noises along the way. To Heather, who really started me on my own intellectual journey, thanks are not enough - her love for her subject could not but have rubbed off.

To the councillors of London who took part in the survey and the interviews a special word of thanks: without their help this book really would not have been possible.

Jim Barry
London, 1991

List of tables

Table 2.1	Response to Postal Questionnaire: London Councillor Survey	13
Table 2.2	Response Based on 912 Survey Population	14
Table 2.3	Response Based on 900 Survey Population (excluding deadwood)	14
Table 4.1	Women's Representation at Local Level: Some Comparisons	67
Table 4.2	Gender of London Councillors: 1964, 1985 and 1990	68
Table 4.3	Proportions of Women Councillors in London: Changes at May 1986 and May 1990 Local Elections	70
Table 4.4	Party Political Membership of London Councillors Surveyed	70
Table 4.5	Party Political Representation in Local Councils: 1985/86	72
Table 4.6	Party Representation in London - GLC, Corporation of London and Boroughs: 1985/86	73
Table 4.7	London Councillor Survey: Length of Party Membership	74
Table 4.8	Councillors' Length of Service as a Councillor	76
Table 4.9	Reasons for Standing as a Councillor	79

Table 4.10	Regular Reading - Newspapers and Journals: London Councillor Survey	82
Table 4.11	Councillors and 'Political Families': London Councillor Survey	84
Table 4.12	Councillors' Age	87
Table 4.13	Councillors by Marital Status and Gender	89
Table 4.14	Councillors' Place of Birth	91
Table 4.15	Length of Time Lived in London: London Councillor Survey	93
Table 4.16	Perceptions of Ethnicity: London Councillor Survey	95
Table 4.17	Councillors' Housing Tenure	97
Table 4.18(a)	Councillors with Dependents Living in Same Household	99
Table 4.18(b)	Who Looks after Child(ren) When They are Sick?: British Social Attitudes	99
Table 4.19(a)	Councillors' Type of School Attended: London Councillor Survey	102
Table 4.19(b)	School-leaving Age	104
Table 4.19(c)	Councillors' Highest Educational Qualification	105
Table 4.19(d)	Percentage of Population with Higher Educational Qualifications	107
Table 4.19(e)	Metropolitan Counties Candidates Survey: Educational Qualifications by Party	108
Table 4.20(a)	Councillor and Spouse by Activity Status	112
Table 4.20(b)	Activity Status of Spouse of Councillor: London Councillor Survey	115
Table 4.20(c)	Part-time Hours of Councillor and Spouse (Spouse in Brackets): London Councillor Survey	116
Table 4.20(d)	Councillor and Spouse by Socio-economic Group	118
Table 4.20(e)	Socio-economic Group of Spouse of Councillor: London Councillor Survey	120
Table 4.20(f)	Metropolitan Counties Candidates Survey: Occupational Status and Occupational Class of Councillors	121
Table 4.20(g)	Councillors' Employment Sector (Public/Private)	122
Table 4.20(h)	Perceptions of Social Class of London Councillors: London Councillor Survey	126
Table 4.20(i)	Self-rated Social Class: British Social Attitudes	127

Table 5.1	Support for the Women's Movement: London Councillor Survey	134
Table 5.2	Degree of Sympathy for the Women's Movement among Non-Supporters: London Councillor Survey	136
Table 5.3	Support for the Women's Movement among Inner London and Outer London Councillors: London Councillor Survey	136
Table 5.4	Perceptions of the Women's Movement: London Councillor Survey	137
Table 5.5	Attitudes to Local Government Women's Committees: London Councillor Survey	139
Table 5.6	Attitudes to Local Government Women's Committees among Inner London and Outer London Councillors: London Councillor Survey	142
Table 5.7	Perceived Priority among other Councillors for Issues Specifically Affecting Women: London Councillor Survey	144
Table 5.8	Councillors' Own Priority for Issues Specifically Affecting Women: London Councillor Survey	145
Table 5.9	Perceived Priority of Council Officers for Issues Specifically Affecting Women: London Councillor Survey	147
Table 5.10	Perception of Changes in Possibilities for Women's Involvement in Local Politics Since the Late 1960s: London Councillor Survey	148
Table 5.11	Explanation of Women's Relatively Low Representation on Local Councils: London Councillor Survey	150
Table 5.12	Perceived Explanation for Relative Under-representation of Women on Local Councils among Inner London and Outer London Councillors: London Councillor Survey	152
Table 5.13	Active Participation in Local Organisations/ Campaigns Before Deciding to Stand for Election as Local Councillor: London Councillor Survey	155
Table 5.14	Women Councillors' Activity in Women's Organisations Prior to Involvement in Party Politics: London Councillor Survey	158

Table 5.15   Involvement of Women Councillors Not Active
              in Women's Organisations, in Campaigns on
              Women's Issues: London Councillor Survey   160
Table 5.16   Current Involvement in Women's Groups or
              Organisations among London Women Councillors:
              London Councillor Survey   161
Table 5.17   Previous Involvement in Women's Groups or
              Organisations of Inner London and Outer London
              Women Councillors: London Councillor Survey   163
Table 5.18   Current Involvement in Women's Groups or
              Organisations among Inner London and Outer
              London Women Councillors: London Councillor
              Survey   164

1 Introduction

Early social theorists tried to formulate invariant laws of society - laws that would hold of all societies, just as the abstracted procedures of physical science had led to laws that cut beneath the qualitative richness of 'nature'. There is, I believe, no 'law' stated by any social scientist that is trans-historical, that must not be understood as having to do with the specific structure of some period. Other 'laws' turn out to be empty abstractions or quite confused tautologies. The only meaning of 'social laws' or even of 'social regularities' is such *principa media* as we may discover, or if you wish, construct, for a social structure within a historically specific era. We do not know any universal principles of historical change; the mechanisms of change we do know vary with the social structure we are examining. For historical change *is* change of social structures, of the relations among their component parts. Just as there is a variety of social structures, there is a variety of principles of historical change.

(C Wright Mills 1959 p.166)

1

It is the destructive, the murderous paper-system, that has transferred the fruit of the labour, and the people along with it, from the different parts of the country to the neighbourhood of the all-devouring *Wen*[1]

(W Cobbett 1830 p.81).

Considerable interest is being shown in Local Authorities in the 1990s, attracting the attention of national politicians and media alike. Local politics looks set to be a burning issue for many years to come which ever party (or parties) is in government.[2]

Yet relatively little has been written on the role of women as recipients of service provision and as local representatives.

This may seem surprising, particularly as local provision is of such importance for women and has been an area of politics where they are represented in relatively high numbers.

Women's interests and needs are often relegated in the hierarchy of importance as other issues and people assume priority. The historical parallels are quite dramatic concerning such things as involvement in the American Abolitionist movement of the nineteenth century and early Socialist and Marxist struggles. Only through the women's movement are women's voices heard more clearly on their own account (Barry 1991).

This book is an attempt to establish the issue of the women's movement as it influences local politics as an item for discussion, an item on the agenda of both local and national politics. The issue is crucial, as highlighted in this examination of the influence of the new women's movement in Britain as a social movement.

Theorists of social movements, particularly those of the new social movements which had their origins in the 'decade of protest', the 1960s, draw attention to the relationship between social movements and political parties. They suggest that social movements are somehow epiphenomenal, that is, that they arise largely from the failings of social democratic and marxist political parties in the West and East either to keep in touch with disaffected members or to move with the temper of the times. They are said to offer a challenge to those parties to take more seriously the issues they raise. Once institutionalised, it is argued, the new social movements will have exhausted their potential and realised their aims through absorption into the traditional machinery of revivified party policy (c.f. Keane 1988, Scott 1990).[3] In this literature, however, the change in consciousness that all this brings about is poorly conceptualised and no mechanism for research is

2

offered.

In respect of the New Women's Movement in Britain researchers are even divided over how far consciousness has changed in recent years. Consider the following:

Like so many tides of social change, which, at their height, seem irresistible, the women's movement has strangely receded from consciousness

(Bouchier 1983 p.1)[4].

By the mid-1980s ... a revolution in consciousness affected women who had never been near a women's liberation meeting

(Coote and Campbell 1987 p.252).

Such contradictory conclusions suggest that researchers tend to make *assumptions* about the issue of consciousness. Rarely, if ever, do they attempt to *explore* the world of taken-for-granted assumptions.

Here, then, a need for empirical exploration. All the more urgent as women's movement activists involved principally in areas of civil society in the 1960s and 1970s move into positions of mainstream political power within the local state through the machinery of social democratic political parties as local authority councillors (Coote and Campbell 1987 p.258).[5]

This study of the effect of the New Women's Movement in Britain on local politics is an exercise in contemporary history; in this sense, history and sociology are the same thing.[6] There are a number of justifications for an exploration along these lines.

First, empirical research gives a voice. The issue of academic and journalistic publishing privilege raises difficult academic, social and political questions of power. Women's access to such media has been limited and highly constrained (Barry 1991). Empirical research enables them to speak, their voices to be heard. We will see that large numbers of women have come into local politics to make their mark. Empirical research enables their voices to be heard thereby empowering them.

Secondly, it enables a consideration of the changing nature of consciousness, of people's ideas and perceptions of the effects of the new women's movement on their understanding and practice of politics. In addition, by taking account of the views of men as well as women, it is possible to analyse the effects more generally, thereby going beyond studies which are gender-specific (Campbell 1987),[7] to the articulation of gender relationships themselves.

Thirdly, by widening the ambit from the British Labour Party to take account of Conservative and other councillors, a consideration of the relationship between social movements and political parties more generally is possible.

* * *

So to the structure of the book.

After a consideration in Chapter 2 of the methodological issues involved in the research, the book proceeds in Chapter 3 to analyse the ways in which women have traditionally been conceptualised in the literature on local politics. To this end a critical review of the academic literature and an original evaluation of three government reports - Maud, Robinson and Widdicombe - are undertaken, revealing priorities of power and privilege.

A major part of the book is focussed around the following two chapters, 4 and 5, which outline the detail of a postal questionnaire survey of *all* female councillors in London, together with a sample of men. The purpose is two-fold. First, to provide much needed information on the social, socio-economic and political background of London councillors. Second, to question conventional wisdom by cross-tabulating party with gender, thereby going beyond the usual party-only tabulations.

Chapter 6 provides details of an in-depth interviewing programme of London councillors which followed the survey, covering all major political parties, women and men. Through this analysis the relationship of women to local politics, and the relationship between the new women's movements and political parties, is explored.

Chapter 7 offers some conclusions.

Notes

1. 'Wen' is the term reserved by Cobbett for use when referring to London.

2. The recent book by Batley and Stoker (1991) considers trends and developments for local government in Europe.

3.   The interested reader is referred to the following in the recent literature on the new social movements: Touraine (1981 and 1985), Offe (1984 and 1985), Cohen (1985), Melucci (1985, 1988 and 1989), Keane (1988), Barry (1990) and Scott (1990). In respect of the new women's movements as social movements: Freeman (1975), Coote and Campbell (1982 and 1987), Randall (1982 and 1987), Bouchier (1983), Dahlerup (1986), Gelb (1986) and Barry (1991).

4.   Bouchier's observation on the next page that the consciousness of the 'Women's Liberation Movement' is 'too potent a force to be smothered' scarcely recovers his position (1983 p.2). The gender difference in respect of the authors quoted here is discussed in Barry (1991).

5.   The move from civil society to the state and the issue of publishing privilege to enable the "voice" of the women's movement to be heard more clearly on its own account is discussed in Barry (1991).

6.   Lichtheim attributes the following remark to a sociologist: 'Sociology ... is history with the hard work left out, while history is sociology with the brains left out' (Lichtheim 1967 p.xviii). Abrams however argues that the two 'are and always have been the same thing' (Abrams 1982 p.x). This goes against Barrett's separation of theory and history (Barrett 1988 p.253).

7.   Campbell also restricts her study to the Conservative Party - see my next paragraph.

2 Methodological considerations

(a) <u>Theory and Method</u>

New social movement theorists like Touraine (1981 and 1985) emphasise the role of human agency in the study of social movements. In many respects this is a reaction to structuralists and post-structuralists who focus on a 'society without actors'.

Whether or not this is an over-reaction is a moot point. Certainly, new social movement theorists like Melucci (1985, 1988 and 1989) point to the dichotomy of structure and action and call for an approach which integrates the two: here, social actors act, move and attempt to bring about change from within structures not necessarily of their own making or choosing.

The study of social movements can therefore not be undertaken as if they exist in a vacuum. Action takes place within historically constituted structures which can facilitate, support, hinder and obstruct.

This kind of research has become well-established in the field of historical sociology where attempts are made to offer analyses that are both logically coherent and chronological. Abrams' work represent this line of thinking perhaps most clearly (Abrams 1982 pp.218-219).

Abrams argues that the dualism of the subject-object, meaning-structure, endlessly formulated, has pre-occupied social and political theorists from Hobbes onwards and sociology from its inception (Abrams 1982 pp.xiii and 228). Through such notions as Marx's concept of ideology and Weber's calculative rationality, the dualism has been perpetuated to the extent that it permeates Western thought. Against this, Abrams argues, 'In the place of the famous assertion of Descartes "I think, therefore I am", we must force ourselves to see the truth of the more modest claim, "I think therefore I think I am", with all that implies' (Abrams 1982 p.229).

This break away from dualism proffers an insight but poses a difficulty. The insight is the perception of the interdependence of people and societies, of actors and social structures reflexively intertwined. The difficulty is the operationalisation, the explanatory grasp of the 'dance' of 'human figuration'.[1]

The metaphor of the dance to explain social action is instructive: different actors[2] dance differently and react in different ways to different partners; furthermore, dancing styles change over time and there are certain rules and customs to be followed and interpreted in various ways. Social actors may even try out new steps, be innovative and change the rules, even invent new dances. In this way, individuality *and* collective behaviour are conjointly explicable.

There is a danger, though, of seeing the people as merely following pre-determined routines, as 'break-dancers'[3] as cheerful and willing robots (Wright Mills 1959 p.189) or even marionettes who dance the lifeless tune of some externally induced logic. But in recognising the routines as ours to follow, in sensing and perceiving the strings by which we move, we come to consciousness of ourselves and society. As Berger so perceptively puts it:

> We see the puppets dancing on their miniature stage, moving up and down as the strings pull them around, following the prescribed course of their various little parts. We learn to understand the logic of this theatre and we find ourselves in its motions. We locate ourselves in society and thus recognize our own position as we hang from its subtle strings. For a moment we see ourselves as puppets indeed. But then we grasp a decisive difference between the puppet theatre and our own drama. Unlike the puppets, we have the possibility of stopping in our movements, looking up and perceiving the machinery by which we have been moved. In this act lies the first step towards freedom
>
> (Berger 1963 p.199).

7

It is precisely this awareness of social location, of the changes wrought historically and struggled with anew, that has proved so difficult to articulate in social theory. Cole and Postgate's conclusion to their historical sweep from 1746 to 1946, in *The Common People*, asks, 'How had the common man [sic] changed in two hundred years?' (Cole and Postgate 1956 p.685). A great deal it seems: freer, healthier, better educated and better clothed. But, 'His mind had changed more than his body', and he was now much wiser. The advances in freedom for a woman were so great, that, 'the whole pattern of her life had changed' (Cole and Postgate 1956 p.686).

Historians have always found it easier to compare snapshots of people at different ends of the process or continuum of change. This has been the project of the Annales School, scholars like Bloch and Febvre who founded the *Annales* journal in 1929.[4] Febvre called for 'A New Kind of History', an interdisciplinary approach to the study of human action which located the sentiments and feelings of an age in the 'mentalite' of its participants (Febvre 1973 Chapter 2).

The influence of *Annales* is clear enough in the work of a number of historical sociologists like Flandrin (1979)[5] and Ginzburg (1980) who seek the meaning of history in artefacts and archives as well as 'hard facts'.[6]

The problems of method raised here are, of course, not new: at the turn of the century positivism provided a rational epistemology at Marburg, whilst at Heidelberg the intuitive grasp of 'cultural totalities' prompted the construction of world-views[7] (Stedman Jones 1971 pp.38-39, Hamilton 1974 pp.39-40 and Hall 1977 p.14).

But these issues and debates have involved more than a question of method: the very nature of the understanding of the social world itself is at stake raising the related issue of values. Proponents of historical sociology tend to be quite well aware that their sociological studies of history are not value-free. There is a strong sense of Weber's concern for the critical rigours of value-freedom, the desire to guard against the excesses of prejudice and bias - doubtless a consequence of Weber's own chaotic social and political milieux (Gouldner 1973 p.10) - but also an awareness that perspectives of the present colour interpretations of the past.

Schutte's review of Ginzburg's work, where she compares American and Italian historians, makes the point well:

... many (though certainly not all) American historians, particularly those working on premodern subjects, retain an unexamined allegiance to one vestige of positivism. They claim, or more often simply assume, that contemporary social problems and political ideologies have nothing much to do with their work as historians. They see their task as philosophically simple, even if technically or methodologically complicated: to reconstruct a past event or situation *wie es eigentlich gewesen*. European historians, Ginzburg included, tend not to be so naive. They are very well aware of the fact that they carry their present commitments and their vision of the future into their version of the past, and they consider it desirable as well as inevitable that they should do so

(Schutte 1976 pp.298-299).

This need not condemn us to partial views of history: the very awareness of perspectives enables the construction of typologies which can be extremely useful in charting the changing processual character of social movements (Barry 1991).

There is, then, a need to consider social movements in all their historical complexity and uniqueness; and whilst this may sound a cautionary note about generalisation, it is an issue to be confronted in the study of all social phenomena. As Abrams explains, 'it is precisely through the unravelling of the uniqueness of events that larger resonances are achieved without vulgarising or losing contact with the experienced lives of the protagonists' (Abrams 1982 p.200).

(b)   The Choice of London

If research into the New Women's Movement in Britain has to be historically specific, a sociology of contemporary history, and to deal with the lived experience of human action, then it has also to be spatially located. There are a number of reasons for this, and for choosing one area like London, foremost amongst them the sheer manageability of research done individually for a book of this kind. To attempt a study of the international magnitude of Castells (1983), for example, would require a research team involving complications of a slightly different order - such things as consistency, team work and the management and co-ordination of collective intellectual endeavour.

London was chosen as the area of study for a number of reasons, manageability notwithstanding. First, I had an interest in London's local government having spent many years working as a clerical, later executive local government officer.[8] Second, living in London made access to the local politicians relatively easy. Third, in the early 1980s the Greater London Council had elevated the profile of women by setting up the first Local Government Women's Committee, soon followed by a number of other London Boroughs (Goss 1984). Fourth, London's local government had experienced a tradition of social democratic politics (Miliband 1982 p.132) - enabling an exploration of the relationship between social democratic parties and the new women's movement in some detail. Fifth, as Flannery and Roeloffs have noted, 'Labourism' has tended to be weaker in the South which may be more amenable to the influences of social movements (Flannery and Roeloffs 1984 p.84).

Of course, every one of these points can be used to argue that the choice of London is a poor one, even that it is likely to prove the existence of social movement influence rather than offer an acid test anywhere near the necessary social scientific rigour. This has to be conceded, though if there is little or no evidence of women's movement activity and influence in London, it is likely to be nowhere else on this argument. Michels chose the German SPD as the object of his research for precisely the same reasons - in his case as an acid test of socialism and democracy (Michels 1911 p.50).

So what is London? In local government terms London has been seen as an autonomous area of local administration since at least 1888[9] when the London County Council (LCC) was set up under the Local Government Act of that year. Eleven years later, some twenty eight Municipal Boroughs were set up, giving London a clear two tier system of administration (though numerous ad-hoc bodies remained). It is interesting that the Local Government Act of 1899 which set up these Borough entities was criticised as breaking London up 'into a collection of twenty-eight power centres', artificially constructed and lacking in 'civic identity' (Byrne 1986 p.80). But a single identity for London remained elusive. In discussing the early twentieth century the City and LCC boundaries, Keith-Lucas and Richards explain:

> Separate boundaries, defining areas much larger than the county, were used for such functions as the Metropolitan Police, the Metropolitan Water Board, for purposes of transport, traffic control, main drainage

10

and electricity. Furthermore, these services were each provided by separate, appointed bodies, unco-ordinated with the county council, and the great differences in wealth between Westminster and Kensington in West London, and Poplar and Bethnal Green in the East End, were exacerbated by much higher rates in the poorer boroughs (Keith-Lucas and Richards 1978 pp.202-203).

London had to await the Herbert Commission and the London Government Act of 1963 for re-organisation into the regional Greater London Council (GLC), Inner London Education Authority (ILEA) and thirty two London Boroughs,[10] and 1985 for the abolition of the GLC[11] followed soon after by the ILEA - a short lived regional identity indeed.

Although it became academically fashionable to see London as a collection of 'strangers' (Eversley 1975 p.103), the idea of London as a 'community', a somehow integrated social and political entity, whether with an outer and inner dimension or a collective whole, is not new - Wheen's evocative *The Battle for London* (1985) published when the GLC came under threat, has a long history. Cobbett's dismissive reference to the all-devouring *wen*, for example, and Dickens' novels (Williams 1985 pp.220-221).

The uniqueness of London, then, has to be accepted and borne in mind when evaluating the findings of the research. The most that can be claimed is that all social research is historically unique and that whilst there are serious limitations concerning generalisation, these are no different to similar problems encountered elsewhere.

(c)   The Survey of London Councillors

The survey findings presented derive from a postal questionnaire sent in the latter part of the 1980s to *all* 456 women councillors in London and a sample (also 456) of men; a total of 912 councillors. The sample was drawn from the inner and outer London Boroughs, the City of London and the Greater London Council (details of councillors having been obtained shortly before its abolition in April 1986). The survey population consisted of 2167 councillors, with the sample chosen covering 100% of all females, and 21% of males,[12] including some councillors who had stood down at the April 1986 elections, alongside many current councillors.

Before undertaking the construction of the questionnaire, informal discussions were arranged with academics, researchers, political activists,

11

councillors and ex-councillors (see Appendix I); a literature review was in hand simultaneously. This approach provided a mass of useful information about which issues were worth pursuing and which hypotheses worth testing.

A pilot questionnaire was then sent out to academics and other interested parties, in order to verify that the questions were easily understandable and the issues raised valid. A second pilot helped refine the questions even further.

Next, copies of the questionnaire were sent to 25 councillors - a third pilot. Although the response rate, 30%, was low the replies confirmed that the questionnaire was ready for use on a larger scale. A copy is provided as Appendix III.

Names and home addresses of councillors were provided by Local Authorities on request, and questionnaires were sent to every female name appearing on the lists, together with the first male name to appear immediately after each woman's name (except where the surname was identical in which case the next male was selected so as to avoid as far as possible any potential consultation between partners which might have biased the findings). Some of the lists were grouped by ward, though most were alphabetical, so the selection of men was random. From these lists, 912 envelopes were addressed by hand and posted. The Questionnaires carried an individual number only - the lists of names and allocated numbers were confidentially filed - and confidentiality was stressed at all times.

Early misgivings deriving from the low response rate of the pilot sent to councillors were not borne out, however, when the survey proper began. Only twelve questionnaires proved to be 'deadwood' (i.e. where a councillor had moved away, was not known at the address, or had died, the envelope being returned undelivered or mailed back by a relative of the deceased). The percentages shown in Table 2.1 are based on a survey figure of 912, representing a response rate of 80.34% (excluding deadwood).

Table 2.1: Response to Postal Questionnaire: London Councillor Survey

	Initial Posting	First Reminder	Second Reminder	Third Reminder	Total	Total%
Deadwood[1]	3	3	2	4	12	1.32
Productive	377	143	55	22	597	65.46
Refusal	24	24	44	26	118	12.94
Other[2]	2	5	1	0	8	0.88
Response sub-total	406	175	102	52	735	80.59
Response b/f	--	406	581	683	--	--
Response running total	406	581	683	735	735	80.59
Non-Response	506	331	229	177	177	19.41
Total	912	912	912	912	912	100.00

([1])   Gone away, deceased, not known at address.
([2])   Other represents queries.

This is an exceptionally high response rate. Widdicombe (1986 p.17) achieved 64% including 3% refusals and McGrew and Bristow (1984 p.70) only 36%, which they argued 'although perhaps slightly low ... [was] ... roughly comparable with that of other such surveys' - they do not give any figure for refusals.

The inclusion of a stamped addressed envelope with each letter and a professionally printed questionnaire which was designed to take no more than ten minutes to complete, undoubtedly helped achieve the very high response rate. So too did persistence: four postings took place over several months and carefully worded accompanying letters, stressing confidentiality, were sent to the respondents *home* addresses (in a handful of cases where no home address was given, the questionnaires had to be sent care of the Town

13

Hall). Considerable time was thus spent in encouraging a high response rate and waiting patiently for replies. Of the eight queries - forms returned with the identifying numbers deleted or torn off - some three were found to be unusable, so the final response can be broken down as follows:

Table 2.2: Response based on 912 Survey Population

	Total number	%
Usable or 'productive'	602	66.00
Not wishing to take part or unusable	121	13.20
Deadwood	12	1.32
Total		80.60

There was no significant difference in the response rate between men and women. Of the 735 questionnaires returned, 372 came from women, 361 from men, with 2 unidentified (these were refusals communicated without the accompanying questionnaire).

Table 2.3: Response based on 900 Survey Population (excluding deadwood)

	Total number	%
Usable or 'productive'	602	66.89
Not wishing to take part or unusable	121	13.44
Total		80.34

14

The 12.94% refusals, however, are sufficiently high to warrant comment - the Widdicombe Enquiry, for example, reported only 3% refusals as we have seen (Widdicombe 1986 p.57). The extremely high refusal rate in the London Survey may have something to do with a strength of feeling about the purpose of the research. The nature of some refusals suggests this to be the case. One male councillor, for example, rang the Departmental Office at Birkbeck College and harangued one of the Research Assistants. In yet another case, a male councillor wrote, saying:

> I cannot see any point in answering pro-left pro-feminist questions. It grieves me that ratepayers and taxpayers' money can be wasted in this way and to what avail? If the Good Lord gave you common sense as well as a brain, why don't you put it to a more constructive use ... ?

Others were a little more concise: 'I do not partake in such research'. These were not isolated cases, but representative of a wider sense of disquiet.

It is not known why the questionnaire generated quite so much concern. The questions themselves were ordered in three sections:

Section 1: 'Political Participation',
Section 2: 'Opinions on Women's Involvement in Local Politics', and
Section 3: 'Now I should be grateful if you would please answer a few questions about yourself'.

Section 1 appeared to offend very few councillors - possibly those who would have been offended by most questionnaires. Section 2, however, raised quite a few temperatures, more than Section 3 which seems to have been seen by the objectors as more an invasion of privacy than anything else.

Section 2 is, of course, precisely the one dealing especially with women. It may be that questions concerning 'the women's movement' were seen as provocative, not the province of a male, or even unnecessary by some of the respondents.

It has not proved possible to discern, from the replies received, any pattern in the disquiet beyond specific objection to Section 2 with some lesser worries about Section 3. This should not detract from the high positive response rate achieved. Indeed, the many good wishes I received from

15

positive responders is indicative of a polarisation of feeling which can only be attributed somehow to the subject matter itself.

The next stage of analysis involved the coding of the completed questionnaires as input data for manipulation using the SPSSx computer package, a statistical package for the social sciences. Although the questions numbered twenty eight in all, with a space for comments, they were coded into fifty five separate responses. *The Widdicombe Report* (1986) made possible comparison of the London Survey with UK Councillors and the population more generally.

Where Widdicombe was not helpful, recourse was had to the *Office of Population Censuses and Surveys Classification of Occupations 1980*, and *The Municipal Year Book* (various editions), and other useful references; where no source is given in the tables which appear in this book, the data derive from the London Survey.

A large amount of data was generated, so much that it has not been possible to present it all here. Instead, the data is used selectively to provide an insight into the background of councillors and highlight certain factors which are seen to affect women specifically, thereby facilitating consideration of the impact of the New Women's Movement in Britain on local politics. For comparative purposes, much of the data is presented in cross-tabulated form showing differences, in particular, between men and women and political party.

Where the percentages are less than a half, they have been rounded down; where a half or above, they have been rounded up. This means that some columns may not add up to 100%.

In some cases, figures are presented for both inner and outer London. Given the socially constructed nature of space, and our perceptions of it, a word of warning may be in order here. Where the London Survey, or *The Municipal Year Book* are used, Inner London conforms to the Inner London Education Authority (ILEA) boundary; where OPCS and Census data are used, however, even in GLC publications, Haringey and Newham appear under inner London, and Greenwich is classified as outer London. The ILEA area has been kept for the London Survey: there is no special reason for this, and it is hoped that confusion will not result from using two slightly different indices.

It would have been useful to conduct a parallel survey somewhere outside London - perhaps another major city, or a rural area - for comparative purposes. Constraints of time, money and manageability precluded this, although it is hoped that the many issues raised will be pursued by other researchers at some time in the future.

This is important because of the relative dearth of material on the impact of women's movements on local politics. The work by Hedlund-Ruth (1984) and Dahlerup (1986) offer potential insights, though it is only Hedlund-Ruth's research in Sweden and Norway which focuses exclusively on local politics.

The usual caveats should be borne in mind when considering the survey data. Amongst others these include limitations relating to the response rate which whilst high compared to other surveys, is still less than total; we shall never know how much the views of the non-respondents would have changed the findings. Further, we are relying on the respondents' understanding of our intended questions, and our interpretation of their replies.

The potential margin for error is sufficiently wide to suggest caution in the interpretation of the results, which represent but one step towards an analysis of the influence of the New Women's Movement in Britain on local politics.

The next step is the clarification of issues raised through the in-depth interviewing programme which followed the survey.

(d)   The Interviews

(d:i)   Selecting the Councillors
It was decided to select councillors for interview from among those who had returned questionnaires. It was apparent from some of the remarks on the questionnaires that many had decided not to stand for re-election and it was thought that the reasons might possibly have some bearing on the research, particularly as one councillor had proffered the remark 'Someone ought to do a research project on why so many councillors are not standing for re-election!'.

But how to select the councillors?

It became clear from analysis of the questionnaire survey results that a wide variety of views existed amongst councillors on women's involvement in local politics, and that these views were differentiated by such things as gender, political party and attitude to the women's movement. It also appeared that a number of issues were particularly salient, such as the question of child-care, and it was thought that age might have some bearing

17

on the identifications made. In all, the following emerged as of crucial importance:

Gender (male/female)
Political Party (Conservative/Labour)
Attitude to the women's movement (supportive/not supportive)
Age (over 40/under 40)
Marital status and children (married/divorced/separated/ widowed)

In order to bring out these issues, it was judged necessary to select interviewees on the basis of these criteria, to endeavour to select ideal-types representing each of several positions.

This meant choosing a sample which was not necessarily representative or totally at random, but indicative of a broad cross-section of views.[13] The following profile of sixteen councillors resulted:

1) Female, Conservative, over 40, supportive*, married with children.
2) Female, Conservative; over 40, unsupportive*, married with children.
3) Female, Conservative, under 40, supportive, married with children.
4) Female, Conservative, under 40, unsupportive, married with children.
5) Female, Labour, over 40, supportive, married with children.
6) Female, Labour, over 40, unsupportive, married with children.
7) Female, Labour, under 40, supportive, married with children.
8) Female, Labour, under 40, unsupportive, married with children.
9) Male, Conservative, over 40, supportive, married with children.
10) Male, Conservative, over 40, unsupportive, married with children.
11) Male, Conservative, under 40, supportive, married with children.
12) Male, Conservative, under 40, unsupportive, married with children.
13) Male, Labour, over 40, supportive, married with children.
14) Male, Labour, over 40, unsupportive, married with children.
15) Male, Labour, under 40, supportive, married with children.
16) Male, Labour, under 40, unsupportive, married with children.
* Supportive, or unsupportive of the women's movement.

At first, Liberal councillors were excluded, given the low absolute numbers in the survey, though they were later added[14] when Labour and Conservative councillors being interviewed expressed surprise and recommended that they be included; no such views were expressed about the Independents, whose decline has been a recent feature of local politics in

Britain, despite their 'resilience' on some local councils (Widdicombe 1986: Research Volume I pp.37-38). In addition, councillors' willingness to be interviewed was taken into account - expressions of hostility were taken as a signal not to approach, as it was felt that councillors would not agree to be interviewed.[15]

Once these ideal-types had been delineated, councillors were selected randomly and their criteria then matched to the ideal-type profile. Where the criteria matched an interview was arranged.

The most difficult to find were:

3)   Female, Conservative, under 40, supportive, married with children.
8)   Female, Labour, under 40, unsupportive, married with children.
11) Male, Conservative, under 40, supportive, married with children.

Indeed, it proved impossible to find a councillor who fitted the criteria under No. 3) above, i.e. a female, Conservative councillor who was under 40 and who had expressed support for the women's movement and was married with children. In this case, a councillor who had expressed 'no particular view' on the women's movement was selected, since she met all the other criteria. In all but one case (No. 1)) a Conservative female who was over 40, who had expressed support for the women's movement and was married with children, interviews were conducted. The gap mentioned is regretted, and was not filled by another councillor who met the criteria. This was because it was necessary to deal with the councillor in question through an official in the Town Hall who, on my behalf attempted, and finally failed, to arrange an interview; this was despite lengthy correspondence during which I supplied the questions in advance at the councillor's request (the only occasion when I was requested to do this). The time taken to respond to my initial request for interview was sufficiently protracted to prevent the choice of another councillor in this category within the duration of the interviewing programme itself.

> I have finally found out that ... [name] ... does not wish to answer the questions you put to her in your letter ... I do hope this does not leave your research with too serious a gap, and I can only apologise for the delay in informing you of this news.
>
> Yours sincerely ...

To the sixteen councillors selected under the above criteria some four single councillors were added (although one had married between completing the questionnaire and interview). These comprised one male and one female Conservative, and one male and one female Labour, together with two Liberal men and two Liberal females (this made twenty four in all). The profiles[16] of the newly selected councillors were as follows:

17) Male, Conservative, over 40, unsupportive, single, no children.
18) Female, Conservative, over 40, who described her attitude to the women's movement as: 'I am a feminist, but not a loony one like the left wing in Camden', single with no children.
19) Male, Labour, over 40, who had not expressed a view about the women's movement, married with no children.
20) Female, Labour, under 40, supportive, single with no children.
21) Female, Liberal, over 40, supportive, married with children.
22) Female, Liberal, under 40, unsupportive, married with child (born between completion of the questionnaire and interview).
23) Male, Liberal, under 40, supportive, Divorced with children.
24) Male, Liberal, who had not supplied his age or expressed his attitude to the women's movement, married with children.

This made twenty three interviews (taking into account the failed arrangements for interviewee No. 1)).

Two further councillors were added to the interviewing programme (making 25 successful interviews in all) because of the nature of the method used to arrange interviews. This consisted of an informal telephone request made to councillors directly, from lists supplied by their local authority, explaining that their names had been chosen at random and seeking a confidential interview in order to explore the findings of the questionnaire survey in some depth. A minimum of one half-hour was requested for each interview. Because of the exceptionally busy nature of councillors' lives, this resulted in messages being left on ansaphones, at offices and at homes with other family members; as some councillors (although few in number) were slow to respond, second choices were sometimes made and councillors approached. In two cases only, this resulted in overlap:

25) Male, Conservative, under 40, unsupportive of the women's movement, married with children.
26) Female, Labour, under 40, not a supporter of the women's movement, married with children.

One further point is worth noting, that an attempt was made to obtain a wide geographical spread. Interviews were finally conducted with councillors in the following Authorities (one interview per Authority unless otherwise stated):-

Greater London Council (two interviews with ex-councillors)
Inner London Boroughs: Camden
                       Greenwich
                       Hackney
                       Hammersmith & Fulham
                       Islington
Royal Borough of Kensington and Chelsea
Inner London Boroughs:Southwark
                       Tower Hamlets (two interviews)
                       Wandsworth (two interviews)
Outer London Boroughs: Barnet (two interviews)
                       Bexley
                       Bromley
                       Enfield
                       Harrow
                       Havering
Royal Borough of Kingston Upon Thames
Outer London Boroughs: Redbridge
                       Richmond Upon Thames
                       Sutton
                       Waltham Forest

This means that two interviews were held with ex-councillors from the defunct Greater London Council, eleven interviews were held with councillors and ex-councillors from nine inner London Boroughs, and twelve interviews were conducted with councillors and ex-councillors from eleven outer London Boroughs. In all, some 25 councillors across twenty one Authorities were represented, providing a wide spatial mix.

(d:ii) The Questions Asked
The issues which formed the substance of the interview schedules were drawn up soon after analysis of the questionnaire data. Some issues, though important, were not developed because of the constraints of time - the experience of women's groups, for example, about which a great deal had already been written.

21

Contact was made with academics, researchers and some councillors and ex-councillors, as well as representatives of the women's sections of the Conservative and Labour Parties,[17] in order to discuss the issues and formulate and refine the questions.

A decision was taken to ask open-ended questions which, it was hoped, in a confidential interview would draw councillors out and help them to express their views freely. Where a question was asked which contained an assumption that a councillors took issue with, a supplementary question was asked - for example, the question 'Is it now easier for women to become councillors, compared to about fifteen years ago?' was asked, because the majority of respondents in the survey thought it was; and councillors were asked in what ways it had become easier, and when. If, however, a councillor replied that they did *not* think it was now easier for women to become elected members, the supplementary question, 'Why do you think the majority of respondents think so?' was asked, as a prompt.

Considerable background data had already been generated by the postal survey, so there seemed little point in asking large numbers of structured questions. The objective was to explore issues in depth, to provide more sensitive, qualitative information. Moreover, an important purpose of the interviews was to interrogate the data from the postal survey - to discuss the findings and hear the views of councillors on these. The following questions were therefore asked of all interviewees usually, though not always, in the order shown:-

Question	Prompt
(a) Is it now easier for women to become councillors, compared to about fifteen years ago?	If yes, in what ways, and when? If no, why do you think the majority of respondents think so?
(b) What problems did you encounter, in your own case, in becoming involved in local politics?	
(c) How did you/have you managed to get around them?	

22

(d) Would you agree that responsibility for family and household best explains why relatively few women become elected members? What could/should be done about this?

If disagree with premise, why did most respondents think this?

How about provision of creches, money or men doing more?

(e) How did you cope with family, household, political and work (if applicable) responsibilities both before and after becoming a councillor?

What changed?

(f) Do you have any ambitions to further your political career; and is politics an alternative to an occupational career?

Does your partner support your political views?

Do you favour councillors being paid?

(g) How would you describe the women's movement? Do you have any examples of where you have come into contact with the women's movement?

What are its aims?

What form does it take?

Have you had any direct experience of it?

(h) What do you think is meant by the term 'radical', used when referring to the women's movement?

Deriving from the 'Left' or from outwith institutionalised Party politics (i.e. Radical Left, or Radical Feminist)?

| (i) | Which issues, affecting women, cross party political boundaries? | Is the 'party line' very strong? |
| (j) | What do you think has been achieved, if anything, by the increased involvement of women in local politics? | Increase in England, Scotland and Wales from12% in 1964, to 19% in 1985, and higher in London. |

It will be seen that some of the questions lead the respondents. Question (d), for example, on its own, gives the respondent little opportunity to consider other factors. To try and counter this, the interviewees were given information from the survey just before this question was asked, in order to set the context: before asking question (d), interviewees were advised that other factors such as the style of politics, lack of confidence and selection by political party were also thought to operate as barriers to women's participation in local politics and that many respondents in the survey (about a quarter) had thought that more than one factor was relevant. This approach, nonetheless, does run the danger of further leading the respondents.

Indeed, the interview as a method of data collection is fraught with many well known difficulties. Strictly structured interviews are little more than personally administered questionnaires, only with a invariably higher response rate, whilst unstructured interviews run the risk of drifting into irrelevant conversation. The approach adopted here is a mid-point between these two ideal-types, with a sequence of pre-determined initial questions, very open-ended and few in number, designed specifically to get interviewees talking openly - in the hope of gaining the unforeseen insights that unstructured interaction can bring. The interview technique was thus largely non-directive and an attempt was made to establish rapport with each interviewee, although it should be noted that the character of the interviews changed as I gained in confidence, and occasionally asked more searching supplementary questions.

Each councillor to be interviewed was told that the research had been funded by the Economic and Social Research Council (ESRC) in the pursuit of a Ph.D. and derived from eighteen years personal experience as a Council Officer and a fascination with the women's movement and feminism generally. In many cases the interview became something of a dialogue, with both interviewee and interviewer asking searching questions of each other. It is contended here that this has added to the richness of the data derived from the interviews, in that the potential for misunderstanding and misinterpretation has been reduced; although it has to be conceded that this openness might have led to respondents telling me what they thought I might wish to hear. The diversity of the views expressed, however, and the obvious sincerity with which the interviewees responded, would suggest this not to be a serious problem.

Another relevant factor was the gender of the interviewer, as well as the status, dress and approach adopted; such factors can be highly significant as evidenced by Labov's research (1969) into the interviewing of youngsters in Harlem, where race was a prominent issue. On one occasion my mode of dress made me feel decidedly uneasy when interviewing a Labour councillor on an inner London Council estate, where poverty was particularly marked. On another occasion, the values expressed and personal problems encountered by one respondent were so close to my own personal situation that it was impossible to distance myself from the research. Such 'problems' as these, however, are common to research of this kind, and a balance of advantage is all that can be claimed: the fact that a *man* was conducting this research is thought, for example, to have aided the interviewing programme, if in a one-sided way, with many respondents expressing curiosity and a wish to know why I had become so involved. Had I been a female who turned up to the interviews in dungarees, the reaction of one Conservative male councillor would doubtless have been different, since he expressed 'fear' of such 'heavies', as he called them. Only three out of all the councillors who were approached declined to be interviewed, with two of these being ex-councillors who said they were excessively busy, but that they would be prepared to be interviewed if I could find no-one else.

There had, as we have seen, been some negative feelings about the research too. One Conservative councillor told me that his party group had met soon after receiving the first questionnaire and made a collective decision not to complete it. That this was not a binding policy decision was evidenced by the councillors' action in returning the form and taking part in an interview. Thank goodness for individuality: 'Their consensus to put it in the dustbin only made me more determined than ever to fill it in!'

(d:iii)   Arranging the Interviews
When arranging the interviews, I offered to travel to wherever was most

convenient for the councillor in question. As it turned out, some nineteen interviews were conducted at the homes of councillors, three at their place of work, one in a Town Hall, one in a cafe and one in the home of a councillors' daughter as it was close to my own home, thereby saving me considerable travelling time (this was at the councillors' own suggestion). I soon began to see the vast differences in housing as I travelled to different areas of London. Many interviews were conducted over weekends since this appeared for many councillors to be their only period of relatively free time, and over Easter itself for the same reason.

With only one exception - a councillor who seemed extremely pushed for time, probably wishing that he had not agreed to the interview - I was given much more time than the thirty minutes I had asked for. Most of the interviews continued for nearly an hour, some going well beyond.

In each case I was made to feel at home, offered refreshment and generally put at my ease - leading me to wonder who was interviewing whom in some instances. In each case, I stressed the confidential nature of the research and asked if the councillor would mind if I taped the interview; an objection was raised in only one case, where I made notes, which I wrote up later that same day. Otherwise the interviews were taped on an unobtrusive Olympus Pearlcorder S810 microcassette recorder, measuring 2" x 4.5". I had, initially, been surprised that the interviewees appeared so co-operative about agreeing to the interviews and recording their views, until one explained, 'What an opportunity: give councillors a chance to express their views like this, and you'll never shut them up'.

So it proved to be: used to public speaking, analytical discussion and debate, the interviews were far from dull; indeed, they were positively illuminating, as we shall see, with more than one councillor passing a comment prefaced by the remark, 'It's a good thing this is confidential'.

Where interviewees are quoted in Chapter 6, some attention has been paid to grammar, to ensure flow of analysis; though some sense of the conversational nature of the interviews has been maintained in order to convey realism. Above all, councillors are not named, nor have allusions been made to personal characteristics or circumstances which might lead others to identify them. Confidentiality remains an absolute priority.

This places severe limitations on the presentation of the analysis of the interviews. Much of the discussion of the interviews whilst appearing impressionistic and speculative is informed by a profound sense of the councillors' own views. This does some disservice to the individual views of councillors, whose interviews were all unique and whose views deserve better representation than is possible given the constraints of confidentiality.

(e)   Concluding Remarks

It has been argued that research into the New Women's Movement in Britain, in common with other social movements, needs to be historically and spatially specific and has to take account of the changing nature of consciousness, the taken-for-granted assumptions about gender. It has been contended that the most appropriate research methods including qualitiative participant observation and interviewing, supported by preliminary discussions and surveys where necessary.

It has been further suggested that this amounts to an exploration in contemporary history for which research strategies must be empirically based if they are to match participants' experience with theoretical proposition. In this, the subjective element of social research is reflexively engaged and no spurious scientific objectivity claimed.

Notes

1.   Abrams borrows the terminology from Elias (1978). See Abrams 1982 pp.231-233.

2.   It is interesting that reference to social 'actors' is commonplace in discussions of human agency - not 'actresses', or a gender-neutral term like 'player'. In their preface Gyford *et al* explain that use of the term 'chairman' provoked 'some lively debate and may be seen as one symbol or symptom of the current politicisation of local government' (Gyford *et al* 1989 pp.ix-xii).

3.   Break-dancing mimics the mechanical jerking of programmed robotics though, like jazz, allows space for individual interpretation. I am extending the metaphor and Abrams' discussion here.

4.   In 1929 they founded *Annales d'histoire economique et sociale,* later *Annales: economies, societies, civilisations* (Burke 1973 p.xii).

5. Flandrin's recasting of Laslett's own data on a Kent village is fascinating and scholarly. Whereas Laslett has argued that the predominance of the nuclear family not only pre-dated industrial capitalism, but may have facilitated its development, Flandrin demonstrates that averages of family size do not help explain the significance of certain families: the few gentry and yeoman families in Laslett's data owned most of the land in the area, gave employment to many and contained around half of the population (servants co-existed with blood-relations) (Flandrin 1979 Chapter 2).

6. Rowbotham's *The Past is Before Us* (1989) is a good example of the documentation of experience in respect of the New Women's Movement in Britain.

7. This was the *nature-geistes-wissenschaften* debate.

8. 1966-1974 with the Greater London Council, and 1974-1984 with the Inner London Education Authority.

9. Byrne notes that London has 'always posed difficulties owing to the rapid and continuous growth of its urban population' - up to the nineteenth century it was thought of as the square mile of the City. It was the special subject of Royal Commissions in the early to middle nineteenth century (Byrne 1986 pp.77-79).

10. The Act brought the bodies into being in 1965. ILEA was in effect a Committee (and Department) of the GLC. The City retained its Corporation status (Byrne 1986 Chapter 5).

11. Abolished in 1986. Similar legislation subsequently affected the ILEA.

12. As we will see when considering Government Reports in Chapter 3 women are under-represented in surveys of local authority councillors. By taking the total population of women councillors in London (with a numerically equal number of men) this bias is eliminated for purposes of analysis.

13. Initially it was decided to select councillors who were married with children; single and child-less councillors were added later for purposes of comparison.

14. This was on the recommendation of Conservative and Labour councillors. Similar criteria for selection were used, though only four Liberal councillors in all were chosen. Their profiles will be outlined shortly. It should be noted that the terms Liberal and Alliance are used interchangeably in this book as various 'middle' groupings including the SDP were in evidence at the time. Given their overall low absolute representation in the research this was thought to be the most appropriate way to proceed.

15. On reflection, this decision is regretted as it may have biased the results of the interviewing programme.

16. The justification for these additions is outlined in notes 13 and 14.

17. The Liberals were unable to assist at this time.

3 Women and local politics

'Silence itself - the things one declines to say, or is forbidden to name, the discretion that is required between different speakers - is less the absolute limit of discourse, the other side from which it is separated by a strict boundary, than an element that functions alongside the things said, with them and in relation to them within over-all strategies. There is no binary division to be made between what one says and what one does not say; we must try to determine the different ways of not saying such things, how those who can and those who cannot speak of them are distributed, which type of discourse is authorized, or which form of discretion is required in either case.'

(Foucault 1979 p.27)

This chapter seeks to demonstrate the ways in women have been conceptualised in the literature on local politics in Britain. A major part of the chapter consists of a critical review of three Government Reports - Maud (1967), Robinson (1977) and Widdicombe (1986). It is argued that, where they are considered at all, women are usually assumed to be the dependents of men, or conceptualised as social roles. It is further argued that the rise of the New Women's Movement has raised the consciousness of (invariably male) authors to women's position, revealing priorities of power and privilege.

(a)   Introductory Remarks

Recent research into the New Women's Movements,[1] which had their origins in the 1960s 'decade of protest', has raised fundamental questions about the nature of politics and democracy, laying great emphasis on the idea of grass-roots participation (Freeman 1975, Coote and Campbell 1982 and 1987; and Dahlerup 1986).

Such concerns can be seen to widen the more conventional liberal view of politics as conciliation and the maintenance of stability and order (Crick 1982 p.14). For the New Women's Movements, politics is about participation in public affairs, where the personal domain and the public arena are equally political. The Women's Movements have introduced more than just a new perspective on politics - they have questioned the very nature of politics itself. But how has the conventional literature of politics considered women, and women's movements?

This is the major focus of this chapter. Not women *in* politics, but women *and* politics; and more specifically women and *local* politics, to reflect the concern with grass-roots participation where women have been relatively well represented.[2]

This will not entail a quantitative head count of women in local politics, nor an evaluation of their place in, or 'successes' in, local politics, but a consideration of how women have been *conceptualised* within the literature of local politics. It will be seen that this is not a semantic problem of definitions, but a concern with changing intellectual fashions and pre-occupations.

(b)   Traditional Pre-Occupations and Current Concerns

Up to the 1960s, the literature on local politics in Britain (and the USA) reflected the pre-occupations of the literature on politics more generally: a focus on governments, constitutions and institutional machinery which brought benefits of efficiency and effectiveness and facilitated the progress of democracy. If democracy was a contest between competing elites, then

31

electoral apathy maintained the framework of individualist liberal freedoms against a tyranny of the majority - a pre-occupation both real and imagined that had exercised liberal and conservative thinkers as diverse as Burke, Tocqueville, J.S. Mill, and Schumpeter.

Whether low turn-outs at local elections were a further guarantor of such freedoms, an indication of the deep ignorance of the processes of local government (Byrne 1986 p.xv), or an appreciation of the 'deadly, dull and irrelevant' activity it sometimes seemed (Maud 1967 Vol.1 p.xii),[3] is a point which is nonetheless little debated in the literature. The concern was with constitutional issues, governmental machinery, boundary areas, and Royal Commissions with their focus on the structures and functions of local government.

The late 1960s saw a watershed in the study of local government. As with the New Women's Movements so the modern phase of work on local government can be traced to the economic, political and social turmoils of this period. As Byrne commented in 1981, 'One thing which can be said with certainty is that local authorities live in exciting times!' (Byrne 1981 p.14); exciting times that can be dated from the late 1960s.

With interest being shown from outside the traditional confines of political science both sociologists and human geographers alike helped re-orient the concerns and focus of local government studies, changing in the process the very vocabulary itself to reflect concerns with local *politics* and the *state*. Studies of the *city*, of the *urban* and *urban social movements* followed, as intellectuals and activists (sometimes one and the same) drew increasing attention to the exercise of power through the social relations of community and local state politics.

So 'political' had the exercise of local politics become (or seemed to have become), that the 1980s witnessed the first serious attempts by a national government to check its powers through a wholesale reconstruction of its funding base - through spending targets, grant penalties, rate capping (Regan 1987 p.39), and the poll-tax, or community charge, instituted in local government in England and Wales on 1st April 1990. The national political turmoil which followed provides further evidence of the high profile 'politicisation' of local politics which looks set to continue for some time.

This chapter will seek to chart the changes undergone in the literature. This will entail a consideration of writings from traditional and more recent political science, government committees of inquiry, and literature which concentrates more on studies of the urban, welfare, the Women's Movement and community politics, as well as that from the so-called 'New Right'.

It will become apparent that there is no clear distinction between these different discourses and that there is often overlap.

Particularly interesting is the relationship between academia and activism.[4] Many social scientists have acted as advisers to local authorities: these include Hilary Wainwright with the Greater London Council's Popular Planning Unit, and many others like Beatrix Campbell who has combined journalism and political activities with scholarly publications. These authors are often socialist or marxist-feminist.

Though it seems improbable that academic publishers such as Tavistock, Routledge and Blackwell would actively seek to encourage a left-wing or feminist bias in their publications, it *is* interesting to ponder a political orientation perhaps more in tune with Verso, Pluto, or the Women's Press. This may have more to do with the higher journalistic profile of some of the authors concerned, or their University or Polytechnic teaching posts. More radical and revolutionary feminist writings on local politics rarely get beyond the pages of journals like *Trouble and Strife* (Carter 1986) or magazines such as *Spare Rib* (Loach 1986a, 1986b and 1986c) - both of which have carried articles on local government councillors.[5]

So how have women been conceptualised in the literature of local politics?

(c)   The Political Tradition

No attempt will be made to summarise the corpus of writings from political philosophy to political science, which I am calling the political tradition, as they have considered women. Such an enterprise is beyond the scope of this book. Since political scientists - many in the Political Studies Association (c.f. Evans et al. 1986) - are already engaged in this process, however, a few comments on the work in progress seem appropriate, before considering the literature on *local* politics more specifically.

Current efforts seek to proceed in four ways. First, the recovery of women's writing from earlier periods in history; second, the effort to attend to women's experiences as new topics for research (e.g. sexual harassment); third, the endeavour to correct mainstream, or 'malestream' bias in existing work; and fourth, the concern to effect a paradigm shift in the way knowledge within a discipline is socially constructed.

This rethinking of conceptual frameworks is not limited to politics.

33

Stacey and Thorne, for example, compare history, anthropology and literature with sociology, and conclude, 'thus far, feminist tools have worked better to criticise than to reconstruct most bodies of theoretical knowledge' (Stacey and Thorne 1985 p.312). It would seem to be early days for this feminist endeavour.

This is hardly surprising given the magnitude of the task. Even within the political tradition, those who do write about women, such as Plato, J. S. Mill and Nietzsche, include both advocates of equality, and outright misogynists.[6]

The point about all this is that the political tradition, in common with other discourses and disciplines, has largely *assumed* the subordination or invisibility of women in society, and eclipsed their experience and achievements in academic literature. As Spender observes, 'women have been excluded as the producers of knowledge and as the objects of knowledge' (Spender 1981 p.1). Even the generic use of the term 'man' to refer collectively to women and men, 'was a rule introduced into (male) scholarly circles in the sixteenth century' (Spender 1981 p.6).

For writers on politics and government prior to the 1970s, this focus on 'mankind' often entailed specific consideration of the institutions and machinery of rule as facilitators of democracy, that 'delicate growth' that required a 'special, carefully controlled atmosphere to survive' (Susser 1974 p.278); that guarantor of liberal freedoms under threat from 'evil men in the Kremlin who promise to bury us...' and '... men of good intentions and good will who wish to reform us' (Friedman 1962 p.201).

This focus on the machinery of government can be found in Hanson and Walles' *Governing Britain*, written in 1969 as an Open University set book, focussing on 'the institutions through which Britain is governed, and the way they work' (Hanson and Walles 1970 p.7). Writings on government and politics in this earlier period focussed their attention on such important matters as Parliament, the Cabinet, Central Administration and Ad Hoc Agencies. When gender *was* considered, it was in terms of voting studies, or the 'battle of the sexes' (Duverger 1964 p.211).[7] The personal was not yet acknowledged to be political and writers such as Wollstonecraft and de Beauvoir went largely ignored.

As with the literature on national government, so too that dealing with the local. A book first published in 1967 - Jackson's *Local Government* - serves to illustrate the tradition which had become established in post-war Britain.[8] Jackson's focus is on the structure, function and organisation of local government, through a consideration of re-organisation, committee administration, finance and central control. The second edition published in 1970 incorporates the Maud and Mallaby Reports, and acknowledges the beginning of a 'most interesting period of change' for local government (Jackson 1970 p.vii). So it was to prove.

But not all local government studies took this a-theoretical, almost academically clinical, approach. The community power studies[9] in America were, in this respect, somewhat ahead of their time in drawing attention to the unargued premises of intellectual concern. These studies are well known to students of political science and political sociology because of the important methodological and epistemological issues they raised.

The debate may be said to have been triggered by Hunter's (1953) study of 'Regional City' - believed to be Atlanta, Georgia - in his *Community Power Structure*. Hunter's approach to the measurement of power in the local community was 'reputational': that is he asked certain groups of local representatives to provide lists of power holders. From this, and a further process of whittling down, he arrived at lists of the most 'important'. Hunter had identified a local group of elite power holders.

The second seminal contribution to this debate came from Dahl's (1961) *Who Governs?*. Dahl's method was altogether more sophisticated in its attempt to remedy the 'conceptual confusion between potentiality and actuality, and the methodological problems of ambiguity and arbitrariness' (Martin 1977 p.46), associated with the reputational approach. Dahl examined such things as the degree of involvement of different individuals in certain local decisions. This focus on the observable decision-making of local notables led Dahl to conclude that, locally, power was diffused.

The major critique of this pluralist approach came from Bachrach & Baratz (1962) in their article 'Two Faces of Power'. They argued that the pluralists had begun 'by studying the issues rather than the values and biases that are built into the political system' (1962 p.950). They enumerated two key defects of the pluralist model: 'One is that the model takes no account of the fact that power may be, and often is, exercised by confirming the scope of decision-making to relatively 'safe' issues. The other is that the model provides no *objective* criteria for distinguishing between 'important' and 'unimportant' issues arising in the political arena' (1962 p.948).

Bachrach & Baratz's focus on 'non-decision-making' underscored the limitations of previous approaches to the study of power. The very agenda itself, on this account, might limit discussion and exclude consideration of certain issues. This critique owed much to Schattschneider's 'mobilization of bias'. As Schattschneider explains, 'All forms of political organization have a bias in favor of the exploitation of some kinds of conflict and the suppression of others because *organization is the mobilisation of bias*. Some issues are organized into politics while others are organized out' (Schattschneider 1960 p.71).

The recommendation for the future direction of research was, however, less convincing than the critique of previous research. How could objective interests be determined, and the tenuous legitimacy which such non-decision-making was somehow to contrive or otherwise facilitate be demonstrated? How could the exercise of power be measured? More recent research adds weight to the view that the concept of power is one of the most slippery in the social sciences, from at least Weber to Foucault, and that its measurement is problematic (c.f. Lukes 1974 and 1986; and Martin 1977).

But what of women in all this - how were they conceptualised? Here, more recent work, urging us to rethink conventional paradigms, is instructive.

Bourque and Grossholtz' (1973) article 'Politics an Unnatural Practice: Political Science Looks at Female Participation' offers some interesting observations on the eclipsing of women in political literature, notably the community power studies. Their opening comments set the scene: 'That politics is a man's world is a familiar adage; that political science as a discipline tends to keep it that way is less well accepted, but perhaps closer to the truth' (Bourque and Grossholtz 1973 p.225).

In considering literature on 'political socialization', 'some classic voting studies', and 'the elite studies, particularly Floyd Hunter, ... Robert Dahl, ... and Robert Presthus', Bourque and Grossholtz identify 'four categories of distortion of the participation of women in politics':-

(i)   **'Fudging the Footnotes'** - where female characteristics or attitudes were cited, but unsubstantiated in the literature cited as the source, 'thus misrepresenting and in some cases falsifying the data';
(ii) **'The Assumption of Male Dominance'** - where, for example, 'women's political attitudes are assumed to be reflections of those of the father or husband';
(iii) The acceptance of **'Masculinity as Ideal Political Behaviour'** - whereby aggression, competitiveness, etc. are held to be the norm; and
(iv) **'Commitment to the Eternal Female'** - wherein female political behaviour is seen as the result of the 'social role as wife and mother,

36

and her mythical status as purity personified'.

(Bourque and Grossholtz 1973 pp.227-229)

The elite studies come in for a drubbing - Hunter's main contribution being that he set a trend subsequently followed by all students of community power: that the people to be studied were 'men'. Bourque and Grossholtz argue, 'The elite studies do not bother to investigate or even explicitly to assert male dominance. They simply take for granted that elite equals male and ignore what chance females turn up in their samples' (Bourque and Grossholtz 1973 p.258).

Studies into local government in this earlier period were thus highly selective in their discussion of structural issues. A contemporary critic, Miliband, observes:

> 'Until the seventies, the subject was predominantly treated in terms of a series of problems which required solution by the application of greater knowledge, more efficient methods of organisation, goodwill or whatever. The most important of these problems appeared to be the conflicting claims of 'efficiency' and 'democracy', to which were linked a variety of other problems, such as the relation of central to local government, the size of areas, internal organisation, finance, personnel, etc.'

(Miliband 1982 p.131).

Miliband's unease derives largely from the exclusion of class analysis, which he seeks to remedy, though his remarks do suggest a more general pre-occupation in the literature with certain structural 'problems', rather than issues of ideology and social relations. The literature lacked, as Gyford has put it, 'any political dimension' (1984 p.1).

This is borne out in Dearlove's review of the literature on the re-organisation of local government prior to the 1970s. Dearlove identifies two traditions of intellectual inquiry on local government: that which positively valued local self-government, and that which embraced 'urban policy science', both of which, he argues, were 'reformist'. He criticises this literature 'which sees governmental reform as bringing the benefit of efficiency, effectiveness and democracy to all at the same time' (Dearlove 1979 p.12). His aim is to draw out the taken for granted assumptions in the literature, within a historical framework.

37

Dearlove's analysis is part of the new tradition of writing on local government, which stresses the political nature of the subject matter under scrutiny and marks a decisive break with the literature of the earlier period he reviews.

Not all recent publications on local politics reflect this politicisation of the literature in the wake of the path-breaking work of Gyford (1976 and 1984), Castells (1977) and Cockburn (1977). The central concerns of writers such as Keith-Lucas & Richards (1978), Byrne (1981 and 1986), Richards (1983) and Hampton (1987) echo the pre-occupations of the earlier period under consideration. Yet there has been a tendency to re-direct research towards the social relationships of local politics, reflected in Collins' (1978) deliberations on the social background and motivation of councillors, and the collection found in Bristow, Kermode and Mannin (eds, 1984), covering such issues as the media, selection of candidates and political recruitment, from which findings such as the embourgeoisement thesis of local politics can be discerned (McGrew and Bristow 1984 p.76).

When we come to consider attempts to rectify the invisibility of women in politics more generally, the activities of members of the Political Studies Association are particularly interesting. Books such as those by Lovenduski and Hills (1981), Randall (1982 and 1987), Lovenduski (1986), and Norris (1987), serve to correct the imbalance, reworking the literature for future generations of students; whilst contributions to the collection by Evans et al. (1986), and the book by Carter (1988), respectively engage the discipline more directly, and judge progress.

The research on women and local politics has followed this pattern, though the focus has tended to be on such things as Women's Committees (Flannery and Roeloffs 1983; Webster 1983; Sofer 1984; Goss 1984; and Button 1984) and participation[10] (Bristow 1980(a), 1980(b), 1982; Hills 1982; Shaul 1982; Forrester 1982; Williams 1985; and Martlew et al. 1985). Hollis (1987) exemplifies the approach as applied to political history.

Hollis begins by noting women's general invisibility, gaining the parliamentary vote only in 1918. But, she explains, 'Women had the local government vote and elected office fifty years before that' (Hollis 1987 p.vii). Hollis reviews the role of women on parishes, vestries, boards and councils of English local government, noting how 'Philanthropic women and suffrage women ... converged in late Victorian England on local government' (Hollis 1987 p.461). Prior to 1918, women argued that their strength lay in their difference to men, their 'loving care' and 'conscientiousness to detail

38

... In time, most men conceded that school and poor law work was suitable for women' (Hollis 1987 p.463). By the 1930s, women's representation had reached between 12 and 15% where it stayed - concealing wide national variations - until the 1970s (Hollis 1987 p.478). In Hollis' work, we see the meticulous attention given to details of representation, acknowledgement of the integration of female responsibilities for family working with part-time politics, the accessibility of local networks for women, and the less intimidating 'style' of local politics (Hollis 1987 p.480).

The literature on participation has similar concerns. The under-representation of women in political office is noted, the reasons usually being ascribed to such things as political 'style', socialisation and/or life-style - acknowledgement is also made of women's lack of confidence.

There is a tendency in this literature to focus on women, who are usually surveyed and interviewed. Two consequences follow from this. First, women are portrayed as almost passive recipients of some ineluctable process beyond their control. Second, the barriers to representation are identified, but not the resistances. The following remark by Hills can be seen in this light:

'since women in Britain continue to define *themselves* in terms of the family rather than their economic role, and *are expected* to shoulder the dual burden of home and employment, the numbers of women *prepared* to enter formal participation in political life can be expected to continue at a low level' (my emphases).

Although Hills continues 'it is only because men have so little responsibility in general for running the home and children that they can afford the time for political activity', a substantial part of the blame is shown to rest with women, almost as co-conspirators in their own subjection and oppression (Hills 1982 p.70).

The study of women's committees in local government is similarly oriented to considerations of representation. Because these are new phenomena, research is barely under way, though it is possible to detect a certain defensiveness about the tentative 'successes', and 'progress' made - for example in the funding of women's groups which are outside the mainstream of traditional politics. Clearly, the potential for liaison between the more socialist-feminist wing of the women's movement in local politics, and the more radical-feminist autonomous women's groups is considerable.

Yet the Local Government Women's Committees are by no means above criticism or threat. *Spare Rib* in July 1987 carried an article 'Birmingham Women's Committee scrapped' (Women Matter, Birmingham 1987).

Perhaps this reflects wider uncertainties about the role and function of such committees, as well as mistrust of their left-wing (Labour) origins, amplified through the media. The high profile of the GLC Women's Committee, before it disappeared along with the GLC itself on abolition in April 1986, left it vulnerable to political attack. Sofer (1984) needed to do little but note the problems that led to the appointment of an internal panel of review in order to cast doubt on the operation of the Administrative Support Unit and the Committee. The Women's Committee was, it seems, not even 'under democratic control. At practically every meeting I have attended, the co-opted members are the largest voting bloc' (Sofer 1984 p.286). Other studies of Women's Committees have attempted to profile prominent women leaders: Merle Amory in *Spare Rib* 171 1986 (Loach 1986c), Linda Bellos in *Spare Rib* 171 1986 (Loach 1986b), and Frances Carter in *Trouble and Strife* No.8, Spring 1986 (Carter 1986) - not to mention Polly Toynbee's hostile profile of Linda Bellos,in the *Guardian* (Toynbee 1987).

The study of women in local politics has thus made women more visible than they were before. It has also drawn attention to the problems faced by women as women, even if there has been a tendency to focus attention almost exclusively on women rather than on the potential detractors from innovative change - men. If, to echo the existentialist concern with free will, women have to make their own history under conditions they have not chosen, this literature has yet to highlight the strategies and barriers continually maintained by men, both material and ideological.

(d)   Official Inquiries and Investigations

Local government has traditionally been regarded as an arm of central government, a plank for central party policy, by successive Conservative and Labour administrations. There are instances where Local Authorities have gone their own way, as in Poplar in the 1920s, and Clay Cross in the 1970s, but by and large, 'local authorities are law-abiding bodies. They do not engage in outright defiance of the state' (Keith-Lucas & Richards 1978 p.177). To a large degree this has remained true, despite media (and some Conservative) protestations about 'loony left' or 'lethal left' social

40

engineering and Marxist entryism (Regan 1987 p.s 19,33,38,47,48 and 50). Certainly there has been some political posturing and some illegality in the 1980s,[11] but the *norm* has been peaceful co-existence in central - local relations.

It is in this sense that the ambivalence shown by political parties to the autonomy of local authorities can best be understood. This is not to suggest that local government has been the puppet of central government or 'agents of Ministers and Whitehall' (Maud 1967 Vol.1 p.xi) - the wide disparity in local provision, poll tax or community charge levels and grant-aid belie such a simple conclusion. It *is* to suggest, however, that party politics has at best paid lip service to participatory democracy at local levels. The Layfield Report (1976) provides a good case in point. An Inquiry into local government finance, set up by a Labour government, it was eventually ignored by a Labour government. As Hampton explains, Layfield proposed:

> 'stark alternatives. Either finance local services from central funds and cease to pretend that local autonomy exists, or increase the ability of local authorities to raise their own income... The government in its response to Layfield (DOE 1977 e) refused to accept the logic of the alternatives presented: they believed, as politicians are wont to do, in the possibility of finding less radical compromises'
>
> (Hampton 1987 p.99 and 101).

Government Reports, as Sir Humphrey in " Yes Prime Minister" has so trenchantly observed, are convenient vehicles for side-tracking the issues: they defuse potentially explosive situations, deferring problems to some future date when solutions can be 'taken on board' and effectively ignored. Commissions and Committees are not entirely without teeth, but their terms of reference are invariably limited, constraining their members from taking the wider perspective. With a de-radicalised agenda, 'official inquiries and investigations...' have been into '... the way our various institutions work and into the possibilities of securing improvements in them.' (Gyford 1984 p.2).

It is not intended to review the gamut of inquiries and investigations here. Instead, the focus will be on the post-war years[12] and the discussion limited to a consideration of three Committees, each some ten years apart. These Committee Reports have been selected because they alone conducted councillor surveys[13] - a consideration of women is thus highly likely to be found in this literature, as women have traditionally been fairly well represented on Local Authorities (at least compared to Parliament). The Committee Reports and accompanying volumes covering the surveys,[14] are as follows:-

(i)   Committee on the Management of Local Government (1967)
        - Vol.1 Report of the Committee
        - Vol.2 The Local Government Councillor
                            (Moss L. & Parker S.R.)
        (England and Wales were covered);

(ii)   Committee of Inquiry into the System of Remuneration of Members of Local Authorities (1977)
        - Vol.I Report Cmnd. 7010
        - Vol.II The surveys of councillors and local authorities (HMSO)
        (England, Scotland and Wales); and

(iii)   Committee of Inquiry into the Conduct of Local Authority Business (1986)
        - The Conduct of Local Authority Business: Report of the Committee of Inquiry into the Conduct of Local Authority Business. Cmnd. 9797
        - The Conduct of Local Authority Business: Research Volume II: The Local Government Councillor. Cmnd. 9799
        (England, Scotland and Wales)

These reports are more generally known by the names of the people who chaired them: The Maud[15] Report (1967), The Robinson Report (1977), and The Widdicombe Report (1986), respectively. The Reports will be referred to by these names henceforth.

(d)   (i) The Maud Report (1967)
Appointed by Sir Keith Joseph in 1964, 'at the request of four of the local authority associations', the Maud Committee was asked 'to consider, in the light of modern conditions, how local government might best continue to attract and retain people (both elected representatives and principal officers) of the calibre necessary to ensure its maximum effectiveness' (Maud 1967 Vol.1 p.iii). The specific concern with calibre followed a general concern

with perceived low standards in local government (Byrne 1986 p.137). The Mallaby Committee on the Staffing of Local Government ran in tandem, concerning itself with officer recruitment and effectiveness; both Committees were 'serviced by the same secretariat' (Hampton 1987 p.73).

The recommendations of the Maud Report reflect the wider pre-occupations of the earlier period of local government literature covering such things as divisions of committee responsibility, salaries for board members, delegation, management, and the relationship between officers and members, as well as indicating a desire to see members playing less of an administrative role. For their deliberations the Committee drew on experience of local government abroad.

The Report's main thrust was managerial - effectiveness and efficiency with a modern corporate image (Cockburn 1977). Perhaps Maud's most radical proposal involved the centralisation of decision-making: committees would be responsible to a 'Management Board', of five to nine members and Principal officers to the Clerk (Maud 1967 Vol.1: paragraphs 158 and 179(a) respectively).

The reaction to the Maud Report was generally unsympathetic though, where favourably received, found itself in tune with practice already in existence or being instituted (Hampton 1987: 75).[16]

So how did the Maud Report deal with women? Largely as if they were invisible, or mere social roles, reminiscent of Bourque and Grossholtz' characterisation. To the Report's credit, some differences between men and women are noted in the survey, though they occur infrequently and in general terms only: the time spent by councillors on public duties, for example, showing that women worked 56.4 hours per month compared to 51.7 hours for men. Further breakdowns are given, by council type, age, education, and socio-economic grouping (SEG), though there is no cross-tabulation by gender. It is worth noting that women were, of course, grossly under-represented among councillors in the survey population anyway. There were only 490 female councillors compared to 3,480 males, representing 12% (Maud 1967 Vol.2: Table 1.1).

Reasons for leaving council service were examined in the Survey, where opportunities for including the gender dimension are missed completely. Table 9.22 provided 'councillors' probable reasons for eventually giving up council work, and ex-councillors' reasons for leaving'. Whilst the reasons were generally gender-neutral, covering things like 'Amount of time given', and 'Frustration of party system', there were others which could be

43

considered 'malestream', in that they might have revealed significant gender differences if presented differently and cross-tabulated accordingly - such things as 'Interference with business or family life', and 'Moving from area'. Further breakdowns are given by age (Table 9.23), education (Table 9.24), SEG (Table 9.25) and length of service (Table 9.26). The important point about the way women were conceptualised is that they were either invisible, seen perhaps as having needs no different to those of men, or (part of the background assumptions of the authors of the Report) assumed to be wives or partners, part of the 'family life' referred to.

Table 9.27, for example, dealt with the question 'Would you stand again for the council in some circumstances?', asked of ex-councillors. One of the responses is classified as 'Yes' - 'If change in domestic or working circumstances'. Some 24% of councillors responded accordingly, yet there was no gender distinction made, nor any attempt to distinguish domestic from working circumstances.

Other tables in the survey are used to compare response by gender, for example Table 2.8 which dealt with the question of how councillors first came into touch with council work, and Table 4.3, which presented preferred aspects of council work. But the researchers did no more than note the differences between women and men, and move on, offering no observation, analysis, or explanation *for* the differences.

The Report itself (Vol.1) parallels the Research Volume (Vol.2) in its representation of women. The discussion of 'Times of Meeting', for example, runs as follows:-

534. The greater part of the written evidence which deals with this subject favours evening meetings. The arguments are that:
   (a)   day-time meetings make it difficult for employees to attend;
   (b)   day-time meetings favour the farmer, the self-employed, and the retired, and discriminate against the young and the wage or salary earner;
   (c)   evening meetings are an inducement to people to serve in local government and to take an interest in its work.

The Report continues in paragraph 535, 'The most important point is ... that the time of meetings of the authority is a principal determinant of the composition of membership of the Council' (Maud 1967 Vol.1 p.149).

44

True, but what of women in all this? The Report's conclusions contained in paragraph 536 are worth quoting at length:

536. Our conclusions are that:
(a) in urban areas evening meetings are more likely to encourage younger people to take part in local government;
(b) the attitude of employers towards release of their staff and the payment of the fixed expenses allowance which we recommend in our Interim Report would make it easier for wage earners to attend day-time meetings;
(c) evening meetings can throw a heavy burden on officers and perhaps make recruitment more difficult;
(d) if meetings are held in the evenings, the authority must face competition from the other distractions of society and the many and varied interests which attract people, not least the demands of home and family;
(e) as far as the rural areas are concerned, evening meetings may involve long journeys often by public transport, in winter months we think evening meetings would be a deterrent;
(f) the time of meetings has a real effect on the attitudes of members toward their local government work and on that of the public who might otherwise participate in it. It is not so much the time of the meetings but their frequency and their duration, and indeed their content, which are of real significance.

(Maud 1967 Vol.1 p.149)

If women were in the minds of the authors it would appear to have been as social roles (point {d}).

Elsewhere, the Report made the assumption that members would be male, sometimes quite explicitly by references to 'he or his wife', when talking of councillors' responsibilities (Maud 1967 Vol.1 p.150). By and large, then, where women were treated at all in the Report and Research Volume, they were characterised as social roles.

(d) (ii) The Robinson Report (1977)
Appointed by the Callaghan government, the terms of reference of the Robinson Report were as follows:

45

'To examine all aspects, other than travelling and subsistence allowances, of the present system of payment under the Local Government Act 1972 and the Local Government (Scotland) Act 1973 of local authority elected and co-opted members, including any anomalies in the system, consideration of its alleged abuses and its social security implications;

to consider alternative systems and their consequences;

and, having regard to the requirements of pay policy and the present severe constraints on local authority expenditure, to make recommendations'.

The members of the Committee were asked to report 'expeditiously' (Robinson 1977 Vol.I p.1). Perhaps this reflected wider concerns about 'integrity' and 'corruption', following close on the heels of the Poulson Affair of 1974;[17] perhaps a reflection of the pragmatic fors and againsts of 'voluntary principles' and the 'calibre' of candidates, one of the central concerns of the Maud Report (1967). The question of payment to councillors had also been the subject of the Wheatley Commission in Scotland (1969) (see Byrne 1986 pp.131-134).

Whatever the impetus behind the initiative, it came at a time when local government had been enjoying a higher profile than hitherto, particularly in London. In 1967, the Conservatives were celebrating victories across the country, being in charge of the GLC, Bradford, Cardiff, Coventry, Leeds, Leicester, Liverpool, Manchester, Newcastle, Nottingham and Southampton. In 1968, they won over all but four of Labour's twenty London boroughs, Barking, Newham, Southwark and Tower Hamlets - and in Newham, it was only the Mayor's casting vote that gave Labour its tenuous hold.[18]

Eye witness reports document the harrowing experience of now *ex*-Labour councillors who could not believe what had happened. But these upheavals were followed by sharp reversals in the early 1970s, when Labour regained much of its lost ground (Gyford 1985 pp.24-28).

Outside London, re-organisation in the early part of the 1970s produced smaller member authorities, and evidence suggested that councillors were spending ever more of their time on Council business (Robinson 1977 Vol.I p.21). All in all, the scene in local government across the country had changed quite dramatically, with less, and different, councillors. Clearly, the upheavals had propelled hitherto unprepared 'youngsters' into previously unwinnable seats, and jettisoned much of what might be termed the 'old-guard'. Further changes, notably within the Labour party in terms of its lifting of the ban on proscribed organisations, but more generally in respect of the interest taken in local government by ever wider groups in the community, resulted in sharply different councillor profiles.

Gyford has documented the changes for Labour, through what he has called the 'new urban left' (Gyford 1983 and 1985): councillors, party activists, community workers and local government officers seeking a 'new local road to socialism' (Gyford 1985 p.17). The involvement of the 'women's movement' was also acknowledged by Gyford. It is indeed interesting to note the large increase in women councillors from Maud (1967): in one short decade, their representation had risen from 12% to 17%, an overall increase of some 42%.

So this was the scene in local government when the Robinson Committee was conducting its enquiries. This is the beginning of what I am referring to as the 'later period', post-war.

In its report, the Robinson Committee noted that the existing system of payments to council members drew its authority from the 1948 Local Government Act, whereby earnings forgone or expenses necessarily incurred were compensated in relation to 'approved duties' undertaken (Robinson 1977 Vol.I p.4). Hampton notes that these allowances had been increased in line with inflation, 'but were never particularly generous' (Hampton 1987 p.115).

The core issues were:-

(a)   the degree to which councillors should be remunerated for their services and their time; and

(b)   whether such remuneration should take the form of an allowance or a salary for what was, in some cases at least, almost a full-time occupation (there were large numbers of councillors in full-time paid employment - some 66% according to Maud (1967: Vol.2: Table 1.6), though no break-down was given by gender - and 'Three quarters ... now economically active', according to Robinson (Robinson 1977: Vol.I p.11)).

The Wheatley Commission (1969) had been in favour of remuneration as a 'substantial part-time salary', but the Robinson Committee rejected this because salaries lacked 'public acceptability: they could affect the structure and operation of local government; and they would be costly'. They

47

continue,

>'Perhaps the greatest single objection is the damage that full-time salaries would do to the principle of voluntary public service, even though we recognise it is unrealistic to expect that nowadays everyone can give freely of their time to the extent demanded by Council activities'

(Robinson: Vol.I p.45).

The Robinson recommendations on this issue can be summarised as follows:

(a)   Abolish the existing attendance allowance
        (Robinson 1977: Vol.I: Paragraph 189);
(b)   Institute a basic annual payment to all councillors
        which 'acknowledges their role as elected members and
        covers expenses (excluding travel and subsistence)'
        (Robinson 1977: Vol.I: Paragraph 194);
(c)   Establish entitlement to a 'financial loss allowance'
        for approved duties (Robinson 1977: Vol.I: Paragraphs
        198 and 199); and
(d)   Inaugurate a 'special responsibility payment'
        for certain appointments, for 'leaders' ie. those chairing
        'the major committees' (Robinson 1977: Vol.I:
        Paragraphs 202-207 and 181-186).

Other sections of the Report summarise the existing situation of councillors, their allowances, and the implications for tax and social security.

Reading through the Report (Vol.I), it is hard not to be struck by the absence of any consideration of women. Once more, women are either invisible or seen as social roles, the implications of which are not even acknowledged, let alone developed. Understandable in the Maud Report, it seems almost unforgivable in Robinson, some ten years after the women's movement had made its impact and some 42% more women were active as local authority members.

A discussion in Chapter 7 serves to illustrate the point. Here, the Committee make clear their belief that:

'it is absolutely fundamental to the effective working of democracy that there should be no unnecessary impediment to the freedom of anyone to put themselves forward for election. Hence we think one important principle is that membership of local authorities should be truly open to all sectors of our society without fear that it will entail financial hardship'.

They noted, 'for example, the continuing under-representation of manual workers on councils', considered the voluntary principle and the problems of the employed councillor including those 'temporarily unemployed or sick'. They did *not* identify any difficulties faced by women[19] (Robinson 1977 Vol.I: Paragraphs 149-154).

Three paragraphs on, women received a mention: 'Even on the same council, the member who loses income as a result of his attendance is much worse off than colleagues who are retired, or housewives, or those who lose no pay (Robinson 1977 Vol.I: Paragraph 157). The implicit assumption of dependency is clear.

The Research Volume (1977 Vol.II) that accompanied the main Report (1977 Vol.I) provided details of two surveys: one 'based on a random sample of councillors in Great Britain', and another 'concerned with the types and rates of allowances available and with the amounts councillors claim' (Robinson 1977 Vol.II p.1). Broadly, the surveys were intended to cover some 50% of all chairs/vice chairs/mayors/deputy mayors, 100% of majority party leaders, and 25% of all other councillors - the chosen sample reflected this.

As with the Maud Research Volume, Robinson noted some differences in gender ratios, but made no attempt at analysis or explanation. The large increase in the number of women councillors from Maud was noted, and the observation made that:

'since 1964 the main increase in the proportion of female councillors has occurred in those aged less than 55 and above this age the highest proportion (19%) is found amongst those aged 55-59. Proportionately more female councillors are found in England than in Wales and Scotland'

(Robinson 1977 Vol.II p.5).

Some 7% are described as 'housewives', the same as for Maud

(Robinson 1977 Vol.II: 10, Table 7). The comment ran: 'Housewives constitute the same overall proportion of councillors as in 1964 but a larger proportion of the economically inactive' (Robinson 1977 Vol.II p.5); once more there was no analysis or attempt to consider why this might be the case, or why more of them were not councillors.

This may have had something to do with the absence of cross-tabulation by gender. Whilst it was interesting, for example, to have noted that only 12% of all female councillors were 'leaders'[20] in 1976, compared to their 17% representation on local authorities (Robinson 1977 Vol.II p.13, Table 16), it would have been of greater moment to consider why - to have at least speculated, or even cross-tabulated gender with 'leader' and other socio-economic characteristics.

Tables 20-50 comprised Section II of the Research Volume and covered 'The councillor's working experience' - of these, Tables 21 and 23 gave comparisons by gender. They dealt with the time spent on council duties by age and sex (age and sex are not cross-tabulated with time spent, but presented separately). The gender differences were small, but perhaps significant: women spent on average 19% of their time on electors' problems compared to 16% for men, and 47% on attendance at or in preparation for council and committee meetings, compared to 53% for men.[21]

The observation on these tables ran 'Women spend a little more time in total than men' (Robinson 1977 Vol.II p.16).

The Robinson Report and its Research Volume thus dealt with women in much the same ways as Maud. This, despite the changed circumstances of the 1970s, and the higher profile of women as elected members.

(d)   (iii)   The Widdicombe Report (1986)
Appointed by the Secretaries of State for the Environment, for Scotland and for Wales, the terms of reference of the Widdicombe Committee ran as follows:

'To inquire into practices and procedures governing the conduct of local authority business in Great Britain, with particular reference to:
(a)   the rights and responsibilities of elected members;
(b)   the respective roles of elected members and officers;
(c)   the need to clarify the limits and conditions governing discretionary spending by local authorities;
and to make any necessary recommendations for strengthening

50

the democratic process'.
(Widdicombe 1986 Report p.17)

No concern with calibre or managerial effectiveness here. Instead, a clear focus on 'practices and procedures'. This undoubtedly reflected the politicisation of local government which had increasingly become an arena of party politics in recent years. Perhaps the polarisation of party politics, a far cry from the 'Buttskellism' of earlier decades, was that much clearer in the 1980s than it had been in the 1970s when the Robinson Committee undertook its essentially pragmatic deliberations.

It is easy to see why this would be a matter of such concern in local government circles. In his foreword, David Widdicombe QC made the following point: 'The formal framework of local government does not recognise the existence of party politics. In law, decisions are taken by the council as a whole, not by the members of the majority party, and officers serve the council as a whole'. He went on, 'The increase in politicisation has placed strains on this statutory framework' (Widdicombe 1986 Report p.15).

Concern about the politicisation of local government, which Widdicombe saw as 'here to stay', had some basis in reality, although the role of the media may well have amplified any general disquiet. The anti-abolition campaigns of the GLC and the ILEA in the early 1980s, Militant activity in Liverpool, and Bristol's free public social security seminar in 1985, could be seen as vehicles for publicising the Labour party's policies (or interpretations of them), on issues which went beyond the conventionally understood jurisdiction of local government (see Regan 1987: Chapter 4). This was not just a re-drawing of the rules by the Labour Party - many Conservative local councils prided themselves on their privatisation of local services, contracting out, and careful husbanding of public money, thereby implementing aspects of Tory Party policy (Ascher 1987).[22] This was noted in the evidence of the National and Local Government Advisory Committee of the Conservative Party to Widdicombe (Widdicombe 1986 Report p.59), and was subsequently given renewed meaning in Bradford.

Quite clearly, central-local relations had undergone considerable strain since the IMF crisis of 1976 (Widdicombe 1986 Report p.53) and the election of a Conservative government in 1979 pledged to (at least) the ideology of monetarist curbs on public spending.

Such politicisation, which it was argued had reached the echelons of some local authorities' senior officers, reflected wider changes in local government - members with professional backgrounds, and officers seen as the political bed-fellows of ruling groups[23] (Regan 1987 pp.43-46).

Byrne sees developments of this kind as responsible for the appointment of Widdicombe, whose interim report recommended the limiting of council authority to engage in party political publicity (Byrne 1986: 120; see also Gyford et al 1989 pp.284-288). The distinction between educational publicity and party political advertising is one that has exercised many since the ensuing Local Government Act of 1986 was hurriedly pushed though Parliament. Nonetheless, this underlying pre-occupation with politics and the parameters of local government remit is evident in the following passage:

'1.3 In announcing the terms of reference on 6 February, the Secretary of State listed a number of items to which he invited the Committee to pay particular attention:
'- ensuring proper accountability for decision taking to elected members and to the electorate generally; and examining possible ways of strengthening local democracy within the existing structure of local government;
- clarifying the status and role of party groups in decision taking;
- ensuring the proper participation and the accountability of individual elected members in the decision taking process;
- examining any problems of propriety which may arise from members' conflicts of interest, particularly where officers of one council serve as councillors of another;
- considering the merits of the development of full-time councillors; and the related issues of the use of members' allowances and the remuneration of councillors generally;
- reviewing the system of co-option of non-elected members;
- studying officers' relationships, particularly in view of their legal and professional obligations, with elected members and political groups;
- clarifying the limits and conditions governing discretionary spending, including use of sections 137 and 142 of the Local Government Act 1972 (and sections 83 and 88 of the Local Government (Scotland) Act 1973) for political purposes in local government, or in relation to bodies set up, and largely financed by, local authorities.' (Widdicombe 1986 Report p.17)

Accordingly, the eighty eight recommendations dealt with limiting powers, audit, surcharge, ombudsman, pecuniary interest, allowances, and codes of practice. The officer should be arbiter, professional manager and adviser - even to party groups - and members' decision-making powers clearly distinguished from their 'deliberative or consultative' role in relation to such matters as police committees. In respect of the officer-member link (twin-tracking), Principal Officers and above should be disqualified from membership of another authority. The recommendations reflect the Committee's interpretation of their terms of reference, constrained by severe limits of time in which to report (one year). They accordingly concentrated on 'principal' councils, matters that applied 'across the range of local government services', and 'all the key issues' rather than 'subsidiary detail' (Widdicombe 1986 Report pp.20-21).

The Report hit the press like a damp squib: David Widdicombe was reported in *The Times* as saying that the Report was not radical, but a call for the re-assertion of the rule of law (*The Times* 20.6.86). In the *Guardian*, Nicholas Ridley, the then Environment Secretary, announced it *was* radical, and promised 'an extended debate on its proposals' (*Guardian* 20.6.86). Certainly, the strict application of the proposed twin-tracking amendments would have banned Bernie Grant from leadership of the London Borough of Haringey, Merle Amory of Brent, and deprived Derek Hatton of his position in Liverpool. Nonetheless, the main body of the Report and its recommendations were not exactly the kind of headline news provided by Gay Rights and Women's Committees in the past.

So how did the Report and Research Volume deal with women? Given the relatively high profile accorded, not least, to Women's Committees by the press and some high-profile local authorities like the GLC, we might reasonably expect a more detailed consideration of women and issues thought to affect them. Certainly, the way the findings are summarised is indicative of the politicised context of the 1980s: 'diversity', 'politics', 'law and reality', 'accountability', and 'initiative', 'all of which' the Report noted, 'were recurring themes in our deliberations' (Widdicombe 1986 Report p.23). The 'growing intensity in political relations between the parties', was also noted, as being 'reflected in a growing polarisation between the ideologies of the Conservative and Labour Parties' (Widdicombe 1986 Report p.33).

Some of the language used in the Report was quite different from that of the previous two Committees - 'territories' instead of 'boundaries' for example, and the use of 'he/she' rather than the generic 'he' - and there are attempts to consider whether stereotypes accorded with the reality of the survey findings. The belief that more women were becoming councillors is shown to be at best overstated, with women under-represented at 5% in the Welsh Counties, and 19% generally (Widdicombe 1986: Report pp.26-27).

The Report could thus be seen to focus a little more clearly on the social relations of local politics than the previous Reports considered here. In tone, style and content, Widdicombe was different, reviewing the changing dynamics of power relationships within local authorities in recent times, noting the changes, offering 'considered' judgments on existing practices, and putting forward 'moderate'[24] recommendations for the future which sought to strengthen the existing framework - clarification of the law and the strengthening of the role of the ombudsman being two cases in point. As with Maud, the symbiotic relationship of officers and members was acknowledged and a clearer demarcation of responsibilities advocated (c.f. Widdicombe 1986: Report p.65 and 66).

There seems little that might be considered radical in all this, in spite of Nicholas Ridley's press comment, though there *was* a concern with the politics of local government rather than with its administration. Despite this, however, the conceptualisation of gender relationships remained poorly developed. Women's under-representation as elected members, for example, was noted, but not explained (Widdicombe 1986: Report p.50). This is curious as there were several references to women's position and under-representation on local authorities in the Report which it is worth acknowledging.

References were made to women's specific presence in the community, in terms of: peace organisations; the representation of women's 'sectional interests' in respect of the EOC; oblique mention of sexual minorities (though the intention may have been to highlight gay orientation as the entry read 'racial and sexual minorities'); and the argument that any proposal to reduce the number of councillors would adversely affect under-represented groups such as women. There was even a reference to compensation for financial loss, which ran, 'It is invidious that a wage-earner and someone looking after a home should put in similar hours but that only the former should be remunerated' (Widdicombe 1986: Report p.193,206,105,173 and 130 respectively).

These scattered references nonetheless remained undeveloped fragments which offered little insight into the Committee's thinking on women. Yet there was one section where their unargued premisses appeared to surface. In their discussion of 'Issues raised by co-option', they acknowledged co-option not only as,

> 'a means by which local authorities can make use of outside expertise and experience which might not be available among elected members and officers. It is also a means of involving the community in local authority proceedings, especially those sections of the community (eg women, ethnic-minorities, council tenants), that are under-represented among elected members; for instance only 19% of councillors are women and only 10% are council tenants'.

But, they noted, co-option was not the only way of achieving this (Widdicombe 1986: Report pp.90-91).

Co-option, it was argued, was non-accountable.[25] Voting and decision-taking should remain outwith the remit of co-option. In any event, it could distort 'the political balance of committees' (Widdicombe 1986: Report p.91). Far better to:

> 'consult outside groups and hold public meetings to explain their policies and seek views ... It would be possible, for example, to appoint a women's advisory committee, whose role was to ensure that service committees took full account of issues of sex equality before reaching decisions'.

If advisory committees seemed inappropriate, advisers might attend meetings (Widdicombe 1986: Report p.92).

Principles of accountability and political balance thus took priority over representation. Although the Committee noted elsewhere that there was no one norm of local democracy (Widdicombe 1986: Report p.103), the one they implicitly endorsed seems a curiously delimited one, one which would indirectly relegate gender to an advisory role with no executive power.

The Main Report thus noted women's under-representation and acknowledged recent developments in the wider society affecting women. It nonetheless failed to explore reasons for women's under-representation, ignored any potential contribution they might make, and failed to offer any suggestion to remedy the imbalance despite its remit to examine 'possible ways of strengthening local democracy'. Issues seen to affect specifically women or women's groups, such as peace issues and women's committees, were treated as peripheral, marginal to the more central issues of political balance, accountability, officer-member propriety, and conventions of local government sobriety.

What then of the Research Volume covering the survey of councillors, providing statistical background to women's under-representation?

The Research Volume reported the increase in women members from 1964 through 1976 to 1986; and noted that 19% 'is still well below the overall population figure of around 51%' (Widdicombe 1986: Vol.II p.19). Further acknowledgements were made of women's differential representation across the many types of local authority; note was *not* taken of the magnitude of the increase in recent years - 42% between 1964 and 1976, and 58% between 1964 and 1986. Perhaps this was a matter of emphasis, perhaps an assumption unexplored.

It is interesting, for example, to consider the construction and objective of the survey.[26] Under 'Design and Purpose of the Study', we find:

'Social and Community Planning Research were invited to carry out a study among the elected members of local authorities in England, Scotland and Wales. The study was conducted by postal questionnaire and was designed to provide:
(i) updated information on the personal characteristics of councillors obtained in the Maud and Robinson studies of twenty and nine years ago respectively;
(ii) data on the working life of the councillor; and
(iii) information on the views and attitudes of councillors towards some of the current issues of importance in local government.'

(Widdicombe 1986: Vol.II p.15)

The final point is a crucial one: 'Some of the current issues of importance in local government'. The issues that were considered were accordingly thought to number amongst those of importance. These included, in the first part of the Volume, personal and occupational characteristics of councillors, their council and political experiences, their working lives, patterns of remuneration, and views and attitudes. A second part of the Volume dealt with members' allowances.

If there appears to be little about women *specifically* in this list, at least the Volume dealt with them collectively along several indices: for example, by type of authority (Table 2.2), age (Table 2.3), marital status

(Table 2.5), activity status (Table 3.2), highest office held (Table 4.3) and so on. Oddly, perhaps, given the tendency to quote statistics from Maud and Robinson for comparative purposes, Table 5.1 in Widdicombe which compares councillors by time spent on council duties did not include gender as is the case of Robinson (Table 21) when interesting, if small, differences were noted. The potential for considering women's special needs was, nonetheless, very great.

This makes it all the more surprising to find no discussion of the implications. The summary of the main findings of the first part of the Volume (Chapter 8), quite properly but mechanically chronicled the statistics and no more - a few more women as elected members, with more of them holding leadership positions. The one obvious opportunity for the Report to break new ground and consider women's issues under 'Views and Attitudes' was not grasped. Instead, issues of influence over decision-making, involvement of citizens in local authority decisions, consultation, co-option, party loyalties, maladministration, organisation and officer recruitment, were considered the more important. It would seem that, of 'the current issues of importance in local government', women and issues affecting them were not a priority.[27]

All in all, then, the Widdicombe Report (as well incidentally as the Government's response)[28] tended to perpetuate the conceptions of women found in Maud and Robinson. There were more statistics differentiated by gender in Widdicombe but, by and large, women were invisible or eclipsed in the government Committee Reports reviewed here. Conceptualised as social roles, or as slightly differentiated versions of men or as their dependents, issues which might affect them were low indeed on the agenda.

(e)   The State, Social Policy and Local Democracy

Ideas have their time. Paradigm shifts are slow to materialise historically. As we have noted, even in more recent literature on the local state, earlier pre-occupations remain. Yet the path-breaking work of the likes of Gyford (1976 and 1984), and Cockburn (1977) does represent an attempt to reconceptualise the ideological parameters of local politics. This intervention from outside the conventions of political science has been joined by sociologists like Saunders (1979) and Dunleavy (1980), and human geographers like Castells (1977, 1978 and 1983). Indeed, the interest shown by protagonists from so many disciplines has led to the opening up of the area to multi and interdisciplinary research.

This has had implications for the study of women, not lost on more radical feminist authors such as Hanmer (1977) and Ettorre (1978), whose purpose has been to locate women's position within studies of the community and the urban, and lay bare the underlying patriarchal assumptions of the scholarship, drawing out implications for social policy.

The parallels between research into local politics, and research into social policy are, indeed, interesting. The context for this has been the theorisation of social policy within a highly charged political environment which has seen writers from both right and left of the political spectrum re-examining the assumptions of the post-war welfare state 'consensus'. At a national level, the Fabian ideas of gradualism and permeation and faith in professional altruism have been undermined by the polarisation taking place in politics generally. Yet this 'attack' (Cochrane 1985), exemplified in the Fowler review has not marked as decisive a break with the Beveridge settlement as at first might appear - rather, it has engendered a critical *rethinking* of the entire position on welfare and social policy (Clarke et al 1987, Part Four).

Deakin identifies three strands of so-called 'New Right' thinking: 'a laisser-faire economic strand; a moralistic position on social policy and a strong commitment to nationalism and the authority of the Nation State' (Deakin 1986 p.7). This approach clearly echoes classic liberalism in its attitude to social policy: the need for a minimal but strong state, with an emphasis on individualism, 'freedom', and the pursuit of self-interest, leading to enhanced national prosperity, a social contract and a spontaneous economic order, echoing from the pages of Locke, Adam Smith and Hayek, in a reworked 'possessive individualism' (MacPherson 1962).

Yet the concern about a 'dependency culture' created by the State, and the missionary impulse to remoralise the family, have considerable implications for women (Ashton 1987 pp.121-123 and 1988 p.27), many of whom are the direct recipients of state services and benefits (London Edinburgh Weekend Return Group 1979), work as its employees, (Barratt Brown 1972) and as we have seen act as its local representatives. Changes, ideological and material (Wilson 1977), in this area thus affect women more directly than any other group. The point here is that women *see* social policy differently to men because of this, because, following the ideas of Gramsci, their social locations intersect political and civil society (Showstack-Sassoon 1987 p.18). This relates not only to their generally subordinate position

58

within the family, which means that they are the ones who have to care for elderly relatives who are returned to the 'community' from state care (McIntosh 1979; Walker 1982; and Wilson 1982), but also to their position within the local community.

If local government has been 'under siege' (Davies 1988), if its reform was the 'flagship' of the Thatcher Administration, then it is women who have been amongst the most directly affected (MacGregor 1988 pp.41-51); and it is women who will continue to be affected as arguments over local political and government rage nationally.

Women have access to networks of local democracy and tend to be represented in greater numbers than they are at national level. They thus participate where, for them, it counts most directly (Kettleborough 1988 p.66). This may result in a different image and understanding of local politics for women, one where participation is seen as involving the meaningful exercise of power. This point has been made most forcibly by radical feminists like Weir (1977), and Hanmer who argues that relatively small undertakings such as Women's Aid can give rise to national movements, highlighting in the process 'the fundamental nature of women's oppression within the family' (Hanmer 1977 p.91).

Such concerns may appear peripheral to politics - inappropriate and ideologically biased - as it has been conventionally defined. For Regan, for example, the focus on women's studies in education has sought to impart 'aggressive feminism' (Regan 1987 p.47), not at all the proper stuff of local government. The one study concerned specifically with women and local politics, using case studies from Norway and Sweden, has noted how representation at this level provides opportunities to rethink traditionally geared political priorities in women's favour (Hedlund-Ruth 1984).

Though contributions from radical feminists have been both instructive and progressive in this respect, it is the socialist and marxist-feminists who have tended to steal the limelight, their access to publishers appearing crucial. Yet it is by no means clear who is centre stage in their theorisation of the relationship between socialism, marxism and feminism - women, or the naggingly elusive proletariat? (Rowbotham 1973; Segal 1979; Barrett 1980 and 1988; and Coote & Campbell 1982 and 1987). The calls for 'Alliances' (Laclau & Mouffe 1985) and 'Rainbow Politics' (Rowbotham 1988) are serious attempts to confront the pragmatic issue of compromise, but raise crucial and related issues of priority.

Such concerns about alliances reflect a wider interest in the proliferation of groups representing particular interests in civil society, which have enjoyed an ascendancy in the wake of the late 1960s era of protest. Whether viewed as new social movements, pressure groups, or as status groupings, these vocal sectoral interests are seen as offering the possibility of some kind of oppositional unity to social forces on the right.

Much academic interest has centred on the spatial dimension of this recrudescence of protest, the 'urban' being seen as the arena within which meaning is socially constructed in bringing together such groups as housing associations, the 'New Urban Left' and urban social movements. But where are women in all this? Theorists of this school of urban politics, such as Saunders, focus on collective consumption and come close to assigning women the role of little more than a neo-Weberian status group. For others, like Castells, more neo-Marxist in orientation, women's involvement in urban protest is relegated to a subsidiary position in a hierarchy of struggle.

Castells' evaluation and ultimate prioritisation of women after twelve years exhaustive cross-national research is worth quoting at length:

> 'Sometimes the conflict was largely connected to the class conflict. On other occasions, it was the power relationship between alternative forms of the state that dominated. In none of the cases observed were the gender relationships at the core of the conflict, in spite of the decisive participation of women in the movements: a striking verification of our hypothesis about the historical hierarchy between relationships of production, power and gender'
>
> (Castells 1983 p.335).

A striking verification indeed - of the low priority accorded to women in recent literature on local politics. In this sense, in the way women are conceptualised and assumptions made, we may say that recent research on local politics mirrors government Committee Reports.

(f)   Concluding Remarks : Values, Hierarchies and Silences

Perhaps hierarchies of priority are inevitable, given the value-ridden nature of social science. Whether in the form of political science, sociology, human geography or government reports, values creep in and lie unexplored. The Great Silences on women in the literature prior to the 1970s say a great deal about women and if the women's movement has had the effect of raising the consciousness of authors to women's position, this has merely revealed priorities of power and privilege.

Much remains to be done if Gouldner's (1973) rejection of Weber's mythical Minotaur of value-freedom is accepted: 'progress' in this sense will come up against the deadening and stifling effects of a scientific community righteously enforcing the outer parameters of its dearly beloved paradigm (Kuhn 1970). Yet if a paradigm shift *is* to be effected, puzzles must be generated.

One of the puzzles of politics has been the arbitrary boundary between the political and the private - a distinction understood in its wider political dimension over thirty years ago by C. Wright Mills (1959 p.15), a distinction questioned by the women's movement of today. In this and in many other respects, the New Women's Movement in Britain represents a challenge to the vested interests of conventional male wisdom.

Notes

1. Consideration of the New Women's Movement in Britain as a social movement is dealt with in Barry (1990 and 1991), as is the question of the 'uniqueness' and 'newness' of the New Women's Movement.

2. Compared to national politics. See Chapter 4.

3. The Union NALGO referred, in its written evidence, to the popular image of local government as an institution that is 'complex, obscure, pettifogging and dull' (Maud 1967 Vol.1 p.91).

4. Dearlove comments: "Professor John Stewart from the Institute of Local Government Studies has deplored the tendency for research to be carried out *into* rather than *for* local government' (Dearlove 1979 p.258). It will be shown that this is not *always* the case.

5. There have been one or two notable exceptions (c.f. Mayo (ed) 1977).

6. See Agonito's (1977) *History of Ideas on Women: A Source Book.*

7. Interestingly, Duverger produced *The Political Role of Women* some nine years before this statement, where he acknowledged an 'antifeminist tradition' as causing serious difficulties for research into women and politics. He further highlighted the need to address the fundamental issues of female subordination, referring to De Beauvoir's *The Second Sex* (Duverger 1955 p.8,9,130).

8. A *few* publications are noteworthy for being 'out of step' with the general custom - e.g. Sharpe's (1962) *A Metropolis Votes*, but such works would seem to be the exception rather than the norm.

9. Literature on national government in some ways paralleled these concerns e.g. Wright-Mills (1956). For an overview of the community power studies and their location within analyses of ideology and legitimacy, see Merquior (1979) Ch.1.

10. See Norris (1986) for study of voting and the American Congress.

11. See Widdicombe 1986 Report p.231.

12. Those after 1960 are helpfully listed in Gyford (1984 p.2).

13. The Royal Commission on Local Government in Scotland (1966-69 Cmnd. 4150, HMSO 1969) conducted a survey covering Scotland only and has been excluded for this reason.

14. All surveys were supplemented with interviews.

15. John Maud later became Lord Redcliffe-Maud.

16. Richards suggests that the importance of the Maud Report lay in its 'educational effect', helping to 'pave the way for the rather less radical Bains Report of 1972' (Richards 1983 p.147), which recommended a 'senior or central committee, advised by a Chief Executive', though the Bains Report did reflect practice already in operation (Richards 1983 p.152).

17. Robinson noted: 'We are aware that many people outside local government regard the system as a great bonanza for elected members' (Robinson 1977: Vol.I p.21).

18. The parallel with Bradford, held by the Conservatives in late 1988 on the Mayor's casting vote with the intention of operationalising privatisation, competetive tendering and free market forces as a blueprint for the future is too important to pass over without comment.

19. Despite a chapter dealing with 'Tax and Social Security Implications', no special consideration was given to women's position. They noted in the context of impending state schemes, differences between councillors 'contracted in' and 'contracted out'. They commented: 'This is a complicated area, and we must leave detailed consideration to those who are expert in the subject' (Robinson 1977 Vol.I: Paragraph 210).

20. Leader was 'defined as Chairman/Mayor, Vice-Chairman/Deputy Mayor, majority party leader and committee chairman/convenor' (Robinson 1977 Vol.II p.6).

21. The hours committed under 'other' reveal a discrepancy between Tables 21 and 23. The *hours* women and men spent per month was 6 and 3 respectively (Table 21), but shown as 5% and 5% in percentage terms (Table 23).

22. For an overview of Conservative Policy, see Chapter 2 in Ascher (1987).

23. Though the practice of involving members in the appointment of officers reduced between Maud and Widdicombe (Widdicombe 1986 Report p.34), there were allegations of patronage, exercised though job advertisements, e.g. in *Labour Weekly* (Widdicombe 1986 Report p.155). Councillor involvement in staff apointments was, although thought to be high at 4%, more a feature of 'small authorities dominated by independent councillors. It is not particularly a feature of party politics at all' (Widdicombe 1986 Report p.34).

24. They rejected 'radical' solutions like 'the adoption of a Ministerial model of government, such as that applying in central government' (Widdicombe 1986: Report p.64).

25. Sofer, as we saw earlier, noted that at GLC Women's Committee meetings she had attended 'the co-opted members [were] the largest

voting bloc' (Sofer 1984 p.286).

26.   Gyford et al (1989) attempt to 'recast' the findings of their research work for Widdicombe 'in a more accessible form' (p.x).

27.   When I met Ken Young, Research Adviser to the Committee, he acknowledged that issues specifically affecting women and ethnic minorities had not been included, given pressure of time.

28.   The Government's response to Widdicombe was published in July 1988: 'The Conduct of Local Authority Business The Government Response to the Report of the Widdicombe Committee of Inquiry' Cmnd. 433, HMSO.

The Reponse was, perhaps, somewhat predictable: proposals for primary and secondary legislation, codes of practice and guidance, the need for Local Authorities to take decisions themselves in some instances, and acknowledgement that some of the recommendations had already been the subject of government action in the Local Government Act of 1988 and the Local Government Finance Bill 'of the current session' (Response: 1988 p.v).

Reading through the main body of the 'Response' (and the specific point by point responses to Widdicombe's eighty eight recommendations pp 43-55), we encounter some of the rebuttals and revisions, though these appear to have reflected pragmatic considerations rather than overtly political orientations. Acceptance, for example, that the attendance and financial loss allowance be replaced with a basic flat rate allowance, 'but not at the levels proposed by the Committee. Total expenditure on the new scheme should not exceed current overall expenditure on councillors' allowances' (Response: 1988 p.48). The belief that levels of remuneration do not deter any 'particular types of person' is explained by the absence of 'evidence' on candidate shortage (Response: 1988 pp.9-10).

The proposal for prohibition of twin-tracking was supported, but for 'chief executives, chief officers and their deputies, as well as certain other council officers in sensitive posts to be identified by each council in accordance with statutory guidelines', rather than for all Principal Officers and above (Response: 1988 p.51). Early reports on the Government's Housing and Local Government Bill, however, suggested that some 90,000 people might be affected, rather than the 10,000 or so envisaged by Widdicombe, if the proposed £13,500 earnings ceiling was imposed (Sanders 1989 p.28).

Proposals for the appointment of an officer 'responsible for propriety generally', and another for 'management co-ordination', were of no great surprise (Response: 1988 pp.17-18).

The remaining responses were equally predictable, with no reference to women specifically, merely confirmation of Widdicombe's stress on sobriety, propriety and accountability as we saw when discussing the attitude to co-option. So it is with the government's response: 'While the contribution of co-opted members to policy formulation can be valuable, it is less clear that accountability is best served if they can take significant expenditure decisions' (Response: 1988 p.5).

4 Councillors in London: Representation and social background

(a)   Gender of Councillors

The June 1987 General Election secured increased female representation in the House of Commons and saw the election of the first black woman MP, Diane Abbott, MP for Hackney North and Stoke Newington. Until 1987, the percentage of women MPs rarely got close to 5% (Stacey and Price 1981 p.141). In 1987, the number rose to 41, or 6.45%.

By contrast, women's representation in local government has been much higher, a factor not unrelated to attitudes within society generally which see the role of local councillor equally suited to women and men; an argument supported by some 85% of respondents in the British Social Attitudes survey (Witherspoon 1985 p.76). Table 4.1 shows[1] how the number of female councillors in the UK has climbed steadily, from 12% in 1964, to 17% in 1976, reaching 19% by 1985. As a percentage of the population this is relatively small, and compares unfavourably with, for example, Sweden (30%) and the USSR (51%). However, women are generally under-represented internationally in local authorities except in the

TABLE 4.1

Women's Representation at Local Level: Some Comparisons (%)

	male	female	N
UK 1964	88	12	3947
UK 1976	83	17	4731
UK 1985	81	19	1552
UK Population	49	51	-
Sweden 1980	70	30	-
Netherlands 1978	87	13	-
Spain 1982	92	8	-
Iceland 1982	88	12	-
USSR	49	51	-

Source: Widdicombe (1986: 19) for UK no absolute numbers
(N) given): Mossuz-Lavau and Sineau (1984: 11 and
corrigendum) - (No absolute numbers given) for
Sweden, Netherlands, Spain and Iceland: and Shaul
(1982) for USSR - No absolute numbers given.

TABLE 4.2

Gender of London Councillors: 1964, 1985 and 1990 (%)

	Male			Female			Nmale			Nfemale		
	64	85	90	64	85	90	64	85	90	64	85	90
Inner London	82	74	70	18	26	30	591	519	489	129	184	215
Outer London	85	80	76	15	20	24	970	970	921	169	241	290
GLC		82	--		18	--		75	--		17	--
City of London		91	88		9	12		147	142		14	19
London Overall		79	75		21	25		1711	1552		456	523
London Councillor Survey Population		27	--		100	--		456	--		456	--

Sources: 1964 figures from <u>Municipal Year book</u> (1964); other figures from <u>Municipal Year Book</u> (1985), London Counciilor Survey, and information provided by Local Authorities in London on request.

USSR and the Eastern bloc - figures are given in the Table for the Netherlands (13%), Spain (8%) and Iceland (12%) - so the UK is far from being the lowest.

National figures nonetheless conceal quite wide variations, with women increasingly represented in urban areas, particularly the London Boroughs, English Metropolitan Districts and Scottish Districts (Widdicombe 1986 p.20). The London figures, for example, though fairly high at 21%, conceal very wide differences as shown in Table 4.2. Table 4.2 contains data collected specifically for the book which henceforth is referred to as the 'London Councillor Survey'.

Moreover, the May 1986 and May 1990 local elections increased female representation in the London Boroughs even further: Table 4.3 shows. outer London representation rising to 24%, and inner London to 30%

The London Councillor Survey reported here took 100% of the female councillor population, together with a numerically equal, but randomly selected, sample of male councillors. This facilitated the development of an approach which enabled:

(a) access to the expressed views of women, who have been generally present in small numbers only in other surveys. Widdicombe, for example, used a 10% sample of a population in which women were already under-represented, constituting only 19% of all councillors (1986 p.15);

(b) specific focus on gender-related issues, thereby correcting the in-built bias of other studies. As we saw in Chapter 3, although one of the main purposes of Widdicombe was to provide 'information on the views and attitudes of councillors towards some of the current issues of importance in local government', issues of gender were not included (1986 p.15);

(c) comparison between women and men, unlike for example the research by Martlew et al. (1985) which concerned itself specifically with women; and

(d) comparison between men and women of different political parties, unlike, for example, Campbell's *The Iron Ladies* (1987), which focussed on Tory women. Table 4.4 shows the breakdown of gender by political party in the London Survey.

TABLE 4.3

Proportions of Women Councillors in London: Changes at May 1986 and May 1990 Local Elections (%)

		Inner London	Outer London	London Boroughs Overall
	N =	703	1211	1914
Before May 1986		26	20	22
After May 1986		30	21	24
After May 1990		30	24	26

Source: Information provided by London Boroughs individually on request.

TABLE 4.4

Party Political Membership of London Councillors Surveyed

	Male		Female	
	%	N	%	N
Conservative	41.1	(117)	39.8	(117)
Labour	49.1	(140)	45.9	(135)
Liberal (b)	7.0	(20)	8.2	(24)
SDP (b)	0.4	(1)	1.7	(5)
Other	2.5	(7)	4.4	(13)
Total (a)	100.1	(285)	100.0	(294)

(a)   Figures may not add up to 100% because of rounding.
(b)   In the Tables which follow Liberal, SDP and Alliance councillors are grouped together under the heading 'Lib'.

70

(b)   Political Representation

Increases in party political affiliation have been a characteristic of local politics, noted from at least the Maud Report of 1964 (Widdicombe 1986 p.19), and swings in party political representation are well established phenomena in both local and national politics. Table 4.5 shows the Conservative Party to have had the majority of seats in the mid-1980s in England, Scotland and Wales: swings to the Labour Party occurred in the May 1986 local elections.

This, however, conceals wide variations in party political representation. In London, for example, the difference between the inner and outer Boroughs is quite marked. Table 4.6 shows eight inner London Boroughs in the hands of Labour, with four Conservative (one of which had no overall majority - Hammersmith and Fulham). In the outer Boroughs, four were held by Labour and fourteen by the Conservatives (in one of which there was no overall majority - Brent), together with two Boroughs where the Labour and Conservative parties depended equally on Alliance support for control (Richmond upon Thames, and Waltham Forest); such Boroughs were 'hung', or 'balanced'. Inner London thus had majority Labour control, with the Conservatives dominant in the outer Boroughs.

As can be seen, Labour also had control of the GLC, although if added together, the seats of all opposition parties (including one vacancy) came to the same number as those held by Labour - forty six.

(c)   Length of Service: Party Membership/Office of Councillor

Although details were not available for national comparison, London councillors were asked how long they had been members of their respective political parties. As can be seen from Table 4.7, most councillors had been party members for ten years or more.

The differences that exist are those between political party, and gender. Labour councillors had significantly shorter service[2] with their political parties than the Conservatives, consistent with increased Conservative recruitment of candidates from the 65+ age group (McGrew & Bristow 1984 p.74).

Particularly marked here is the difference between Labour and Liberal women and Conservative women: some 63% of Labour and 75% of Liberal women had been members for less than twenty one years, this was true for

71

TABLE 4.5

Party Political Representation in Local Councils: 1985/86 (%)

	England,(1) Scotland and Wales	London(2)	London Councillor Survey*
N =	1491	2167	602
Conservative	40	50	40
Labour	33	41	48
Liberal/SDP/Alliance	10	7	9
Other (3)	16	2	3
Total	100	100	100

(1) Source: Widdicombe (1986: 38)

(2) Source: Municipal Year Book (1986: 764); adapted for percentages. The figures include GLC, Inner and Outer Boroughs. The City of London has "no party politics".

(3) Includes Independent, SNP, Plaid Cymru, Ratepayers/Residents Associations and vacancies

*   This indicates the degree of representativeness of the London Councillor survey sample in terms of party political affiliation: there is a slight bias towards under-representation of Conservatives and over-representation of Labour, caused by the weighting of the sample towards women. In analysing the results of the London Councillor Survey, the two populations of men and women will generally be treated separately.

72

TABLE 4.6

Party Representation in London - GLC, Corporation of London and Boroughs: 1985/86 (1)

(a) Greater London Council: Lab.46; C.41;L.1;SD.3;V.1   Total Seats: 92
      Corporation of London (City): Has no party politics   Total Seats:161

Abbreviations: (a) Party Representation
IND=Independent.C=Conservative.LAB=Labour.L=Liberal.SD=Social Democrat.
ALL=Lib/SD Alliance.RA=Ratepayers Residents Association.O=Others, including members not declaring any affiliation (*Ind.Lab. +Ind.C.V.=Vacancies)
(b) London Boroughs. (I)=Inner London(within ILEA area).(O)=Outer London Borough(with own education services).

London Boroughs (32)	IND.	C.	LAB.	L.	SD	ALL	RA.	O.	V.	Seats
Inner London (12)(I)										
Camden		26	33							59
Greenwich		16	43	2		1				62
Hackney		3	50	6				*	1	60
Hammersmith & Fulham		23	21	3				3*		50
Islington			49			3				52
Kensington & Chelsea (Royal)	1	39	14							54
Lambeth		26	34		4					64
Lewisham		28	39							67
Southwark		8	50			3		3*		64
Tower Hamlets	1		30	19						50
Wandsworth		33	26			2				61
Westminster City	1	42	15					1+	1*	60
(b) TOTAL - Inner London	3	244	404	30	4	9	–	7	2	703
Outer London (20)(O)										
Barking & Dagenham	2	3	36	3			3		1	48
Barnet		47	13							60
Bexley		38	14			9			1	62
Brent		31	31	3					1	66
Bromley		50	5			5				60
Croydon		62	5				3			70
Ealing	2	34	30			3		1+		70
Enfield		47	19							66
Haringey		23	36							59
Harrow		40	6	13			4			63
Havering		37	12			5	9			63
Hillingdon		57	10			2				69
Hounslow		27	33							60
Kingston upon Thames (Royal)		38	3			9				50
Merton		43	13				1			57
Newham			56	1	3					60
Redbridge		49	12			2				63
Richmond upon Thames		24		26		2				52
Sutton		41	7			8				56
Waltham Forest		25	25	7						57
(c) TOTAL - Outer London Boroughs	4	716	366	53	3	45	20	1	3	1,211
TOTAL Inner & Outer (b) + (c)	7	960	770	83	7	54	20	8	5	1,914
TOTAL GLC, Inner & Outer (a) + (b) + (c)	7	1001	816	84	10	54	20	8	6	

(1) Source : <u>Municipal Year Book</u> (1986 : 764) (adapted)

TABLE 4.7

London Councillor Survey: Length of Party Membership (%)

	Cons		Lab		Lib		Total	
	m	f	m	f	m	f	m	f
N =	116	115	140	135	20	24	278	287
0 - 3 years	0	0	0	1	0	4	0	1
4 - 9 years	11	6	10	23	20	46	12	19
10 - 20 years	40	34	50	39	60	25	46	35
21 years or more	49	60	40	37	20	25	42	45
Total	100	100	100	100	100	100	100	100

only 40% of Conservative women. When we take membership of twenty years or more, 37% of Labour women were in this category, 25% of the Liberals and 60% of the Conservative women. 94% of the Conservative women councillors had been party members for ten years or more.

This quite clearly has something to do with age: female councillors tend to be older than male, though this is more marked within the Conservative Party, whose councillors are generally older than Labour and Liberal (see also Barron et al 1987 p.258). More will be said of the age profiles later.

When we consider councillors by length of service (Table 4.8), we find no significant difference between Conservative and Labour party, or gender, using a chi-squared test; though Liberal men tend to have fewer years of service, as do Liberals generally and women (particularly in Scotland). The other point worth noting is that Conservative women councillors tend to have longer service than women from the other political parties, though the difference is not marked; we have already noted that they tend to be older, and have been party members longer than any other group.

The tendency not to remain for more than ten and rarely beyond twenty years in local politics, with the concomitant that service tends to be two, or perhaps three, terms of office is borne out by evidence from the Widdicombe Report for the years 1964, 1976 and 1985, and by Martlew for 1983 in Scotland. It is also worth noting that many councillors in the London Survey indicated that they would not be standing again.

Given the average period of two or three terms, it is an interesting question why councillors decided to stand for office in the first place. If local politics is a major stepping stone to parliamentary office,[3] a route where the 'art' of politics is learned, and the participants become socialised into the political community, we might expect to find such ambitions voiced by councillors at the outset.

(d)   Reasons for Standing as a Councillor

Table 4.9 shows the results of a question asked of councillors to do with 'the how' and 'the why' of standing for election. The question asked was 'why did you decide to stand for election as a councillor?', and the answers were coded according to both the means (of being able to stand for office) and the goals mentioned.

TABLE 4.8

Councillors' Length of Service as a Councillor (%)

	Widdicombe for:(1)			Scottish (2) Councillors		London Councillor Survey for:							
	1964	1976	1985			Cons		Lab		Lib		Total	
	m + f	m + f	m + f	m	f	m	f	m	f	m	f	m	f
N =	3930	4691	1536	742	115	117	116	140	133	20	24	285	291
0 - 3 years	26	28	25			2	2	6	10	25	38	6	9
4 - 9 years	31	35	40	56	67	56	56	56	63	70	54	58	58
10 - 20 years	39	26	32	28	24	28	33	25	20	5	8	25	25
21 years or more	9	10	3	16	9	15	10	14	8	0	0	13	8
Total	105*	99	100	100	100	101	101	101	101	100	100	102	100

(1) Source: Widdicombe (1986: 35)
(2) Source: Martlew (1985: 63)
* Note: The figures given in Widdicombe are accurately transcribed here
    except for the total – in Widdicombe the total is incorrectly given as 100

Given the fact that this question was open-ended the method of coding was given special attention, and was designed to allow the responses to 'speak for themselves', without the suffocation of a rigid categorisation.

To this end, a random sample of fifty replies were extracted for consideration to see what, if anything, they had in common. Patterns *were* discerned in the overall coding process. As the final result shows, the categories elicited were appropriate due to the low number of residual 'other' factors.

In mentioning 'means', or facilitators for office, the most common reason advanced was that councillors had been *asked* to stand: no Liberal men made any mention of 'means' at all, though the Liberal female councillors asked to become involved constituted 50%. This stands out as the main facilitator, with many Labour and Conservative councillors being encouraged by others. For some, time becoming available was clearly important, though not overwhelmingly so. The ability to undertake the onerous duties of Council office, however, is clearly related to family issues for women: whilst only 8% of male Labour councillors suggested that they stood for election because the family had grown up, and no Liberal or Conservative male councillors referred to this, female councillors were more likely to mention this: some 13% of Conservative, 24% of Labour, and 25% of Liberal women councillors advanced this reason.[4]

This issue of selection by invitation raises questions related more specifically to 'sponsorship'. In contrasting two ideal-types of social ascent through education, sponsored and contest mobility, Turner noted that sponsorship offered the chosen an early route into elite membership in a society. Selection, he argued, was followed by 'sponsored induction' into this 'private club' (Turner 1960 p.122 and 123). Such concerns echo the preoccupations of the early elite theorists about 'infiltration' and 'restocking of ruling classes' (Pareto 1966 p.162 and Mosca 1939 p.68).

Turner's work raises two important issues of special relevance here. First, that selection tends to work *against* the absorption of previously under-represented groups. Second, that it must operate early on in the socialisation process if it is to succeed in successfully orienting the new social recruit; delay can cause 'strain' which may result in non-assimilation (Turner 1960 pp.134-5).

Turner's focus of attention was education and, more specifically, schooling, but his concerns do offer two insights into the position of female councillors. First, that lack of sponsorship may help to account for their under-representation in local politics, compared to their size in the population.[5] Second, that the delay in participation *affects* their assimilation into the 'private club' of local party politics. The material constraint of responsibility for family and household, as we will see later, affects women's ability and readiness to stand for office quite strongly. Perhaps it also affects the values they will have assimilated by the time they do take up office, with a weaker party identification leaving space for social movement influence.

Before moving on to consider *why* councillors decided to stand, it might be worth noting the results of a survey by McGrew and Bristow (1984) of candidates for the Metropolitan Counties. Although the differences between Metropolitan Counties and London may have a prejudicial effect, and whilst candidates are clearly not the same as councillors, the Metropolitan Survey provides a useful benchmark against which to compare the London Councillor Survey.

As McGrew and Bristow argue 'the two dominant motives for standing were the desire to further one's party organisation or policy and the desire to serve the community' (1984 p.83); Table 4.9 (c) shows the overall results of their survey.

They suggest that the role of 'community service' for Conservatives 'sat conveniently' with their 'emphasis upon local issues'; whilst for 'many Labour candidates party policy and efficacy underpinned their orientation towards council service', though 'perhaps more surprisingly, respondents provided little evidence of any serious ideological commitment to societal change' (op cit. p.84).

So, for McGrew and Bristow, Metropolitan County candidates seek largely to further their party organisation or policy, and to serve their communities without pushing to 'change society' in any significant way. The issue of 'political apprenticeship' is also taken up by McGrew and Bristow, but this is secondary, though related to, the analysis of motivation, and will be pursued later.

TABLE 4.9

Reasons for Standing as a Councillor

(a) <u>HOW</u> - Means or facilitators mentioned: London Councillor Survey %

	Cons		Lab		Lib		Total	
	m	f	m	f	m	f	m	f
N =	26	31	26	38	3	4	55	79
Family grown up	0	13	8	24	0	25	4	18
Asked to	73	65	73	63	0	50	75	66
Time available	12	16	8	3	0	0	9	8
Other	15	7	12	11	0	25	13	9
Total	100	101	101	101	0	100	101	101
Mean not mentioned	0	0	0	0	100	0	0	0

(b) <u>WHY</u> - Goals mentioned: London Councillor Survey %

	Cons		Lab		Lib		Total	
	m	f	m	f	m	f	m	f
N =	102	105	126	124	18	23	251	263
To help others	4	14	3	6	0	4	3	9
To serve the community	26	19	14	12	28	26	20	16
Local issue important	14	19	17	14	6	17	15	16
To aid the party	24	12	33	21	33	22	28	17
For power	23	24	29	22	22	26	26	23
For women	0	0	0	18	0	4	0	9
Other	11	11	6	8	11	0	8	10
Total	102	99	102	101	100	99	100	100

(c) Metropolitan Counties Candidates Survey:
Candidates' Ranking of Motives for Candidacy

	First	Second	Third	Fourth
Conservative	Community service	Personal ambition	Party support	Token ambition
Labour	Party support	Community service	Personal ambition	Change society
Liberal	Party support	Community service	Token candidacy	Personal ambition
Overall	Party support	Community service	Personal ambition	Token candidacy

Source: McGrew & Bristow (1984: 84, Table 4.11, no absolute numbers in Table).

Turning now to the London Councillor Survey, it is not easy to offer simple interpretations on Table 4.9 though three points are worth making. First, 18% of Labour women councillors and 4% of Liberal women councillors said that they had stood for office to benefit women in some way. No man mentioned this, or its male parallel, and no Conservative woman.[6] Involvement in different types of women's groups may account for this, though more will be said of this later.

Secondly, more men than women said they stood for election to aid the party: the possibility of local politics being seen as a route to a political career of some kind, perhaps to prospective parliamentary candidate as we noted earlier, might be relevant here, suggesting an important distinction between male and female aspirations.

Thirdly, an issue arises if we divide the categories in the following way:

		Total % m	f
(a)	To help others To serve community Local issue important	38	41
(b)	To aid the Party For power	54	40
(c)	For women	0	9

This is a useful grouping, since the distinction between 'To aid the party' and 'For power' was often difficult to maintain despite what McGrew and Bristow argue and presented quite serious coding problems. Included under my 'For power' category, for example, were the following comments:

'the attraction of political activity'
'natural progress to get involved'
'desire to achieve concrete results from political
            beliefs = *praxis*'
'to force through change'
'to further the interests of the working class'
'desire to get things done'

'because I'd be better than the previous lot'.

This means that, discounting those who mentioned that they stood 'For women', there is a fairly even split between a desire for the exercise of political power, and a wish to become involved for reasons more related to the locality, with the former only marginally more important. This was a point that arose in the interviewing programme which followed the survey, with many councillors seeing local politics as an end in itself, rather than a means to achieving some other goal. This point is elaborated in Chapter 6.

If we include the 'For women' category with those related to the locality,[7] we can discern an important difference between men and women, with women slightly more oriented to 'community' issues, something argued by Martlew (1985) and Barron et al (1987) but missed by McGrew and Bristow. Martlew's remarks are made in the context of councillors' involvement with organisations prior to engagement with local politics, and suggest 'the importance of community politics as a recruitment path for female councillors ... [who] ... may not seek power as an end in itself' (1985 p.52 and 60). More will be said of this later, after we have considered whether other factors have played a part in this process, particularly the family background. First, we might pause to see just how important local issues *are* to councillors, in terms of their local reading.

(e)   Regular Reading - Newspapers and Journals

A question was included to see whether there were any differences between political parties, and men and women, in terms of what they read (Table 4.10). The question was 'which newspaper(s) and journal(s) do you read on a regular basis?' Rather than go into any great detail about the type of newspapers or journals, however, it was decided to code the responses by the number of items read regularly, and the mention of 'local' and 'womens' reading. This means that comparison with national reading habits is not possible, nor necessarily desirable since this was not the purpose of the question. The intention was, rather, to seek differences in regular reading in terms of local and women's issues.

Little difference emerges. It could be argued that Liberal councillors read less than their Labour and Conservative counterparts, though it might be unwise to draw any firm conclusions from this. Most councillors would seem to read between one and three items regularly.

TABLE 4.10

Regular Reading - Newspapers and Journals: London Councillor Survey (%)

Number of items
read regularly

	Cons m	f	Lab m	f	Lib m	f	Total m	f
N =	117	115	140	134	20	24	285	289
None	3	4	0	2	0	8	1	3
1 - 3	58	53	60	57	70	75	61	57
4 - 6	26	28	27	23	10	13	25	25
Over 6	14	16	14	19	20	4	14	16
Total	101	101	101	101	100	100	101	101

Local Reading

	m	f	m	f	m	f	m	f
N =	117	115	140	133	20	24	285	288
Mentioned	22	18	16	22	15	21	18	20
Not mentioned	78	82	84	78	85	79	82	80
Total	100	100	100	100	100	100	100	100

Women's reading

	m	f	m	f	m	f	m	f
N =	117	115	139	133	20	24	284	288
Mentioned	1	10	0	7	0	4	0	7
Not mentioned	99	90	100	93	100	96	100	93
Total	100	100	100	100	100	100	100	100

Nor is there any significant difference in party political or gender terms in local reading, for example, of local papers. Around 20% of both male and female councillors, for example, said that they read local newspapers on a regular basis. This would support the suggestion that no firm conclusions can be drawn about party differences in terms of local/community issues versus party loyalties in contradistinction to McGrew and Bristow. Both gender, and survey coding factors, play a far more important role than they acknowledge.

This contrasts with the findings on 'women's reading', in that a much lower percentage mention reading women's publications. The kind of reading noted here included *'Woman's Own'*, 'various women's magazines', *'Cosmopolitan'* and *'Outwrite'*. The way the question was worded, however, may be responsible for this relatively low response - perhaps use of the term 'magazine' might have prompted more mention. As it stands, only 1% of Conservative male councillors mentioned that they consulted 'women's reading' on a regular basis, with no Labour or Liberal men. By contrast, 10% of Conservative women councillors mentioned 'women's reading', 7% of Labour women, and 4% of Liberal women. This is a relatively high response given the wording of the question, and, even though the absolute figures are low, represents a clear difference in gender terms. Though this is unlikely to surprise anyone, the absence of male readers does suggest a taken-for-granted world of assumptions within 'women's reading' on which men do not draw; this is clearly true even for publications as widely different as *Woman's Own* and *Outwrite* (a lesbian publication which recently closed down, Laws 1989 p.31).

(f)   Councillors and 'Political Families'

Consideration of the motivations for elected membership would be incomplete without looking at the influence of the family since the literature would suggest this plays an important role in the lives of elected members generally (Stacey and Price 1981 pp.156-8). Such influence can clearly work in contradictory ways: as an obstacle to participation, or as a spring to action.

Respondents in the London Councillor Survey were asked whether any member of their family had ever been involved in politics. As Table 4.11 shows, some 59% of female, compared to 47% of male councillors, answered 'yes', suggesting the importance of role models and direct experience for

TABLE 4.11

Councillors and 'Political Families': London Councillor Survey (%)

(a) "Have any members of your family ever been involved in politics?"

| | Cons | | Lab | | Lib | | Total | |
	m	f	m	f	m	f	m	f
N =	115	116	133	132	20	24	276	289
Yes	42	55	53	65	50	42	47	59
No	58	45	47	35	50	58	53	41
Total	100	100	100	100	100	100	100	100

(b) "If 'yes', who?"

| | Cons | | Lab | | Lib | | Total | |
	m	f	m	f	m	f	m	f
N =	74	94	111	131	13	19	198	244
Mother	20	19	20	22	23	26	20	21
Father	35	20	36	37	15	16	34	24
Partner	18	28	17	19	23	16	18	22
Other Female Relative	7	10	10	11	8	11	9	10
Other Male Relative	20	23	17	21	31	32	19	23
Totals	100	100	100	100	100	101	100	100

(c) "How were they involved in politics?"

| | Cons | | Lab | | Lib | | Total | |
	m	f	m	f	m	f	m	f
N =	38	52	61	69	8	13	107	134
As M.P.	11	6	0	0	0	23	4	5
As Councillor	32	31	20	29	13	46	23	31
Local/central Candidate	3	6	3	3	50	8	7	4
Member of Political Party	42	44	44	28	38	15	43	33
Member of Trades Union	13	13	33	41	0	8	23	77
Totals	101	100	100	101	101	100	100	100

women (particularly in the Labour Party - though the Labour councillors featured higher in their response to this question anyway).

Councillors were then asked to enter details of the family members so involved. This question produced a wide variety of responses, with some councillors mentioning several family members whilst others moved on to the next question.

The absolute numbers of Liberal respondents is too low to make comment worthwhile, but it would appear that for Conservative and Labour councillors the influence of parents is considerable with many fathers of councillors having been involved in politics. Next come mothers, more or less equal with partners and other male relatives. Fathers are also mentioned more often by male councillor respondents. This would seem to confirm the inportance of role models for all councillors and is not surprising.

What is surprising is the number of mothers and other female relatives mentioned (nearly one third, excluding wives) when women's actual representation in local and antional politics is so much lower than that of men.

In respect of involvement, councillors' family members were predominantly members of political parties and councillors themselves. There were no Labour councillors with family members as MPs though some 11% of Conservative men and 6% of Conservative women had MP family connections (again, low absolute numbers were recorded for the Liberal respondents). As would be expected more Labour councillors then Conservative mentioned Trade Union as well as other political activity.

All in all, the higher profile of women family members in the lives of London's councillors is greater then might have been expected given their lower representation in formal parties compared to men.[8]

(g)   Councillors by Age and Gender

Having considered the political composition and experience of councillors, it is worth pausing to consider their social background - to build up a profile of councillors in London in order to see how far, if at all, 'elected members as a group are ... highly unrepresentative of the overall population' (Widdicombe 1986 p.19). This means looking at such things as the age, marital status, place of work, and housing tenure of councillors in London.

We noted earlier that Conservatives generally and Conservative women in particular tended to have longer service as councillors than any other group, and that they had been party members for longer (Tables 4.8 and 4.7 respectively). Table 4.12 confirms that they also tend to be older (33% over 60 years of age compared to 16% for Labour women and 8% for Liberal women).

The age profiles shown here were difficult to tabulate for purposes of comparison, since the decile categorisation used in the London Councillor Survey differed from Widdicombe: this has been partly compensated for by using an OPCS County Monitor for Greater London, which enable further comparison with the region itself.

These problems, however, render comparative analysis problematic, though by taking note of the following observations from the Widdicombe Report, we may be able to derive *something* of value from comparisons with the London Councillor Survey. The Report noted that:

(a)   'in all authorities, with the exception of the Welsh Counties and Districts and the English Shire Districts, there has been an increase in the number of elected members aged less than 45' (1986 p.20);

(b)   this is 'most marked in the metropolitan areas, London Boroughs and Scottish districts, where it has been coupled with a decrease in those aged 60 or over' (ibid.);

(c)   'Almost half of Liberal councillors were under 45, compared to less than 20% of Conservatives, and less then one in ten Independents' (op cit.p.38); and

(d)   'the changes [between 1964 and 1985] may be summed up as councillors as a body becoming more *diverse*, rather than younger' (op cit.p.22).

As Widdicombe further remarks 'the increase in the proportion of younger councillors in the metropolitan areas would appear to explain the image of the councillor as distinctively younger than before, as recent publicity has centred to a great extent on these authorities' (op cit.p.20).

So London, in common with other metropolitan areas, has a larger than average proportion of younger councillors, confirmed in Table 4.12 for members up to 30 years of age, when compared with Widdicombe for members up to 34. We can also see that London has a smaller percentage of councillors over 60 years - with 2% more women than men, (23% and 21% respectively), compared with 29% of women and 37% of men councillors

86

TABLE 4.12

Councillors' Age (%)

(a) Official Surveys

	Greater London(1) m + f	Widdicombe(2) popul- ation 1985		G.B. Councillors 1964		1976		1985		Scottish Counci- llors(3) 1983	
		m	f	m	f	m	f	m	f	m	f
N =	6608598			3445	485	3848	795	1245	289	744	115
< 35 years	51	32	29	5	2	9	8	6	9	-	-
< 31 years	-	-	-	-	-	-	-	-	-	4	0
< 61 years	82	75	67	-	-	65	70	62	67	70	68
> 60 years	18	25	33	-	-	35	29	37	29	30	32
Total	100	100	100	-	-	100	99	99	96*	100	100

(b) London Councillor Survey

	Cons		Lab		Lib		Total	
	m	f	m	f	m	f	m	f
N =	117	112	140	132	20	24	285	286
< 35 years	-	-	-	-	-	-	-	-
< 31 years	5	5	4	8	15	8	5	7
< 61 years	76	67	81	84	95	92	79	77
> 60 years	24	33	19	16	5	8	21	23
Total	100	100	100	100	100	100	100	100

(1) Source: OPCS County Monitor Reference CEN81 CM56 (1982: 9). No breakdown
        by gender.
(2) Source: Widdicombe (1986 : 21). No absolute figures for population.
(3) Source: Martlew (1985 : 63)

Note: "-" indicates no entry, due to incomparability of data
        * 96% is the figure recorded in Widdicombe (1986: 21).

nationally; in other words, the age profiles of women councillors in London are similar to those of men councillors there, unlike councillors elsewhere.

(h) Marital Status

More councillors, generally, tend 'to be married than in the population as a whole ... primarily a reflection of the different age structure of councillors - more in those age groups are likely either to be married or to have been married' (Widdicombe 1986 p.22). Yet London councillors do differ in this respect as Table 4.13 shows, in that the numbers married reflect more closely the population with slightly more men married than women, 64% - 59% respectively in the population, compared to 67% - 61% among London councillors. They are more likely to be single, divorced, separated or widowed, when compared to councillors elsewhere.

London Liberal councillors deserve special mention: nearly twice as many men are single, divorced, separated or widowed, compared to women (45% - 26%), though the general trend is just the opposite: female councillors in this category clearly outnumber the male. The low absolute numbers of Liberal councillor respondents, however, means that this might not be representative of Liberals generally.

We noted earlier that Conservative female councillors tend to be older, to have been party members longer than any other group, and to have given longer service as councillors. Any conclusion that this might have meant a greater involvement of widowed Conservative female councillors (given the difference in life expectancy between the sexes (Haralambos 1986 pp.304-306), is shown to be hasty and ill-conceived, judging from Table 4.13. Indeed, what is interesting is the party difference: if the Conservative Party is the party of the 'family', Labour may be the party of the serially monogamous partnership. This conclusion was borne out in the interviews, when Labour councillors frequently mentioned difficulties in relationships with their partners, some explaining that they had been divorced, and were now re-married, a factor not accounted for in either of the surveys mentioned in Table 4.13.

TABLE 4.13

Councillors by Marital Status and Gender (%)

	Widdicombe (1)						London Councillor Survey:							
	Population 1985		Councillors- 1976		1985		Cons		Lab		Lib		Total	
	m	f	m	f	m	f	m	f	m	f	m	f	m	f
N =	not given		3902	816	1250	300	115	116	138	134	20	23	281	291
Single	29	22	6	8	6	5	17	21	20	24	30	17	19	21
Married	64	59	90	75	88	76	73	63	62	53	55	74	67	61
Divorced/ Separated/ Widowed	8	19	4	17	6	18	10	16	17	23	15	9	14	19
Total	101	100	100	100	100	99	100	100	99	100	100	100	100	101

(1) Source: Widdicombe (1986: 23)

89

(i)   Place of Birth and Time Lived in London

It is not possible to compare London councillors with councillors more generally as data are not available, though it *is* useful to see how generally representative a group of people they are and to consider the differences between them. This is facilitated by Table 4.14.

The first thing to note is that Greater London has a high proportion of residents who were born outside the UK; this is particularly so for inner London with 24% of such residents. The number of London councillors born outside the UK is half this figure, though still about twice the Great Britain average of 6%.

When looking at party differences, we find more Liberal and Conservative councillors born in England, compared to Labour (around 90%-80%). The other differences appear to be related more closely to gender, although party remains an important variable.

Some 8% of Labour women come from Ireland, twice that of Conservative women, Conservative men and Labour men (no Liberals came from Ireland), and more Labour men come from Scotland and the New Commonwealth and Pakistan (6% and 10% respectively) than any other category of councillor. These aside, other small differences do emerge. For example, 5% of male Liberal councillors came from the Old Commonwealth and 3% of Labour females. We can also see that more Conservative and Liberal female councillors (5% and 4% respectively) were born in the New Commonwealth and Pakistan; the other groups - Labour men notwithstanding - are less well represented. There were no Liberal councillors born in Scotland, or in Ireland, whilst 4% of Liberal women were born in the European Community, compared with only 1% of Labour women, and no other councillors. These figures are very small, and do not lend themselves to generalisation.

When we consider town of birth we note that only about half of all London councillors were born in Greater London, with nearly 40% born outside the South East area. This may be a little surprising, given that only about 15% of all councillors in the London Councillor Survey were born outside England, but may well confirm a kind of 'London effect'. If London *is* acting as a kind of magnet, it may well be attracting certain kinds of people from elsewhere. A point worth acknowledging in this respect is the higher than average percentage of women in London local politics which we saw earlier (Tables 4.2 and 4.3), and the higher than average educational

TABLE 4.14

(a) Councillor's Place of Birth: Country: London Councillor Survey (%)

	Cons m	Cons f	Lab m	Lab f	Lib m	Lib f	Total m	Total f
N =	115	114	137	134	19	24	278	289
England	90	89	79	81	90	88	85	86
Scotland	0	2	6	3	0	0	3	2
Wales	1	2	2	2	0	4	1	2
Ireland	4	3	4	8	0	0	4	5
Old Commonwealth (Australia/ Canada/New Z.)	0	0	0	3	5	0	1	1
New Commonwealth + Pakistan	1	5	10	2	0	4	5	4
European Community	0	0	0	1	0	4	0	1
Other	4	0	0	1	5	0	2	0
Total	100	101	101	101	100	100	101	101

(b) Councillors' Place of Birth: Region: London Councillor Survey (%)

	Cons m	Cons f	Lab m	Lab f	Lib m	Lib f	Total m	Total f
N =	115	112	137	134	20	24	279	286
S.East/Greater London	57	54	52	43	50	42	54	48
S.East/Outer Met.	6	6	7	10	10	4	7	8
S.East/Outer S.E.	7	4	4	4	0	13	5	5
Other	30	37	37	44	40	42	34	40
Total	100	101	100	101	100	101	100	101

(c) Population Born Outside the UK (%)

	London Councillor Survey m	London Councillor Survey f	Inner (1+2) London Population	Outer (1+2) London Population	Great (1+2) Britain
N =	32	31			
Ireland/Old Commonwealth(Aus. Canada.New Z.)/New Common + Pakistan/ European Comm./and Other	12	11	24	15	6

(1) Source: OPCS County Monitor Reference CEN81 CM56 (1982: 10)
for all countries outside UK. (No absolute numbers given).
(2) Note: 4% Inner London Population, 3% Outer London and 1% GB, born in
Ireland.
12% Inner London Population, 8% Outer London and 3% GB, born in New
Commonwealth and Pakistan.
Source: Census, 1981 Key Statistics for Local Authorities in Great
Britain Ref. CEN81 KSLA (1984: 30). (No absolute numbers given).

qualifications possessed by London councillors, which will be considered shortly.

Before jumping to the conclusion that local politics is the causal factor, or magnet, however, we should pause to consider Table 4.15, which is concerned with the length of time lived in London, cross-tabulated by gender and area. Here, there is virtually no difference between men and women, with some three-quarters of both having lived in London for over 20 years. We saw earlier (Table 4.8) that councillors' service tends to be two or three terms of office, so it would look as if *people* are attracted by London, perhaps by the political milieux, but still by London in some way, and only after they have been there for some time do they venture into the waters of local politics. Hardly the 'carpet-baggers' they were labelled by Michael Heseltine in the early 1980s!

One final point. Cross-tabulation of gender with area on this issue does produce an interesting finding: that over twice as many female councillors (24%) have lived in inner, compared to outer London (11%), for between 10-20 years, closer, as we have seen, to the period of office more commonly associated with elected membership. The figure of 24% for female councillors in inner London is also considerably higher than the 15% recorded for men.

(j)   Perceptions of Ethnicity

It is appropriate, in considering origins of councillors, that we look at their perceptions of their own ethnicity. A question was included in the London Councillor Survey which asked, 'which ethnic group would you say you belong to, if any?'

When considering the individual responses to this question, it soon became obvious that a wide variety of perceptions had been adumbrated, which differed from the following classification used by the Commission for Racial Equality:[9]

Ethnic Minority	White
1. African	1. U.K. origin
2. Caribbean/W.Indian	2. European
3. Pakistani	3. Other
4. Bangladeshi	
5. Indian	
6. Other	

92

TABLE 4.15

Length of Time Lived in London: London Councillor Survey (%)

	Inner London m	f	Outer London m	f	Total m	f
N =	113	125	150	140	282	284
0 - 3 years	0	1	0	0	0	0
4 - 9 years	8	8	1	3	4	6
10 - 20 years	15	24	20	11	18	19
over 20 years	77	66	79	85	77	75
currently living outside London	0	1	0	1	0	1
Total	100	100	100	100	99	101

Because of this a sample of some 50 answers were extracted and examined for patterns. The cross-tabulation in Table 4.16 is the result. As with categorisations shown elsewhere in the data, the residual 'other' category has a relatively small percentage of responses, so the classification would appear to be reasonably appropriate, although only just so in this case as it should be borne in mind that the overall 16-17% shown under 'other' is relatively high compared to other residual categories in the London Councillor Survey. Clearly, perceptions of ethnicity differ widely and are not *easily* classifiable. Some of the responses categorised under 'other', for example, were:

> Jewish,
> Caucasian,
> Church of England, and
> Asian

Further, as Fitzgerald explains, 'many people born in the New Commonwealth or Pakistan are not black, and ... black people in this country are increasingly being born in this country ...' (1984 p.15).

Any conclusions which might be drawn from the data should therefore be tentative. Bearing this in mind, Table 4.16 *does* reveal some interesting perceptions.

First, it was only Labour councillors (men and women at 4% and 3% respectively) who said that they thought they belonged to a 'Black' ethnic group; included in this categorisation were those who entered simply 'Black' in answer to the question, as well as those who added something to the 'Black' i.e. 'Black British', or 'Black Jamaican'.

Secondly, there was a greater tendency for Conservative councillors to refer to themselves as 'British and Indigenous' or having a 'UK identity' (i.e. English, Scottish ...) and for Labour councillors to refer to themselves as 'White', 'White caucasian', or 'White C of E'. As with the 'Black' categorisation, those who mentioned their colour as 'White' plus something else were classified under the 'White' category.

What this means is unclear - it is tempting to suggest that the Labour councillors had a tendency to equate ethnicity with 'race' or 'colour' and the Conservatives to equate it with 'nationality' or region. Apart from this, there appears a myriad of perception about ethnic identity - particularly interesting in that around 85-86% of London councillors were born in England, as we saw in Table 4.14.

TABLE 4.16

Perceptions of Ethnicity: London Councillor Survey (%)

	Cons		Lab		Lib		Total	
	m	f	m	f	m	f	m	f
N =	104	105	133	123	19	23	263	268
White + (1)	30	22	41	55	26	22	35	38
Black + (1)	0	0	4	3	0	0	2	2
UK Identity	17	18	17	11	5	9	16	15
British and Indigenous	11	12	6	5	5	4	9	8
European	6	1	5	2	11	4	5	2
Not Recognised	16	31	11	15	21	39	14	23
Other	20	16	17	10	32	22	19	14
Total	100	100	101	101	100	100	100	102

(1) Included in the 'White +' and 'Black +' categories are those
     describing themselves as either 'White' or 'Black', or White or
     Black together with some other characteristic, e.g. 'Black Jamaican'.

The relatively high percentage of 'not recognised' responses may bear witness to this, though it is far from clear what is meant by so high a response, which included those who had gone to the trouble of deleting the question. This may indicate a strength of feeling about the issue itself - indeed, one female councillor wrote 'none of your business'. It was precisely *because* a strength of feeling was anticipated that the term ethnicity was used; and it may be that the strength of feeling was not sensitive to the niceties of that distinction. In any event, such conclusions are mere speculation and in need of further development.

The final point worthy of consideration in this respect is the difference in the proportion of men and women who did not recognise an ethnic identity for themselves (14% and 23% respectively). Women are almost twice as likely *not* to recognise ethnicity, in all three political parties. Conversely, the tendency for men to associate themselves with an ethnic identity may say something more about men than ethnicity: some kind of need for collective status, which women feel less strongly about? This, of course, is the issue of 'reference groups'.

(k)   Housing Tenure

The Widdicombe Report explains that the:

> 'proportion of owner-occupiers has ... increased from 66% in 1964, to 76% in 1976, and 85% in 1985. However, although the proportion of owner-occupiers within the general population (now 57%) has increased significantly over the last twenty years, the rate of increase among councillors has been at a faster pace'.
>
> (1986 p.22 and 23).

Figures for housing tenure from the London Councillor Survey are given in Table 4.17. From this table we see that London councillors differ little from councillors generally, with owner-occupiers being around 79% of the total. This, however, conceals a significant party difference: with the owner-occupation of Labour councillors ranking 15% to 20% lower than Conservatives and Liberals. This may well be related to the greater Labour presence in inner London, where owner-occupiers represent only 27% of all householders. Indeed, other data derived from the Survey differentiates in spatial terms the levels of owner-occupation for London councillors as

TABLE 4.17

Councillors' Housing Tenure (%)

	Population(1) Inner London m + f	Population(1) Outer London m + f	UK Pop-ulation m + f	Widdicombe (2) 1964 m + f	Widdicombe (2) 1976 m + f	Widdicombe (2) 1986 m + f	Cons m	Cons f	Lab m	Lab f	Lib m	Lib f	Total m	Total f
N =	964,934	1,542,722	9995	3970	4607	1550	116	113	136	134	20	24	280	289
Owner Occupier	27	62	57	66	76	85	94	91	65	67	95	83	80	78
Council Rent	43	23	32	16	16	10	1	0	21	25	5	13	11	14
Private: Rent/Rent Free	30	15	11	18	8	4	5	5	10	5	0	0	7	4
Other(3)	-	-	-	-	-	-	0	4	4	4	0	4	2	4
Total	100	100	100	100	100	99	100	100	100	101	100	100	100	100

(1) Source: OPCS County Monitor Ref. CEN81 CM 56 (1982: 14) for Inner and Outer London
(2) Source: Widdicombe (1986: 23)
(3) Includes Co-Operative rented, tied house, housing association.

Note: Neither Widdicombe nor the OPCS County Monitors have an 'Other' category, so it may be prudent to collapse the London Councillor Survey figures into the 'private rent/rent free' category. They remain separated here for purposes of presentation.

97

follows:

GLC	86%
City	80%
Outer London	89%
Inner London	67%

Conversely, we find more Labour councillors living in accommodation rented from local authorities - and again, we find such accommodation associated with inner London residents more generally.

The major conclusion to be drawn about housing tenure, then, is that Labour councillors tend more closely to reflect their constituents and the population generally than the other parties, but that *no* party exactly reflects the people they purport to represent. Councillors are a privileged group when it comes to housing: particularly marked is the mere 1% of Conservative male councillors who live in rented council accommodation; no Conservative women are recorded here.

This is mitigated if we take account of privately rented accommodation, though surveys tend to group such housing with rent free and 'other'. The 'other' category, shown separately for the London Councillor Survey, included 'with my parents', co-operative rented, tied houses, Housing Associations, and so on. If we lump all these together, we find women disproportionately represented here, together with Labour men. It would be difficult to draw any firm conclusions from these data, based on gender, since political party seems to be the more salient variable.

(l)   Dependents Living in Same Household

The London Councillor Survey went on to ask councillors whether they had any children, how many they had, their ages, and how many of these lived with them. Additionally, they were asked if they provided care for anyone else in their household, such as elderly parent(s) or disabled adult(s). The results have been compiled in Table 4.18 (a).

Comparison with other councillors is not possible due to the absence of data, and comparison with Greater London is only possible for households containing any number of children under 5 years of age. This must sound a cautionary note for any conclusions.

98

TABLE 4.18 (a)

Councillors with Dependents Living in Same Household (%)

	Greater London(1) Population m + f	London Councillor Survey: Cons m	Cons f	Lab m	Lab f	Lib m	Lib f	Total m	Total f
N =	296949	80	79	88	85	12	16	186	193
With any number of children under 5	12	15	8	24	17	33	13	20	11
With any number of children 5-16 years	–	30	17	24	34	42	38	28	26
With any number of children over 16 years	–	55	76	52	49	25	50	52	62
Total	–	100	101	100	100	100	101	100	99
N =		115	111	131	128	20	23	274	279
Providing care for elderly parent/ disabled adult etc. (as a % of all councillors)		13	15	11	14	5	4	11	13

(1) Source: OPCS County Monitor Ref. CEN81 CM 56 (1982: 13)

Note: Percentages of councillors with any children: Cons 30%, Labour 34%, Liberal 40% (London Councillor Survey).

TABLE 4.18 (b)

Who Looks After Child(ren) When They are Sick?: British Social Attitudes (%)(1)

	Reported by men	Reported by women
Mainly the men	2	–
Mainly the women	56	70
Shared equally	42	29
Total	100	100

(1) Source: Witherspoon (1985: 57) – no absolute numbers given.

99

What is clear from the data available, however, is that a higher proportion of male councillors in London have children under 5 living in their households - 20% for male councillors, as against 11% for women. Far fewer Conservative councillors are recorded here, particularly Conservative women at 8%, perhaps a reflection of the age profiles discussed previously: Conservative women tend to be older, and may well have entered electoral politics when their children had grown up. We saw from Table 4.9 that 13% of Conservative women councillors said that the family being off their hands was a reason for engaging in politics more actively; this is confirmed by the high 76% of Conservative women who said they had children *over* 16 years of age.

More generally, far fewer female than male councillors had children under 5 living with them, suggesting difficulties for such women, whose absence is reflected in local politics. This may be the result of responsibility for household and family resting more with women - in 1984, for example, women constituted some 90% of single parent families (EOC 1987 - see also Joshi 1988[10]).

From this point on conclusions are more tentative and relate specifically to differences between London councillors. Few Liberal men, for example, have children over 16 years of age - a factor related, perhaps, to their younger age profile (see Table 4.12). Also, more Labour women than men have children between 5 and 16 years, a factor which may be related to the care functions of the education system, enabling more time for participation (though this is not related to the ability to attend meetings, which are often held in the evenings). Barron et al found that Labour women county councillors were more likely than Conservative women 'to enter the Council while their children were young' (Barron et al 1987 p.258).

Thus far, we have been considering material distinctions in terms of care, though any differences in the way men and women *perceive* their role as carers for dependents may well be at odds with the reality they perceive for themselves. Table 4.18(b) from the British Social Attitudes Survey shows that men tend to exaggerate their responsibilities when, for example, reporting who looks after sick children.

So, given the role of women as 'primary carers' (see also Walker 1982 p.26), it is surprising to find so little difference between men and women in percentage terms, when caring for elderly parents and disabled adults; indeed, using a chi-squared test, we find no significant difference. A number of female London respondents mentioned that they *had* provided care for someone in the household other than children, but that they no longer did: this may reflect the reality of the time commitment necessary for political participation, and be the reason for such a low percentage in the Table. In other words, women's role as carers for very young children, elderly parents and disabled adults acts as a barrier to their representation in local politics.

(m)   Education

Gender is often seen as an important factor in terms of Education. As one Conservative female councillor put it:

'My parents did not think education beyond the '3Rs' and such like of much importance for girls'.

So how salient a variable is it in the education of London councillors?

From an initial perusal of Table 4.19(a), it would appear that in terms of schooling, gender is a more salient variable than party: women are more likely than men to have attended independent/private schools (35%-27%) and, conversely, men went more frequently to state secondary schools than women (69%-64%).

To jump to this conclusion, however, would be hasty. First, a chi-squared test reveals *no* significant difference. Secondly, party differences, and party/gender inter-relationships, complicate the picture. Indeed, on closer examination it becomes evident that Labour councillors (male and female) are more likely to have attended state secondary schools than councillors from any other political party; and Conservative councillors (more particularly women) to have attended independent/private schools.

It is not possible to generalise from this, however, due to the absence of comparative research, so conclusions about the type of school attended are speculative. It may well be that education more generally correlates quite highly with social class, though exploration of this will have to wait to the next section.

For the time being, no other conclusions seem possible from Table 4.19(a); even the 'other' category, which included 'Church of England', 'Grammar School abroad' and 'orphanage', is of little significance at 4% for men and 2% for women.

<u>TABLE 4.19 (a)</u>

<u>Councillors' Type of School Attended: London Councillor Survey (%)</u>

| | Cons | | Lab | | Lib | | Total | |
	m	f	m	f	m	f	m	f
N =	113	112	134	133	20	24	274	286
State Secondary	59	48	78	77	65	71	69	64
Independent/ Private	38	50	16	21	30	29	27	35
Other	3	2	6	2	5	0	4	2
Total	100	100	100	100	100	100	100	101

When considering councillors by age left school, however, comparison is made possible by data from The Widdicombe Report. Here, we see that councillors in general, and London councillors in particular, have a far greater tendency to leave school at an age later than the average for the population; the figures are outlined in Table 4.19(b).

Perhaps the most striking contrast is among those completing full-time education at 18 or over: only 5% of the population left school at age over 18 years, compared to 24% of councillors nationally, and 56.5% of councillors in London. In other words, councillors generally are five times more likely to finish education at over 18 years than the population, whilst London councillors are eleven times more likely to stay on beyond the age of 18.

Echoes of Turner's elite 'private club' have special resonance here. If Widdicombe can remark that 'the disparity between councillors and the general population is clearly illustrated' (1986 p.23), then the disparity for London councillors is even more marked.

There is also a party and a gender difference. First, the Liberals are more likely to continue full-time education beyond the age of 18 years, and secondly, Liberal and Conservative men, together with Labour women, stay on longer than Conservative and Liberal women and Labour men. The significance is, of course, that those who stay on beyond 18 enter further and higher education with the increased facility for educational qualifications.

Given the older age profile for Conservatives, particularly Conservative women, it might be thought that they would tend to have left school *earlier* than Labour and Liberal councillors: that this is not the case may well be related to the type of school attended - 50% of Conservative women attended independent/private schools.

When considering the highest educational qualification attained {Table 4.19(c)}, we note further disparities between councillors and the population. Only 5% of the population possess degrees, higher degrees or their equivalent, compared to 22% of councillors generally, and 43.5% of councillors in London. In other words, councillors generally are over four times more likely to have degrees, higher degrees or equivalent, than the population, and London councillors over eight and a half times more likely. Hardly representative of the population they serve, a concern expressed in the Maud Report (see McGrew and Bristow for discussion 1984 pp.71-72) - perhaps a sign of the meritocracy, or the professionalisation of local politics.

TABLE 4.19 (b)

School-leaving Age (%)

| | Widdicombe (1) | | London Councillor Survey: | | | | | | | |
	Population	Councillors	Cons m	f	Lab m	f	Lib m	f	Total m	f
N =	15212	1557	116	107	129	127	19	24	271	276
14 or under	31	19	5	7	19	11	0	4	12	9
15	31	19	10	8	11	9	0	21	10	10
16	25	22	17	18	12	15	11	13	14	16
17	7	16	8	19	5	6	5	4	7	11
18 or over	5	24	60	49	53	60	84	58	58	55
Totals	99	100	100	101	100	101	100	100	101	101

(1)   Source: Widdicombe (1986: 24)

TABLE 4.19 (c)

Councillors' Highest Educational Qualification (%)

	Widdicombe (1)		London Councillor Survey:							
			Cons		Lab		Lib		Total	
	Population	Councillors	m	f	m	f	m	f	m	f
N =	15843	1479	111	101	130	126	19	23	267	264
Degree/Higher degree/ equivalent	5	22	44	22	52	52	58	44	49	38
Higher qualification below degree	8	9	20	15	10	16	16	13	14	15
GCE A Level	6	8	8	6	6	6	16	0	8	6
ONC/D	-	5	1	1	1	0	0	0	1	1
GCE O Level	17	25	5	12	6	5	5	13	5	8
CSE (other than Grade 1)	14	1	0	1	1	1	0	0	0	1
Other	-	7	12	28	9	8	5	9	11	16
None	48	23	11	16	15	13	0	22	12	15
Total	98	100	101	101	100	101	100	101	100	100

(1) Source: Widdicombe (1986: 24)

Table 4.19(d), enables comparison of the population by gender, though only for persons with above GCE A-level. We see that slightly more males than females hold such 'higher educational qualifications' (14%:12% for Great Britain, and 16%:13% for outer London) but that women rank slightly higher in inner London (16% compared to 15% for men). London councillors generally possess higher educational qualifications {see Table 4.19(c)}.

Widdicombe points to councillors in the London Boroughs and the Metropolitan counties as the ones with the highest qualifications - both at 39%, well above the average (1986 p.25). In this respect, it is worth considering an aspect of the survey of candidates carried out by McGrew and Bristow, reproduced as Table 4.19(e). Here, we see Liberal and Labour councillors possessing a degree or above, at 49% and 42% respectively, with Conservatives trailing well behind at 27%. The Conservatives have the majority of GCE O and A-levels, Teachers Certificates, HNCs and HNDs (with the Liberals a close second 53% and 45% respectively), whilst Labour have the majority of Industrial Apprenticeships and the largest percentage with no formal qualifications at all.

Comparison with the London Councillor Survey, however, is problematic for two reasons. First, McGrew and Bristow do not break down their categories by gender and, secondly, the qualification profiles differ: Industrial Apprenticeships, for example, have been coded under the 'other' category shown in Table 4.19(c). Nonetheless, some comparisons *are* possible.

For example, more Liberal and Labour councillors possess degrees and above than Conservative {Table 4.19(c)}. The breakdown by gender for the London Councillor Survey, however, reveals some fascinating distinctions. Whilst male councillors in London are more likely to have gained a degree or higher degree than females (49%:38%), Labour women are as highly qualified as Labour men: both stand at 52%.[11] The percentage of Liberal men, 58%, is higher than that for Labour men and women, with Liberal women standing at 44%. Trailing behind both Labour and Liberal men and Labour women, are Conservative men at 44% (the same as Liberal women), with Conservative females at *half* that figure - 22%.

The relatively low proportion of 22% for Conservative women may have something to do with their being older than other councillors: given the relatively recent expansion of higher education, which reflected changed attitudes to participation in education (with significant impact on women), we might well expect the oldest sector or group to be the least qualified. The

TABLE 4.19 (d)

Percentage of Population with Higher Educational Qualifications (1)(2)

	m	f
Great Britain	14	12
England and Wales	14	12
England	14	12
Greater London	15	14
Inner London	15	16
Outer London	16	13

(1) Source: Census 1981 Key Statistics for local authorities in Great
             Britain Ref. CEN81 KSLA (1984: 30) - no absolute numbers
             given.
(2) Note: The Census 1981 Definitions Booklet (ref. CEN81 DE) (1981: 30),
          defines higher level qualifications as follows:

'Higher level qualifications are those commonly obtained at age
18 or over by study at a level above General Certificate of
Education (Advance Level). They are categorised into three levels,
a, b, and c:

level a - higher university degrees

level b - first degrees and all qualifications of first degree
            standard and all qualifications of higher degree
            standard (other than such degrees themselves which
            appear in level a).

level c - qualifications that in general satisfy the three
            requirements of: obtained at age 18 or over; above
            GCE (A) Level; below first degree level. Level c
            includes most nursing and teaching qualifications
            (though persons who have taken a degree in education
            appear in level b).

A qualified person holds at least one qualification at level a, b or c'.

TABLE 4.19 (e)

Metropolitan Counties Candidates Survey: Educational Qualifications by Party (1)

	No formal qualification		Industrial Apprenticeship		GCE O/A Level		Teachers Cert. HNC/HND		Degree		Total
	N	%	N	%	N	%	N	%	N	%	N
Conservative	13	(18)	1	(1)	20	(27)	19	(26)	20	(27)	73
Labour	29	(19)	12	(8)	21	(14)	25	(17)	62	(42)	149
Liberal	6	(7)	0	(0)	19	(22)	20	(23)	43	(49)	88
Total	48	(15)	13	(4)	60	(19)	64	(21)	125	(40)	310

(1) Source: McGrew & Bristow (1984: 77, Table 4.8); absolute numbers shown under N with percentages given in brackets. No breakdown by gender given.

high representation of Conservative females with O-levels and 'other' qualifications (included here were matriculation and nursing qualifications, for example) and no qualifications at all is also explained by this factor.

The relatively high number of Labour women with degrees and above is also worthy of special mention: Widdicombe notes that the younger the councillor group, the more likely they are to 'possess degree level qualifications', than councillors elsewhere (1986 p.26): though the highly qualified nature of Labour females is particularly marked, and may offer some evidence that educated Labour women are choosing local politics as an outlet for the furtherance of their objectives. We have already noted, for example, that Labour women are no less nor more likely than other women to stand for election for reasons related to the locality (Table 4.9). They are, however, highly influenced by the experience of female family members in politics, if not significantly more than others from other political parties, though they are *far* more likely to stand for election 'for the benefit of women'.

We will consider the views of these Labour women councillors in more detail later, when we come to consider their views on the women's movement generally and on Local Government Women's Committees more specifically, as well as their route to local politics.

(n)   Employment and Social Class

In order to ascertain the employment pattern of London councillors, they were all asked the following questions both for themselves and their spouses: 'Please enter your current occupational status ... if part-time, number of hours per week'. The coding presented some difficulties because of the existence of different social class occupational classifications, so recourse was had to the *OPCS Classification of Occupations,* to enable coding in respect of:

(a)   activity status; and
(b)   social class and socio-economic group (SEG).

To convert (b) into a form compatible with Widdicombe, for comparative purposes, the *OPCS General Household Survey* was consulted for the collapsed version of this classification, which is as follows:

109

Descriptive definition	SEG numbers
Professional	3, 4
Employers and managers	1, 2, 13
Intermediate non-manual	5
Junior non-manual	6
Skilled manual (incl. foremen and supervisors) and account non-professional	8, 9, 12, 14
Semi-skilled manual and personal service	7, 10, 15
Unskilled manual	11

(1980 p.229)

This resulted in a seven point classification, to which was added an eighth category for armed forces and not known, into which were recorded SEG groups 16 and 17.

The next stage entailed a visit to the Low Pay Unit, who advised on coding for part-time hours: 0-7, 8-15, 16-30, and other (used in practice for recording over 30), being consistent with legislation and employment practice in respect of employer-employee obligations.[12] This was followed up by checking the *New Earnings Survey Part f*, 'Hours, Earnings of Part-time women employees, types of collective agreement', which gave the following breakdown of hours:

Not over 8, 8-16, 16-21, 21-24, 24-26, 26-28, 28-30.

(1985 p.F38, Table 181)

The shortened categories 0-7, 8-15 and 16-30 were thought appropriate, since this breakdown conformed to the distinctions noted by the Low Pay Unit in their leaflet 'Part-time workers - Your Wages - Your Rights', in their discussion of legal rights at work:

'if you normally work 16 hours or more or have worked between 8 and 16 hours in the same job for five years or more you also have the following rights at work ...'

The leaflet goes on to outline the rights, which need not detain us here. The distinction was embodied in coding for the London Councillor Survey.

110

Table 4.20(a) brings out the harsh realities of economic life in Britain in the 1980s: relatively high levels of unemployment, and considerable part-time working. The debates about how many unemployed there 'really' are will be sidestepped here, for obvious reasons: *comparison* of data is more meaningful for our purposes.

In considering the activity status of councillors and their spouses, it is interesting to note the fall in full-time employment for councillors generally, between 1976,[13] and 1985. This clearly reflects the bleak economic context of Britain in the 1980s, and is to be expected. The correlative rise in the percentage of those describing themselves as retired, however, is not matched by an increase in the number of councillors over retirement age. This is explained away by Widdicombe as the consequence of early retirement and redundancy, so that those 'between say, 55 and 64, ... having poor prospects of obtaining further employment, considered themselves as retired' (1986 p.28).

This may well be true, but retirement is *not* a characteristic feature of London councillors, except for Conservative women, of whom 24% are retired, a higher proportion than councillors more generally; this is hardly surprising, given that they *are* older - and that we have noted the generally younger age profile of the other groups of London councillors. Indeed, what *is* characteristic of London councillors is precisely high levels of full-time employment, compared to councillors elsewhere, and in Greater London as a whole - though the disparity between the male and female population is interesting, with 75% of males working full-time in inner London, compared to 46% of females, whereas in outer London we see 83% of males working full-time compared to 41% of females, a spatial polarisation.

However we read these figures, males predominate in full-time employment, and females in part-time - right across the board. The only other points that jump out of the data relate to the relatively low number of Conservative women working full-time (39%) and the relatively high number of Labour women (63%). Consideration of party and gender complexities such as these would doubtless have led Hills to at least qualify her conclusion that 'overall, women who are housewives are not over-represented in local councils, but women in full-time employment are under-represented' (1982 p.69).

The relatively low number of Conservative women in London working full-time compared to Labour women, has, as we have noted, a great deal to do with their age - 24% are retired against 15% of Conservative women

TABLE 4.20 (a)

Councillor and Spouse by Activity Status

PART I Councillors by Activity Status (%)

| | Population (1) | | | | Widdicombe (2) | | |
	Inner London m	Inner London f	Outer London m	Outer London f	1976 m + f	1985 m	1985 f
N =	789266	749112	1329382	1239186	4717	1246	290
Working full-time	75	46	83	41	65	62	26
part-time	2	15	1	19	7	4	14
Unemployed			10 m	7 f (3)	2	4	3
Retired					16	28	15
Permanently sick/ disabled					0	1	0
Looking after home/family					7	0	40
Other/Not applicable					3	0	1
Total	–	–	–	–	–	100	99	99

PART II

Councillor and Spouse by Activity Status (Spouse in Brackets): London Councillor Survey (%)

	Cons m	Cons f	Lab m	Lab f	Lib m	Lib f	Total m	Total f
N =	117(82)	103(67)	136(90)	130(73)	20(11)	24(17)	281(189)	273(170)
Working full-time	78(29)	39(63)	78(52)	63(73)	80(27)	54(71)	78(40)	51(69)
part-time	7(40)	18(6)	2(18)	15(4)	15(36)	17(6)	5(29)	16(5)
Unemployed	0(0)	2(2)	4(2)	6(3)	0(0)	8(12)	2(1)	4(3)
Retired	15(5)	24(30)	16(14)	12(21)	5(0)	8(12)	15(10)	17(23)
Permanently sick/ disabled	0(0)	0(0)	0(0)	0(0)	0(0)	0(0)	0(0)	0(0)
Looking after home/family	1(22)	17(0)	0(12)	2(0)	0(36)	13(0)	0(19)	11(0)
Other/Not applicable	0(4)	1(0)	0(1)	2(0)	0(0)	0(0)	0(2)	2(0)
Total	101(100)	101(101)	100(99)	100(101)	100(99)	100(101)	100(101)	101(100)

(1) Source: OPCS Couny Monitor Ref: CEN81 CM56 (1982: 11 and 12), for working, full and part-time.
Economic statistics from the 1981 cens s, Statistical Series: No.31 (1984: 20, GLC, London),
for unemployed (absolute numbers not given)

(2) Source: Widdicombe (1986: 28 and 29).

(3) Note: For Greater London as a whole.

112

councillors elsewhere, yet it also has a great deal to do with their status within the household as 'looking after home' - some 17%, twice the proportion of Liberal women, and eight and a half times that of Labour women. This would seem to reflect a more general pattern of 'housewifery' for Conservative female councillors at 40%, who may see local politics as an alternative career to paid employment. It may be that the older age profile of female councillors in London means that more are retired, and that they would be describing themselves as housewives if they were younger. Nonetheless, even the 'relatively' low figure can be seen as high, given the amount of responsibility being assumed in local politics.

The relatively high number of employed Labour women councillors is more difficult to explain, though an answer would seem to lie in the educational qualifications they hold. We noted from Table 4.19(c) that Labour women councillors have the highest proportion with degrees and above of any female group of councillors, and are equal to male Labour councillors in this respect. They would seem to be using their qualifications to secure full-time employment (63% were in full-time employment), though at a rate less than Labour males (78% were in full-time employment) - still a wide gap, though narrower than that between males and females of other political parties.

Other factors that might be explored relate to the differences in part-time working among men, with the Conservatives three and a half times as likely to work part-time than Labour (7%:2%), and the Liberals seven and a half times (15%); the differences in unemployment, with no Conservative or Liberal men recording themselves as unemployed and one Labour man calling himself 'unwaged'; and the differences in looking after the home/family. On this final point it is worth noting that for the men, no Labour, only 1% of Conservatives and 5% of Liberals classed themselves as househusbands, whilst for the women, 17% of Conservatives, 2% of Labour and 13% of Liberals described themselves as housewives. The relatively low 2% for Labour women is explicable in terms of their increased propensity to engage in paid employment.

The 'other' category was used largely for those unwilling to answer this question on the questionnaire, or had independent means.

This leads on to a consideration of the activity status of the spouses of councillors: the figures are shown in brackets in Table 4.20(a), and separately in Table 4.20(b), for purposes of analysis. The data would seem to 'fit' with the activity status profile of councillors in London: no details are available for comparative purposes for councillors elsewhere. As expected, London women councillors have predominantly full-time working husbands - less for Conservative women who are generally older, and whose husbands are therefore more likely to be retired. For London male councillors, relatively few of their wives work full-time - except among Labour male councillors, where just over half of their wives have full-time paid employment. Such factors would appear to be entirely explicable in social class terms, and there are no surprises here.

There are some differences - Liberal women have more unemployed husbands and the wives of Conservative and Liberal male councillors are more likely to be found looking after the home/family than Labour male councillors' wives, but this is to be expected certainly for Conservative men's wives. In any event conclusions about the Liberals suffer from the low absolute response. The major implication to be drawn from Table 4.20(b), is that male councillors tend to have wives who work part-time, look after the home/family, or are retired, whereas female councillors have husbands who work full-time, or are retired. Party differences pale into insignificance when seen in the light of the contrast between males and females.

Before considering the socio-economic groups, we might pause to look at the part-time hours of councillors and their spouses - Table 4.20(c).

Given the trigger points at which legal rights become available for part-time workers noted earlier, we might expect to find a large number of councillors working below 8 and 16 hours per week, if employers are using this 'flexible' system of employment to their full advantage.[14] Increases in part-time working have been clearly documented by Atkinson (1984) who argues that such employment fits into peripheral rings of a firm's contractual orbit encompassing employees who have 'plug-in' and 'plug-out' jobs, including subcontracting, job-share, agency and homeworking. A whole literature is being built up around notions of 'flexibility' and 'the flexible firm' suggesting caution in the drawing of any firm conclusions from the data about manipulation of occupational contracts as an employer-led strategy (e.g. Pollert 1987 and 1988; Batstone 1988 p.200). In any event the phenomena 'reserve army of labour' (Marx 1867 pp.781-94) and 'dual-labour market' (Barron and Norris 1976) are not new.

Interestingly, the figures in Table 4.20(c) do not lend support to Atkinson's thesis - well over half of part-time working councillors and spouses work in excess of 15 hours per week. Any other generalisations from the Table are problematic. For example, some 60% of the husbands of

114

TABLE 4.20 (b)

Activity Status of Spouse of Councillor: London Councillor Survey (%)

	Cons		Lab		Lib		Total	
	m	f	m	f	m	f	m	f
N =	82	67	90	73	11	17	189	170
Working - full-time	29	63	52	73	27	71	40	69
- part-time	40	6	18	4	36	6	29	5
Unemployed	0	2	2	3	0	12	1	3
Retired	5	30	14	21	0	12	10	23
Permanently sick/ disabled	0	0	0	0	0	0	0	0
Looking after home/family	22	0	12	0	36	0	19	0
Other/Not applicable	4	0	1	0	0	0	2	0
Total	100	101	99	101	99	101	101	100

TABLE 4.20 (c)

Part-Time Hours of Councillor and Spouse (Spouse in Brackets): London Councillor Survey (%)

	Cons m	f	Lab m	f	Lib m	f	Total m	f
N =	8 36	13 29	2 51	19 14	4 10	4 4	14 106	38 48
0-7 hours	13(7)	0(0)	0(7)	0(60)	25(0)	0(0)	14(6)	0(33)
8-15 hours	25(28)	23(50)	0(29)	21(0)	0(25)	25(0)	14(27)	24(11)
16-30 hours	25(55)	54(50)	100(57)	74(40)	75(75)	75(100)	50(58)	66(56)
Other	38(10)	23(0)	0(7)	5(0)	0(0)	0(0)	21(8)	11(0)
Total	101(100)	100(100)	100(100)	100(100)	100(100)	100(100)	99(99)	101(100)

female Labour councillors who work part-time work under 8 hours per week. The relatively low *number* of such husbands in this particular category may have something to do with this, however - only 4% overall being involved in part-time work {Table 4.20(b)}- so the drawing of conclusions based on such low figures would be unwise.

We now move on to the socio-economic grouping of councillors - Table 4.20(d) - which includes figures for their spouses in brackets; figures for spouses are separated out in Table 4.20(e). Details of Metropolitan County councillors and candidates from the McGrew and Bristow Survey are reproduced as Table 4.20(f) for comparative purposes. Here, then, we have information on the population, councillors generally, London councillors and their spouses broken down by party and gender, and Metropolitan County councillors and candidates.

So what might we expect to find from the figures? It has been argued that a trend is discernible 'towards a more professionalised (or more middle class) local political elite ... in all parties ... [supported] ... by the fact that a majority of each party's candidates hold some form of higher educational qualification' (McGrew and Bristow 1984 p.76). We *have* noted the high levels of qualification held by councillors, particularly those in London, and evidence is given in Table 4.20(f) for very high levels of non-manual councillors and candidates in the Metropolitan Counties.

The claim that increasing private business interests are pervading local authorities at the political level (op cit.p.76) was not specfically pursued in the London Councillor Survey as the distinction between public and private has become blurred due to privatisation.

The returned questionnaires were nonetheless coded by employment sector. The results are given in Table 4.20(g). The absolute numbers for London respondents is relatively - but not too - small (two hundred and thirty eight, or 40% of the total - absolute numbers given in brackets in the Table), since many responses were not amenable to classification under either public or private headings - 'clerk', 'manager', and 'secretary' are just a few examples.[15]

The findings are, as it turns out, unremarkable. More Labour Councillors work in the public sector than councillors in the other parties, and more Conservative councillors in the private sector. The gender differences are probably explicable by reference to the low absolute numbers of classifiable responses for females. If there appear to be slightly more London Councillors in the public sector than councillors elsewhere, or the

TABLE 4.20 (d)

Councillor and Spouse by Socio-economic Group (%)

PART I

	London (1) Population		Widdicombe (2) Population	Councillors
	m	f		
N =	1979810	1391030	not given	1347
Professional	23	10	3	9
Employers & Managers			11	32
Intermediate Non-manual	22	58	9	18
Junior Non-manual			18	10
Skilled manual/ own account non professional	30	4	23	16
Semi-skilled manual and personal service	14	17	18	4
Other (3)	11	10	16	12
Total	100	99	98	101

(1) Source: Economic statistics from the 1981 census, Statistical Series No.31 (1984: 72, GLC, London).

(2) Source: Widdicombe (1986: 30).

(3) Includes Unskilled Manual/Armed forces/N A.

118

TABLE 4.20 (d)

PART II

	Cons m	f	Lab m	f	Lib m	f	Total m	f
N =	82(50)	52(36)	95(59)	87(51)	17(6)	14(10)	199(118)	162(106)
Professional	21(8)	6(11)	6(5)	8(10)	24(0)	14(30)	14(6)	7(14)
Employers and Managers	54(26)	29(56)	43(22)	23(33)	53(0)	21(30)	48(22)	25(40)
Intermediate Non-manual	12(26)	23(19)	25(32)	41(35)	24(50)	29(10)	20(31)	34(26)
Junior Non-manual	5(8)	8(3)	3(14)	9(2)	0(17)	14(10)	4(12)	9(3)
Skilled manual/ own account non-professional	6(2)	6(11)	13(2)	0(10)	0(0)	7(10)	9(2)	3(11)
Semi-skilled manual and personal service	1(14)	10(0)	2(12)	2(6)	0(17)	7(10)	2(13)	5(4)
Other(1)	1(16)	19(0)	7(14)	16(4)	0(17)	7(0)	4(14)	17(2)
Total	100(100)	100(100)	99(101)	99(100)	101(101)	99(100)	101(100)	100(100)

(1) Includes Unskilled manual/Armed forces/N A.

TABLE 4.20 (e)

Socio-economic Group of Spouse of Councillor: London Councillor Survey (%)

	Cons		Lab		Lib		Total	
	m	f	m	f	m	f	m	f
N =	50	36	59	51	6	10	118	106
Professional	8	11	5	10	0	30	6	14
Employers and Managers	26	56	22	33	0	30	22	40
Intermediate non-manual	26	19	32	35	50	10	31	26
Junior non-manual	8	3	14	2	17	10	12	3
Skilled manual/Own account non-professional	2	11	2	10	0	10	2	11
Semi-skilled manual and personal service	14	0	12	6	17	10	13	4
Other(1)	16	0	14	4	17	0	14	2
Total	100	100	101	100	101	100	100	100

(1) Includes Unskilled manual/Armed forces/NA

TABLE 4.20 (f)

Metropolitan Counties Candidates Survey: Occupational Status and Occupational Class of Councillors (%) (1)

	Employee	Self-Employed	Retired
Conservative	29	48	24
Labour	82	2	16
Liberal (2)	95	–	5
Total	77	7	16
(N=172)			

	Councillors		Candidates	
	Manual	Non-Manual	Manual	Non-Manual
Conservative	5	95	16%	84
Labour	21	79	21%	79
Liberal	9	91	12%	88
Total	17	83	17%	83
	(N=162)		(N=526)	

(1) Source: McGrew and Bristow (1984: 92 Table 4.16)

(2) McGrew and Bristow's original error in transcribing Labour for Liberal in their published article has been corrected here.

TABLE 4.20 (g)

Councillors' Employment Sector (Public/Private) (%)

| | Population not given | Councillors(1) | London Councillors - London Councillors Survey(2) | | | | | | | |
| | | | Cons | | Lab | | Lib | | Total | |
			m	f	m	f	m	f	m	f
N=	943									
Public	37	36	4(10)	4(9)	21(50)	14(33)	3(6)	2(4)	28(66)	20(46)
Private	63	61	21(50)	8(20)	11(26)	5(13)	4(10)	3(7)	36(86)	16(40)
Not stated	-	3	75	88	68	81	93	95	36	64
Total	100	100	100	100	100	100	100	100	100	100

(1) Source: Widdicombe (1986: 32)

(2) Note: the numbers in brackets for the London Councillor Survey indicate the number of classified responses, or N.

122

population in general, this is entirely consistent with Widdicombe's findings for the London Boroughs and the Metropolitan Counties (Widdicombe 1986 p.32).

Consideration of the socio-economic grouping of male and female councillors and their spouses in Table 4.20(d) with figures for spouses separately tabulated in Table 4.20(e) permits consideration of what I will call the embourgeoisement thesis of local politics, without getting too bogged down in the debate in respect of social class analysis over women's place in stratification studies (e.g. Goldthorpe 1983 and 1984; and Stanworth 1984). This is important because in this debate women are usually positioned within the family, the central unit of study, as effectively mirroring their husband's social class position. Goldthorpe has defended this positioning by arguing that the classification system ranks sales work above skilled manual - if the parameters were re-drawn combining sales with semi-skilled manual, then any cross-class complexities pale into insignificance in the face of the explanatory power of traditional class analysis and 'stable' familial collectivities.

Yet these debates tell us little about social relationships *within* families. They may not be a haven in a heartless world, but the locus of struggle, of unequal power relationships (c.f. Hartmann 1981, Barrett and McIntosh 1982). As Dex puts it:

> '... what use will a single dimensional class analysis have which treats women's class as mediated by their husband? It enables a head-count analysis to be made, but what is left out of the category is as important as what is included, so a single class classification tells us little about social relationships'.

> (Dex 1985 p.171)

In order to take account of social relationships it has been necessary to break down our population of councillors by male, female, party and spouse, into socio-economic groupings to facilitate an analysis of different occupational experiences.

Widdicombe explains that historical comparison of councillors' socio-economic status is problematic, given changes in the way that the Registrar General has classified socio-economic groupings,[16] but that 'In common with the findings of the Robinson Study of 1976 ... more councillors were in non-manual jobs than the general population and substantially more in professional or managerial employment' (1986 p.29). Widdicombe goes on to note that this is related to the low age profiles of councillors (op cit p.30).

If we turn now to Table 4.20(d), we see that councillors generally *are* unrepresentative of the population as a whole, and that London councillors are even *more* atypical - though London councillors more closely reflect the higher socio-economic profile of Greater London. Here, amongst the higher groupings, both party and gender differences abound. It may be that we can discern a general leaning to embourgeoisement in social class terms, though this is shown to be highly conditioned by political party and gender.

First, male councillors in London are disproportionately represented in the Professional/Employer/Manager category, clearly mediated by party - Conservatives 75%, Labour 49%, and Liberal 77%.

This is not the case for female councillors: some 35% of Conservatives, 31% of Labour and 35% of Liberal women were in these categories - a greater consistency in gender terms, with gender for women only *marginally* refracted by party - surprising given the high level of qualifications possessed by Labour women councillors. In these categories, therefore, the gender variable has greater explanatory power than party.

This is less marked for the Intermediate/Junior non-manual categories, with party playing an important role for both men and women, although gender is still significant. The figures are, for males: Conservatives 17%, Labour 28%, and Liberal 24%; whilst for females, Conservatives 31%, Labour 50%, and Liberal 43%.

If we now consider the various manual and personal service occupations, we find party playing an important role: no Liberal male, quite high numbers of Labour men, and relatively high numbers of Conservative females recorded under semi-skilled manual and personal service - probably reflecting their increased role as 'housewives'.

In turning to the socio-economic groupings of councillors' spouses, we find what might be termed a mirror image of the councillors categories: more women councillors in the Professional/Employer/Manager categories have husbands in the same group,. than male councillors whose wives predominate in the lower categories. The findings for Liberal councillors in this respect suffer once more from low absolute numbers in the Survey, and little can be interpreted from these statistics.

So, what does a consideration of Table 4.20(d) tell us? First, that councillors in general, and London Councillors in particular, are unrepresentative of the London population, though Labour Councillors reflect their constituents' socio-economic groupings a little more closely.

Secondly, that a weak version of the embourgeoisement thesis of local politics is discernible, but that, as with Goldthorpe's more general critique of the cultural convergence thesis, political and social values play too important a role to be dismissed (1971 pp.336-338; see also Haddon's Foreword to Kerr et al's [1960] classic thesis on convergence).

Thirdly, that a more significant factor than party mediates social class: that of gender.[17]

Consideration of the socio-economic profiles of councillors would not be complete without a look at councillors' perceptions of their own social class. This is facilitated by Table 4.20(h).

As expected, we find more Conservatives and Liberals describing themselves as upper/professional, middle/middle class, and more Labour councillors reporting themselves as working class. This is interesting, since the socio-economic profiles shown in Table 4.20(d) are not quite so clear cut. Take Labour male councillors as an example. The non-manual/manual divide for this group is 77%:22%. Yet some 40% classified themselves as working class.

Gaps between perceptions of social class and occupational classification are not unknown in sociology, indeed it is precisely the balance between objective criteria (the job) and subjective perceptions of occupations (the general standing within the community) which goes to make up the Registrar General's classification. But the gaps between Table 4.20(d) and Table 4.20(h) would appear to go beyond the niceties of classification, and may well reflect deep rooted ambivalences or strengths of feeling about social class, as well as class changes between generations given the expansion of the tertiary sector and education since the Second World War.

It was precisely because of this that the question included in the Survey read 'Which social class would you say you belong to, if any?' The relatively high numbers of those classified under uncertain or outdated would seem to confirm the ambivalence, though the terms working class and middle class are clearly far from dead.

The method used for classifying the responses was the one used before in the London Councillor Survey: a random sample of 50 entries were analysed for patterns. The large number of working and middle class responses clearly speak for themselves.

There is another interesting finding from Table 4.20(h): over one and a half times more women than men saw the notion of social class as

TABLE 4.20 (h)

Perceptions of Social Class of London Councillors: London Councillor Survey (%)

	Cons		Lab		Lib		Total	
	m	f	m	f	m	f	m	f
N =	113	110	137	133	19	22	276	282
Working CLass	10	11	40	33	5	18	25	22
Middle Class	38	37	20	29	37	32	29	33
Upper/Professional Middle Class	13	7	8	5	16	0	11	7
Uncertain	12	19	20	22	16	9	16	19
Outdated	9	19	5	8	16	14	8	13
Other	18	6	7	3	11	27	11	6
Total	100	99	100	100	101	100	100	100

126

TABLE 4.20 (i)

Self-Rated Social Class: British Social Attitudes (1)

	%	N
Working	48	(789)
Upper-Working	19	(319)
Upper-Middle/Middle	27	(438)
Poor	3	(47)
Dont Know/Not Answered	3	(53)
Total	100	1646

(1) Source: Young (1985: 3)

127

outdated - this category included those who said they did not recognise the term, or went to the trouble of deleting it - though using a statistical test of the difference between proportions we find that a variation of 5% could be explained by chance. Nonetheless, it is worth noting that marginally more women than men saw their social class as uncertain - answers such as 'upper proletarian', 'alienated', 'can't locate myself', or other generally ambivalent or hesitant responses were recorded here. Apart from Liberal women, who were more unlikely to go under the 'other' category than any other group, Labour and Conservative female councillors were more likely to regard social class as outdated, or be ambivalent in their attitudes towards it.

Table 4.20(h), thus offers a cautionary note for the interpretation of surveys generally such as the one reproduced as Table 4.20(i) from the British Social Attitudes Survey (1985) which do not cross-tabulate responses. Here, we see large numbers of the population referring to themselves as working or upper working class, whereas the London Councillor Survey would suggest this to be a factor more related to Labour Party supporters, and perhaps men more generally.

(o)   Where Next?

So far the social background and political representation of London councillors has been outlined, cross-tabulated by party and gender. This has been largely a descriptive exercise, though necessary in order to sketch out comparative similarities and differences between councillors and the populations they serve. It helps to fill the gap in published literature on the background of London councillors.

What patterns have emerged?

It would appear that councillors generally are asked to stand for office. London does seem to act as a kind of magnetic attraction, though most London councillors assume office only after they have settled for a while, then serving two or three terms. They are younger, more likely to own their own homes, have full-time employment and be better educationally qualified than their constituents and most other councillors. Whilst most councillors are married, London councillors more closely reflect their constituents' profiles.

There are party differences. Labour councillors, for example, are more likely to have jobs in the public sector that Conservatives; and whilst generally likely to be in non-manual occupations, are more likely than

Conservatives to be in manual jobs.

But it is the gender differences which have been most noticeable. Women, for example, are more likely to be asked to stand for office when dependents are gone, the family grown up - there are, therefore, less women councillors than men with children under five years of age. Many women, accordingly, participate in local politics at a later stage than men - this is particularly marked for Conservative women. This suggests a potentially weaker assimilation of party political values.

Women also draw on a world of experience which would seem to be quite different in kind to that of men. The large number of female role models within the family, their reading of women's magazines and their desire to benefit women and their communities is indicative. In addition, they are less likely to identify with ethnicity or social class.

We have also considered the educational qualifications and occupations of male and female councillors. Women's occupations are more likely to be part-time and lower in the socio-economic ranking - this, despite their educational qualifications which for Labour women are directly equal to those of Labour men, and higher than male London councillors generally.

The next step in the analysis is to see how these similarities and differences are translated into the experiences of becoming a councillor, and how they affect the perception of activities and identities encountered in political life. This is the focus of the next chapter.

Notes

1. Percentages are generally used in the Tables which follow - absolute numbers are shown as 'N'. 'm' indicates male, 'f' indicates female.

2. The use of a chi-squared statistical significance test has been used here. For this test and for all chi-squared tests in this book a 5% level of significance is used. This means that there is a one-in-twenty possibility that the proposition can be explained by sampling factors, or chance.

3. 'experience in local government has frequently proved to be a stepping stone to national politics: as many as one third of MPs are or have been local councillors' (Byrne 1986 p.7).

4.   There is a significant difference here, using a statistical test of the difference between proportions.

5.   It might be contended that invitation helps overcome lack of confidence and that their participation rate is thereby higher than otherwise would be the case. The question of confidence is dealt with later.

6.   Barron et al also noted that some county councillors stood to put forward a 'women's viewpoint' (Barron et al 1987 p.35).

7.   The difference is significant according to a statistical test of difference between proportions.
     If added to category (b) the difference is far less marked - indeed what then is striking is the similarity between women and men.

8.   Stacey and Price remark 'the importance of coming from a political family may be relatively greater for a woman then for a man, because of the strong weight of tradition against women entering politics' (Stacey and Price 1981 pp.157-58). Even this would seem to underestimate the female influence noted here.

9.   The following appeared in the *Census Newsletter* in February 1989:-

     'As a result of further consultation, the Government has decided that a modified form of the question on ethnic group will be included in the 1989 Census Test. The new form is slightly different from that proposed in the White Paper *1991 Census of Population* (CN 430) published in July 1988 (and reported in *Census Newsletter no.6)*. The changes, shown below, are designed to make the question more acceptable to the public and to provide better information.

Original form of question proposed in White Paper:	Modified form of question to be used in census test:
Ethnic Group	*Ethnic Group*
Please tick appropriate box	Please tick appropriate box
-- 1 White	-- 1 White

-- 2 Black	-- 2 Black-Caribbean
-- 3 Indian	-- 3 Black-African
-- 4 Pakistani	-- 4 Black-Other
-- 5 Bangladeshi	(please describe)
-- 6 Chinese	....
-- 7 Any other ethnic	....
group (please	-- 5 Indian
describe)	-- 6 Pakistani
....	-- 7 Bangladeshi
....	-- 8 Chinese
	-- 9 Any other ethnic
	group (please
	describe) ....'

(Source: OPCS *Census Newsletter*, No.8, 14 February 1989 p.3).

10. Joshi notes lower activity rates for mothers, particularly those who had a child under five (Joshi 1988 p.9). She presents details from the General Household Survey (published reports) (Joshi 1988 p.30, Table 2).

11. A statistical test of the difference between proportions confirms that this is significant.

12. Ascher (1987) notes that, in the National Health Service context, contract employer strategy may be influenced by eligibility for national insurance payments. In referring to the Autumn Statement 1985 (London: HM Treasury 1985 p.32), she notes: 'In November 1985 the Government raised the national insurance threshold from £35.50 to £38 per week. Contract cleaners paying NHS wage rates of £1.90, for example, could thus employ workers for up to 20 hours a week (at basic rate) without being eligible for national insurance payments' (Ascher 1987: footnote 14, p.279).

This clearly variable element has not been taken into account in the London Councillor Survey, since details of hourly rates of pay (indeed salary generally) were not sought. It was considered that this was a large issue and that detailed consideration was beyond the scope of the research. Consideration of hours was thus accorded priority. Any supposition about employer strategy in respect of part-time workers should therefore be cautious.

13. The remuneration of councillors was, of course, the concern of the Robinson Report which was dealt with in Chapter 3.

14. The caveat in respect of National Insurance eligibility noted earlier in the chapter (note 12) suggests caution in any conclusion deriving from the following analysis.

15. Where a company had comparatively recently been privatised, such as British Telecom (1984/85), the respondents' employment was classified under "public".

16. For an outline, see footnote in *OPCS Classification of Occupations 1980* (1980 p.x).

17. Joshi notes that, for women, occupational 'downgrading after childbearing is apparent in a variety of British data sets ... domestic constraints force women to take jobs that are convenient, even if they don't make full use of their potential. At the lower end of the market, the risk of job-downgrading declined the longer the absence from employment' (Joshi 1988 pp.20-21).

5   Experience and participation

(a)   <u>The New Women's Movement in Britain</u>

Having analysed political representation, and the educational, social and socio-economic background of councillors, we may now move on to a consideration of the nature and perceptions of the New Women's Movement in Britain.

Dahlerup suggests that empirical enquiry might usefully ask the 'interesting questions ... who actually works for feminist goals, no matter in which context ... [and] ... how many of these women consider themselves part of the Women's Movement?' (1986 p.6).

Councillors in the London Councillor Survey were asked whether they regarded themselves as supporters of the Women's Movement (Table 5.1). There was no significant difference between men and women on this question, 60% of men and 56% of women answering yes. The difference lay in membership of political party: this was especially true for Conservative and Labour women (only 16% of Conservative women compared to 89% of Labour women saying they supported the women's movement). The support

133

TABLE 5.1

Support for the Women's Movement: London Councillor Survey (%)

		men	women
	N =	255	267
"Would you regard yourself as a supporter of the Women's Movement?"	YES	60	56
	NO	40	44
	Total	100	100

Those answering "Yes":

	Cons m	f	Lab m	f	Lib m	f
N =	96	104	135	127	17	24
	29	16	84	89	65	58
Total	22		87		61	

134

of Conservative women for the Women's Movement appears low indeed although, of those who were not prepared to express support, some 29% indicated that they were sympathetic to it (Table 5.2).

Of the relatively small proportion of Labour women (11%) who did not regard themselves as supporters of the Women's Movement, 84% were sympathetic. Conservative women thus came out quite clearly as non-supporters of the Women's Movement: only 16% said they supported it and of the rest, 27% of these were not sympathetic to it. On the other hand, it may be surprising to some that among these London councillors, 29% of Conservative men and 16% of Conservative women *did* regard themselves as supporters; and that among those Conservatives who were not supportive, 35% of the men and 29% of the women were sympathetic.

Table 5.3 breaks these figures down for inner and outer London, though no firm conclusions can be drawn here: we can only note, for example, that Conservative women from inner London were more sympathetic than those from outer London.

This view of the Women's Movement by Conservative female councillors deserves more than a passing glance, however, since a number of those who were not supporters, nor sympathetic to the Women's Movement, took the opportunity provided on the questionnaire to make comments, such as:

'I am a "feminist" but do not actively support any particular movement.'

'I believe men are there to look after women. I adore Margaret Thatcher. I believe very few women have the capabilities to enter politics.'

Remarks such as these show different understandings of the term 'Women's Movement'. Indeed, the points made beg the question of what the councillors though they were being asked to express support for. Another question (Table 5.4) was asked about the nature of the Women's Movement; this question was asked *after* the one about support. As can be seen, the categories provided for their views in terms of (a) Liberal, (b) Socialist/Marxist, and (c) Radical perspectives, with a fourth more wide ranging definition (d), and a residual category (e) for other views. Little difference emerged, most councillors believing the movement to be radical,

TABLE 5.2

Degree of Sympathy for the Women's Movement among Non-Supporters: London Councillor Survey (%)

	Cons		Lab		Lib		Total	
	m	f	m	f	m	f	m	f
N =	81	96	53	43	8	15	148	166
Sympathetic	35	29	83	84	75	47	54	46
No view	26	26	8	2	13	13	18	18
Not Sympathetic	22	27	4	0	13	20	15	19
Other	17	18	6	14	0	20	14	18
Total	100	100	101	100	101	100	101	101

TABLE 5.3

Support for the Women's Movement among Inner London and Outer London Councillors: London Councillor Survey (%)

	Cons				Lab				Lib			
	male		female		male		female		male		female	
	%	N	%	N	%	N	%	N	%	N	%	N
Inner London	29	(28)	23	(31)	89	(72)	94	(78)	33	(3)	57	(7)
Outer London	28	(61)	15	(69)	80	(56)	84	(44)	73	(15)	63	(19)

TABLE 5.4

Perceptions of the Women's Movement: London Councillor Survey (%)

"Which of the following do you think best describes the Women's Movement (tick only one)?"

	Cons m	Cons f	Lab m	Lab f	Lib m	Lib f	Total m	Total f
N =	95	97	134	130	18	22	253	262
(a) It concentrates on women's legal rights and equal opportunities	17	15	5	4	6	14	10	9
(b) It attempts to work with other groups in attacking fundamental social inequalities, of which women's exploitation is a part	7	2	17	17	11	14	13	12
(c) It pushes for a radical change away from a male-dominated society	27	29	34	30	33	41	30	30
(d) It attempts to deal with all matters of concern to women (from equal opportunities to patriarchy)	21	21	32	38	33	23	28	29
(e) Other	27	33	12	12	17	9	19	20
Total	99	100	100	101	100	101	100	100

or embracing a wide variety of perspectives - which of course includes radical. Hedlund-Ruth noted beliefs about the Women's Movement being 'militant' or 'extreme' (Hedland-Ruth 1984 p.29).

Such perceptions may have something to do with initiatives for women, such as Local Government Women's Committees, originating from the left and the portrayal of left initiatives generally in the media. As one Conservative woman councillor put it:-

'I am a feminist, but not a loony one like the left wing in Camden'.

In any event, it may sound a cautionary note in respect of identification of the New Women's Movement in Britain with a political party, and would be a strategic question for movement activists seeking to use or co-opt the existing channels of institutional party politics to further their aims. Bodies like the 300 Group, for example, might well seek all party support, though in the London Councillor Survey only 4% of women respondents said they currently belonged; this figure included no Labour Party members as we shall see later.

(b)   Local Government Women's Committees

Perceptions of the New Women's Movement in Britain as somehow 'radical' were thought to be worth pursuing. Dahlerup argues that 'interaction between the challenging movement and those working inside the political system is crucial to the strength of being outside' (1986 p.15 and 240).

This presents a somewhat false dichotomy, since those 'inside the political system' can be considered as *part* of the New Women's Movement in Britain - it all depends on the definition used. The institutional distinction, however, is valid, since movement activists may *well* be using pre-existing, established party political mechanisms, to further their aims. In order to see if perceptions about the radical nature of the movement are more related to initiatives by the left, or groups and individuals which are not affiliated to political parties, a question was included in the London Councillor Survey to elicit attitudes to Local Government Women's Committees, which, as we have seen, were initiated by the Labour Party. Table 5.5 shows the results.

Some generalisations are possible about these findings, but with qualifications. First, there were relatively few respondents who thought that Women's Committees had been a successful innovation - but more women

TABLE 5.5

Attitudes to Local Government Women's Committees: London Councillor Survey (%)

	Cons		Lab		Lib		Total	
	m	f	m	f	m	f	m	f
N =	97	93	135	127	16	23	253	253
Successful Innovation	3	11	33	44	6	4	19	27
Too early to pass judgement	20	20	39	35	25	44	30	29
Largely Unsuccessful	51	32	21	9	44	44	34	23
Other	27	37	8	13	25	9	17	21
Total	101	100	101	101	100	101	100	100

than men, and more Labour Party supporters than Conservative thought them a success.[1] But before we jump to the conclusion that they have *not* therefore been successful we should note two things:

(a) that nearly a third of all respondents thought it was 'too early to tell', this figure including 20% of both Conservative men and women, and a high proportion of Liberal women; and

(b) that many of those who passed comments on their choice added caveats such as 'they still have a long way to go', and 'I feel that the PR aspect has not been successfully handled'.

So we should be cautious before we dismiss such committees even though one third of the women and nearly a quarter of the men said that they thought women's committees had been largely unsuccessful.

Secondly, the fifth or so of respondents who are recorded under 'other' were often those who indicated that they had no direct experience of women's committees and did not, therefore, wish to pass judgement. One woman who ticked 'other' said 'I have never heard of them' (this may have been a dismissive remark, or genuine ignorance). Other comments, though few in number, suggested some unease - 'they've made it easier to pass the buck'.

Thirdly, the party and gender differences noted earlier deserve special comment since the results do not suggest a clear perception about women's committees, perhaps because of their relatively recent appearance.

The party differences are reasonably clear: Labour Councillors feel it is either too early to judge women's committees, or that they have been successful; we could interpret this as meaning that where they have been established they have fulfilled or are fulfilling their promise, but that it is too early to tell how successful they might be in the long run. This, of course, raises the question about 'success' itself, and it is not clear what the councillors thought was meant by this term - and that they may, anyway, have all used different criteria. The raising of consciousness may mean success for one councillor, whilst another might be expecting to see material changes before judging. The other point about party differences is that Conservatives and Liberals tend to regard women's committees as largely unsuccessful; though many in their ranks think it perhaps a little too early to condemn them.

The gender differences, however, though refracted by party, are a little clearer: women are more likely to regard women's committees as a successful innovation than men, who are more likely to see them as largely unsuccessful.[2] This is particularly interesting for Conservative female councillors who are nearly four times as likely to regard them as successful as Conservative males: and for Liberal women who are almost twice as likely to feel that it is too early to pass judgement, compared to Liberal men.

So what can we conclude from Table 5.5? First, that party differences in attitudes to Local Government Women's Committees are fairly well established: given the fact that they are the product of Labour Party initiatives, it is hardly surprising to find Labour more favourably disposed towards them. Secondly, that gender can sometimes operate independently of party even if mediated by it, in that women, of whatever political party, are more likely to be favourably disposed towards women's committees, or to be less dismissive in their judgement. The New Women's Movement in Britain *may* be playing more pervasive a role than would have been expected.

We turn now to Table 5.6, which differentiates attitudes by party, gender, and inner/outer London - given the high profile of inner London women's committees, we might expect the expression of attitudes to be based on direct experience, though the larger number of Labour Boroughs in inner London may account for differences. So, what are the results? They are that Labour councillors are *more* favourably disposed to women's committees in inner London, and Conservative and Alliance councillors less favourably inclined. In other words, a political polarisation is evident where Women's Committees have been particularly active; with greater geographical distance and less immediate exposure, more councillors are prepared to reserve judgement - particularly noticeable for Labour and Alliance women councillors.[3]

(c)   Priority for Issues Specifically Affecting Women

Given the earlier arguments about the diffuseness of the New Women's Movement in Britain and the findings just considered which relate to Local Government Women's Committees as initiatives from the left, it is becoming apparent that party and gender interact in a curious, and often by no means clear, way. Party differences, which are to be expected given the long established adversarial nature of institutionalised politics in Great Britain, seem to be mediated or refracted by gender. Indeed, it is becoming clear that

TABLE 5.6

Attitudes to Local Government Women's Committees among Inner London and Outer London Councillors: London Councillor Survey (%)

	Cons				Lab				Lib			
	male		female		male		female		male		female	
	IL	OL	IL	OL	IL	OL	IL	OL	IL	OL	IL	OL
N =	32	58	29	60	75	53	82	42	3	14	6	18
Successful	3	3	0	15	40	23	48	36	0	7	0	6
Too early to tell	13	22	24	20	31	47	28	50	0	29	17	50
Largely unsuccessful	56	47	35	30	23	21	10	7	100	36	67	39
Other	28	28	41	35	7	9	15	7	0	29	17	6
Total	100	100	100	100	101	100	101	100	100	101	101	101

Note: IL = Inner London
      OL = Outer London

factors related to gender are sometimes *so* pervasive, that it can be argued that gender is mediated by party.

To see whether this translates into action over issues which specifically affect women, questions were asked about the kind of priority given to such issues: the results are shown in Tables 5.7, 5.8 and 5.9. Any conclusions drawn from these tables must be speculative however, given the highly nebulous character of the wording 'issues specifically affecting women'.

Nonetheless, despite the ambiguous wording of the question Table 5.7 offers some interesting insights. Specifically, we find 60% of Labour women councillors who see other (male) councillors according low priority to women's issues - and no Liberal male or female councillors who see other male councillors giving a high priority. We can also see that Labour men and women were more inclined to see other female councillors giving an enhanced priority to these matters.

More generally, however, two interpretations stand above the rest. First, that nearly half of all councillors thought that other councillors sometimes gave a high and sometimes a low priority to women's issues. Secondly, that gender highly conditions the responses: that councillors generally recognise that it is other female councillors who tend to give a higher priority to issues specifically affecting women. The implications of this are not immediately obvious, though it could be contended that increases in women's representation would enable greater representation of their interests.

What then do the councillors themselves feel about the priority accorded to women's issues (Table 5.8)? Given the perception that whilst male and female councillors may vacillate it is women councillors who tend to give a higher priority to women's issues, we might well expect to find something similar, i.e. a large percentage of councillors suggesting that things be left as they are, and more females than males arguing for a higher priority. So what do we find?

We do find large percentages for the *status quo* 37% of all councillors; and a pattern highly conditioned by *party*, with over 70% of both Conservative female and male councillors opting for the *status quo*.

We also find very high percentages arguing that women's issues be given a higher priority than they are at present. This too is conditioned by party, with 81% of Labour men and 92% of Labour women arguing that the priority should be higher. Before we jump to the conclusion that party has primacy over gender, however, we should not forget that the *issue* here

143

TABLE 5.7

Perceived Priority among other Councillors for Issues Specifically Affecting Women: London Councillor Survey (%)

	Men Councillors								Women Councillors							
	Cons		Lab		Lib		Total		Cons		Lab		Lib		Total	
	m	f	m	f	m	f	m	f	m	f	m	f	m	f	m	f
N =	100	88	134	121	17	21	257	243	74	93	105	129	16	24	201	260
(a) Relatively HIgh	5	7	14	8	0	0	10	7	27	17	45	36	6	13	34	27
(b) Relatively Low	40	36	42	60	47	52	42	51	30	20	12	14	25	21	20	17
(c) Sometimes High, Sometimes Low	55	57	44	31	53	48	48	42	43	62	43	50	69	67	46	55
Total	100	100	100	99	100	100	100	100	100	99	100	100	100	101	100	99

144

TABLE 5.8

Councillors' Own Priority for Issues Specifically Affecting Women: London Councillor Survey (%)

	Cons m	Cons f	Lab m	Lab f	Lib m	Lib f	Total m	Total f
N =	99	96	138	128	18	24	261	260
Higher	17	20	81	92	78	67	56	61
Lower	11	5	2	1	6	0	6	3
Leave as it is	72	75	17	7	17	33	38	36
Total	100	100	100	100	101	100	100	100

concerns gender. Moreover, it may be that rather than being surprised that so few Tories (18.5%) plump for a higher priority for women's issues than obtains at present, perhaps some would be surprised that so *many* would argue for an increase in the priority accorded to women! One Tory woman, for example, argued that 'safety, ease of travel on buses, and shops for small children' were important.

Councillors do not operate in a vacuum: their work is conditioned by the bureaucratic machinery through which policies are realised. A question was therefore included in the survey about the kind of priority given to women's issues by Council Officers, the bureaucrats (Table 5.9). Before considering the results two caveats are in order: first, we must not forget the nebulous wording of 'issues specifically affecting women', and once again be cautious in our speculations; and secondly, we must be mindful that *many* councillors saw officers as 'under orders!'. Another councillor in the same vein, remarked 'council officers do as the majority party requests them to'.

This last point, however, may be a little overstated since officers can frustrate, facilitate, discourage or enable, depending on a variety of factors. So what do we find from the survey? That Conservatives were more inclined to see officers as according a relatively high priority to women's issues, though councillors generally see officers as according a low priority, or no priority at all (sometimes high, sometimes low).

There is relatively little difference here, in either gender or party terms. A comment by one of the male Labour councillors who saw no special priority being given either way made an interesting point:

'Especially as we have an extraordinarily low number of senior female officers. The Brotherhood really does exist!'

It turned out from the subsequent interviewing programme that the councillor in question was referring to the Masons (Saunders noted the postponement of council meetings in Brighton 'because they clashed with Masonic Lodge meetings', 1979 p.349); though the implication is clear - the male brotherhood 'really does exist!'

(d)   Is It Now Easier for Women to Become Councillors?

Thus far we have examined how the New Women's Movement in Britain has permeated local politics in terms of attitudes to women and women's

146

TABLE 5.9

Perceived Priority of Council Officers for Issues Specifically Affecting
Women: London Councillor Survey (%)

	Cons m	Cons f	Lab m	Lab f	Lib m	Lib f	Total m	Total f
N =	99	85	133	127	17	24	255	250
Relatively High	20	27	14	9	6	17	15	16
Relatively Low	28	20	44	50	53	54	39	40
Sometimes High Sometimes Low	52	53	42	40	41	29	46	44
Total	100	100	100	99	100	100	100	100

147

TABLE 5.10

Perception of Changes in Possibilities for Womens' Involvement in Local Politics Since the Late 1960s: London Councillor Survey (%)

	Cons		Lab		Lib		Total	
	m	f	m	f	m	f	m	f
N =	107	109	138	129	18	24	270	279
Easier for women	64	55	67	55	61	58	65	56
Harder for women	1	4	1	4	0	0	1	3
About the same	36	41	32	41	39	42	34	41
Total	101	100	100	100	100	100	100	100

issues, and been translated into action through the increased representation of women councillors. Yet we have also noted potential barriers to the achievement of objectives relating to women's issues, particularly the 'male brotherhood', mediated by established party political machinery and institutionalised local authority bureaucracy.

But why are increasing numbers of women being elected now, and is it easier for them to become elected than it used to be? Are women struggling through against similar or increasing odds, or are there facilitators operating here? A question was included in the London Councillor Survey which asked whether it was easier for women to become councillors compared with about fifteen years ago. The results are shown in Table 5.10.

The most startling point about Table 5.10 is the absence of party difference: most councillors think it is now easier for women to become elected members, over a third think it is about the same, and virtually no one thinks it is now harder. Yet on closer examination, the gender difference becomes clear: more *male* councillors (65%) tend to think that it is now easier than female councillors (56%). Now, this is not a startling difference, but it *is* consistent right across the three political parties, though with a slight convergence between Liberal males and females and it is statistically significant using a chi-squared test. In other words, women are somewhat less convinced of improvement than men. Indeed, if we present Table 5.10 in a slightly different way, we have:

		%
Easier for	male	65
women	female	56
Harder, or	male	35
about the same	female	44

That is, nearly two thirds of men think it is now easier for women to become elected members compared with about fifteen years ago, whereas close on a half of female councillors think it is now harder or about the same.

So what factors are at work here? If men see more changes, what precisely is it that they think has changed? A question was included in the Survey to see which factor(s) best explained why it was that relatively few women became elected members. As we can see from Table 5.11, respondents were asked to tick only *one* of a series of factors mentioned.

TABLE 5.11

Explanation of Women's Relatively Low Representation on Local Councils: London Councillor Survey (%)

"Which one of the following best explains why relatively few women become elected members (tick only one)?"

	Cons		Lab		Lib		Total	
	m	f	m	f	m	f	m	f
N =	107	109	136	133	17	24	267	284
(a) Women are less likely to be selected by their political party	7	7	8	11	6	4	8	9
(b) Women see the 'style' as politics as being inappropriate for them	9	1	12	10	18	21	11	7
(c) Women lack confidence	5	17	10	9	18	17	8	13
(d) Responsibility for household and family takes priority	51	50	52	41	47	46	51	44
(e) Other	29	26	18	30	12	13	23	27
Total	101	101	100	101	101	101	101	100

150

Before moving on to look at the results shown in Table 5.11, however, a word of explanation is in order about the choice of factors given to the respondents.

Much of the literature on the under-representation of women in local politics suggests that women are unwilling or unable to stand (c.f. Bristow 1980 p.1019). This is for a variety of reasons, related to:

(i)   anticipation of discrimination (Martlew 1985 p.48 and 50);
(ii)   less education and job experience (Shaul 1982 pp.496-7), and the resultant power imbalance (Martlew 1985 p.49);
(iii)   exclusion from networks of political and business influence, leading to isolation (Shaul 1982 pp.496-7);
(iv)   'personality traits' such as passiveness and nurturance (Shaul 1982 pp.496-7), deriving from socialisation (Martlew 1985 p.49), and male stereotyping (Shaul *op cit*);
(v)   the style of politics. One female councillor is reported by Martlew as saying 'We're intimidated by points of order etc ...' (Martlew 1985 p.59);
(vi)   lack of selection by political parties. As McGrew and Bristow observe, the Conservatives were 'considerably more likely to nominate women than were Labour (20% compared with 16%) although they were more often nominated for less winnable seats, resulting in 15% of Conservative councillors compared with 13% of Labour' in the Metropolitan Counties (McGrew & Bristow 1984 p.75); and
(vii)   family and household responsibilities. This can result in a lack of time and energy (Shaul 1982 pp.496-7), and less flexible 'time budgets' (Martlew 1985 p.49), with concomitant difficulties in reconciling domestic, economic and political roles (*op cit* p.55). The family may even *discourage* participation (*op cit* p.53).

Due consideration was given to these points and a list of four categories constructed, as shown in Table 5.11. Judging from the findings in the pilot survey these seemed to be the most salient, and mutually exclusive, though it was thought that the style of politics and lack of confidence could be related.

TABLE 5.12

Perceived Explanation for Relative Under-representation of Women on Local Councils among Inner London and Outer London Councillors: London Councillor Survey (%)

	Cons				Lab				Lib			
	male		female		male		female		male		female	
	IL	OL	IL	OL	IL	OL	IL	OL	IL	OL	IL	OL
N =	32	68	31	74	73	56	82	46	3	15	7	19
(a) Less likely to be selected	6	6	3	8	10	9	9	11	0	7	14	0
(b) Style of politics inappropriate	16	7	0	1	12	13	12	7	0	20	14	21
(c) Lack of confidence	3	3	16	18	8	11	11	7	33	13	14	16
(d) Responsibility for Family and Household	38	59	39	57	48	54	35	50	33	53	43	47
(e) Other	38	25	42	16	22	14	33	26	33	7	14	16
Total	101	100	100	100	100	101	100	101	99	100	99	100

Note: IL = Inner London
      OL = Outer London

The responses quite clearly indicate that it is thought to be specific responsibility for family and household that hampers participation: as one woman councillor commented 'Women do not have housewives'. Some 24% cited *more* than one factor, suggestive of a constellation of constraints, many of these classing themselves under 'other' which is probably why this category covers around one quarter of all responses; though most were prepared to plump for family and household responsibilities as the major one. Particularly interesting is the clear awareness by male councillors of the material nature of this barrier to participation.

Differences in political party are relatively marginal: slightly more Liberals (male and female) tend to cite the style of politics and lack of confidence, than do councillors from the other parties, but the differences are not large. Some 21% of Liberal females compared to only 1% of Tory females cite 'style', though this may be related to the different age profiles, educational characteristics, and socio-economic profiles of these women: as we know, Tory women are older, and less educationally qualified, and they do cite lack of confidence as frequently as do the Liberal women. It is difficult to be other than speculative about these supplementary findings.

The salience of some of the factors is illustrated by the following responses:

(i)   selection:
       'Until recently few women offered themselves for consideration' (male respondent)

       'Men exclude them' (male respondent)

(ii)   style of politics:
       'Politics is confrontation, compromise and competitiveness' (male respondent)

       'Women are naturally diffident and do not care for the rawness of politics' (female respondent)

(iii) lack of confidence:
       'Apathy, fear of criticism' (female respondent)

       'They become too emotionally involved' (male respondent)

(iv) family and household
       'My wife says so! She is always right!' (male respondent)

       'Women do not have housewives' (female respondent)

The dominant factor is, nonetheless, perceived to be responsibility for family and household; all political parties, and all males and females tend to agree on this, with men citing this barrier more frequently than women. This is confirmed as representative of both inner and outer London in Table 5.12.

Perhaps this is something of a truism, but it does sit somewhat uneasily with men's greater tendency to suggest that it is now easier for women to become elected members compared to about fifteen years ago. Perhaps the diffuseness of ideas about women's 'liberation' and equality have effected a change more ideological than real.[4] Men tend to exaggerate their role in caring for sick children (Witherspoon 1985 p.57) - perhaps too, they tend to exaggerate the ease with which women become elected members. Yet when presented with a question slanted differently - not 'do you take your share of household responsibilities to enable your wife greater freedom in the public world?', but 'Why do relatively few women become elected members?' - men's awareness of the barriers to women's participation in local politics becomes crystallised.

It may well be that men of opposing political persuasion agree, though for quite different reasons: Labour men seeing it as a regrettable reality that is amenable to adjustment or change (though perhaps not for them), Conservative men with references to 'Mother Nature', believing it to be a necessary and immutable fact of life, one Tory man remarking that 'unless men are to start *having* children society will always be male dominated'. The interviewing programme carried out subsequently and reported in the next chapter would suggest this to be the case. This is not to let Labour men off the hook. In the case of all three political parties the question needs to be asked what men are doing about household and family responsibilities, given their understanding that these factors militate sharply against women's participation.

So, what does a consideration of barriers to women's representation in local politics tell us? Above all it tells us that there is a clear awareness amongst councillors of all political parties that responsibility for family and household is the most important obstacle to women's participation, and that men are especially well aware of the nature of this material barrier.[5]

154

TABLE 5.13

Active Participation in Local Organisations/Campaigns Before Deciding to Stand for Election as Local Councillor: London Councillor Survey (%)

	Cons m	f	Lab m	f	Lib m	f	Total m	f
N =	116	114	140	133	20	24	284	288
Active	61	73	79	87	70	71	71	79
Not active	39	27	21	13	30	29	29	21
Total	100	100	100	100	100	100	100	100
N =	69	81	110	115	14	16	200	224
Involvement in:-								
One group	61	49	42	37	64	75	51	44
Two groups	20	24	22	24	7	6	20	22
Over two groups	19	27	36	39	29	19	30	34
Total	100	100	100	100	100	100	101	100
N =	69	80	106	111	13	16	195	219
Type of group:-								
Women's group	0	16	1*	14	0	25	1	16
Aid giving/ Charity	4	10	2	1	8	13	3	6
Shared interest	28	25	39	35	31	6	35	29
Specific issue	29	15	39	34	23	25	33	26
Party affiliated	29	26	15	14	39	25	22	20
Cultural and Religious	7	8	3	2	0	6	4	5
Other	3	0	3	0	0	0	3	0
Total	100	100	102	100	101	100	101	102

* Note: One Labour man indicated that he was involved in setting up a Women's Aid Refuge.

The need for a partner, available and supportive (a wife!) emerges as the most salient factor in participation:

'Wife takes a lot of stick for me when I am out, also acts as a messenger' (male respondent).

'The only reason that I can be a councillor is that my husband helps out at home - without his support it would be impossible' (female respondent).

'I'm not standing again as I intend to share the responsibility of bringing up children' (male respondent).

Quotes such as these underline the need to investigate the divisions of responsibility within the domestic sphere, and the mechanisms used by women and men councillors to cope with the conflicting demands of political, domestic and other priorities. These issues, raised by the Survey, are explored in the next chapter.

(e)   Involvement in Organisations, Groups and Campaigns, as a Route to Participation

We have noted so far that despite perceptions to the contrary (particularly men's perceptions) the route to participation in local politics is, for women, strewn with ideological and material stumbling blocks. A complex of factors would appear to be responsible for this: notably male resistance, family and household chores, less frequent selection by political parties, and lack of confidence stemming from socialisation.

Yet we have also noted that women *are* entering local politics in increasing numbers and that, when there, hold views and positions sometimes at odds with the men in the political parties they represent. They are, as with male councillors, somewhat unrepresentative of the populations they serve, but they do have a number of things in common: higher educational qualifications than women in general, greater experience of paid employment and, often, politically active mothers or other female relatives who seem to have provided a reference point or role model. They are also more likely to engage in politics when dependents such as children are 'off their hands'.

But how do they come to be involved specifically in local politics?

156

What is their channel, and does it differ from men's? To what extent, if at all, does the New Women's Movement in Britain affect the route to participation for these women?

Martlew argues that female councillors tend to be 'goal oriented rather than ideological in their political involvement', highlighting the 'importance of community activities both as a route into council work and as a continuing and particularly important aspect of the activities of women councillors' (Martlew 1985 p.65).

This is so, he argues, because:

'community based politics ... revolve primarily around "nurturance" issues (for example, child care, housing, etc.). Such community activism not only relates more closely to the experience of such women but it is also less formalized and can be more easily assimilated within their "time budgets"'

(Martlew 1985 p.49)

Accordingly women are 'more likely than men to have been involved in community councils, tenants associations and marginally more so in ratepayer bodies. Men were more likely than women to be involved in a business or in union organizations' (Martlew 1985 p.52).

This emphasis on community politics might be thought to sit easily with arguments about sectoral cleavages and collective consumption (Saunders 1979; Dunleavy 1980; and Castells 1977, 1978 and 1983). As women are recipients of such things as public housing and transport, so may they be potential vanguardists in the mobilisation of urban social movements.

Yet does this hypothesis really hold up to scrutiny? What if women were involved in 'women's groups', 'women's organisations' or 'women's campaigns', which appeared to be less influenced by so-called consumption issues, and more by the raising of their own consciousness, or issues like abortion with far-reaching implications for both men and women, which are assimilated only with difficulty into the restricting concept of collective consumption?[6]

Tables 5.13 to 5.18 were designed to test this hypothesis. Table 5.13 asked respondents if they had been active in any local organisation or campaign, before deciding to stand for election. As we can see, 79% of the women and 71% of the men said they had been so involved; Labour councillors had been more inclined to be involved, though the gender

TABLE 5.14

Women Councillors' Activity in Women's Organisations Prior to Involvement in Party Politics: London Councillor Survey (%)

"Were you an active member of any women's group or organisation before you became active in party politics?"

	Cons	Lab	Lib	Total
N =	116	135	24	291
Yes	29	38	29	33
No	71	62	71	67
Total	100	100	100	100
Number of groups:- N =	33	51	7	4
One group	70	59	100	66
Two groups	15	24	0	19
Over two groups	15	18	0	15
Total	100	101	100	100
Type of group(s):- N =	32	50	7	92
New women's group	16	66	71	47
Traditional women's group	69	6	14	30
Women's section	13	28	14	22
Other	3	0	0	1
Total	101	100	99	100

Note: One Labour male indicated that he was involved in one new women's group.

difference is clear - women were involved more often than men (a statistically significant difference using a chi-squared test). Of those who were involved, most (nearly 50%) were active in one group, though nearly a third were active in more than two groups.

Respondents were then asked to name the groups, for which a classification had to be found. As with all the Tables in this section, a sample of fifty responses was analysed for patterns: the categories shown are the result. Interestingly, most councillors were involved in shared interest (i.e. Trade Unions, Tenants Associations) and specific issue groups (i.e. CND, Environmental), particularly Labour men. Females mentioned women's groups and aid-giving voluntary or charity organisations more frequently and the Conservatives party affiliated bodies more often than Labour. These propositions are statistically significant using a chi-squared test. Whilst men appear to mention party-affiliated bodies more often then women, a chi-squared test reveals no significant difference.

The responses, however, tend not to suggest marked differences in the pre-political experience of women when compared to men - except, of course, for women's groups. It is to this that we now turn.

Tables 5.14 to 5.18 were addressed to female respondents only, since it was their experience that was then being sought. Table 5.14 asked women councillors whether they had been active members of any women's groups or organisations before they became active in party politics. This specific question obviously focussed their minds, and the number mentioning women's groups jumped from the 16% mentioned in Table 5.13 to 33% - with Labour females being most involved, 38% answering 'yes' to this question. So, a third of women had been involved in women's groups - usually one group as we can see from Table 5.14. When asked what *type* of group, an interesting split occurred: of those involved, 66% of Labour women and 71% of Liberal women indicated that they had been in new women's groups like local Consciousness-Raising (CR) groups, and 69% of Conservative females indicated membership of traditional women's organisations such as the Mother's Union and the League of Jewish Women. Nearly one quarter of women (mostly Labour) had been members of a women's section of another organisation, such as a Local Government Women's Committee.

TABLE 5.15

Involvement of Women Councillors Not Active in Women's Organisations, in Campaigns on Women's Issues: London Councillor Survey (%)

"If no, were you involved in any campaigns over women's issues?"

	Cons	Lab	Lib	Total
N =	99	102	19	235
Yes	8	48	0	25
No	92	52	100	75
Total	100	100	100	100

	Cons	Lab	Lib	Total
N =	8	47	1	56
Type of Campaign:-				
Political Rights	25	23	0	23
Services for women	25	13	0	16
Abortion	13	30	0	27
Economic	25	9	0	11
For children	0	19	0	16
Other	13	6	0	7
Total	101	100	0	100

Note: Four Labour men indicated that they were involved in four separate campaigns: Political rights, Abortion, Economic and For children.

160

TABLE 5.16

Current Involvement in Women's Groups or Organisations among London Women Councillors: London Councillor Survey (%)

"Are you now a member of any women's group or organisation?"

		Cons	Lab	Lib	Total
	N =	112	134	23	286
Yes		34	52	17	40
No		66	48	83	60
Total		100	100	100	100
	N =	38	68	4	114
Type of Group(s):-					
New women's group		8	34	50	26
Traditional women's group		42	6	0	18
Women's section		29	49	0	40
Local Government Women's Committee		3	10	0	7
300 Group		8	0	50	4
European group		8	2	0	4
Other		3	0	0	2
Total		101	101	100	101

161

Of those who were not involved in women's groups or organisations, some 25% were active in campaigns over women's issues (Table 5.15) - this was especially true for Labour women, with 48% of these councillors having campaigned, whilst among Conservatives the comparable percentage was only 8%, the Liberals indicating that they were not involved in any such campaigns at all. Interestingly, abortion figured prominently for those involved in these campaigns, with Labour women at 30%, followed by Political Rights campaigns such as 'Lesbian Rights', 'for women's suffrage while a schoolgirl' and 'lobbying MP to support the Sex Discrimination Bill'. Also important for Labour women were services for children like pre-school playgroups (arguably a collective consumption issue if provided by the state). The Conservative women were more likely to be found campaigning on economic issues like tax reforms and services for women - usually health screening - as well as for political rights. One Tory woman said that she 'wouldn't touch them with a greasy barge pole', though this was far from being a typical remark. One said 'not *before* elected - after, yes'.

Another question asked women if they were currently members of any women's group or organisation; the results are given in Table 5.16. Here we find some 40% of women currently members, with more Labour women, and few Liberals; most of these are members of *one* group.

When we analyse Table 5.16 in detail we find Conservative women still predominantly in traditional women's organisations, though the percentage has dropped from 69% prior to involvement in party politics to 42% after (though we must bear in mind that there are now 34% indicating involvement compared to 29% previously). If we lump together Local Government Women's Committees, the 300 Group, and European groups (all relatively recent innovations), Labour women's membership of new women's groups has dropped from 66% before becoming a councillor to 46% after election (though in percentage terms, more of them are involved, the proportion increasing from 38% to 52%). The doubling for both in terms of membership of women's sections of other organisations may help to account for this: as women become involved in politics, so perhaps they reduce membership of their autonomous women's groups, and join women's sections. We can only speculate about this.

The final point worthy of note in Table 5.16 is the membership of the 300 Group referred to earlier. Here, we see 8% of Conservative women, and 50% of Liberal women claiming membership. None of the Labour

162

TABLE 5.17

Previous Involvement in Women's Groups or Organisations of Inner London and Outer London Women Councillors: London Councillor Survey (%)

	Cons		Lab		Lib	
	Inner London 7	Outer London 24	Inner London 32	Outer London 17	Inner London 3	Outer London 4
New women's group	14	17	75	53	100	50
Traditional women's group	57	75	6	6	0	25
Women's section	14	8	19	41	0	25
Other	14	8	0	0	0	0
Total	99	100	100	100	100	100

Note: One Labour male reported membership of a new women's group.

TABLE 5.18

Current Involvement in Women's Groups or Organisations among Inner London and Outer London Women Councillors: London Councillor Survey (%)

	Cons		Lab	
	Inner London	Outer London	Inner London	Outer London
N =	8	27	43	25
New women's group	0	11	35	32
Traditional women's group	50	44	2	12
Women's section	0	37	44	56
Local Government Women's Committee	13	0	16	0
300 Group	0	7	0	0
European group	25	0	2	0
Other	13	0	0	0
Total	101	99	99	100

councillors reported membership of this group. An interesting finding for a group which purports to be non-party political.

Consideration of Table 5.17, brings little in the way of surprises. Involvement in traditional women's groups for Tory women was higher in outer London prior to elected membership, and in new women's groups Labour women's involvement was greater in the inner boroughs. So too for Table 5.18: membership of Local Government Women's Committees and European groups is higher in inner London, and for the 300 Group greater in the outer boroughs. These tables tell us little that we might not have inferred from party differences.

So, what can we conclude? It would appear that women's involvement in women's groups prior to elected membership is *much* higher than might have be expected: a third of all women were involved in women's groups, and of the two thirds who were not, a quarter had been active in campaigns over women's issues. In other words 50% of *all* the responding women councillors in London had been involved in women's groups and/or campaigns before becoming active in party politics.

Conservative women are to be found in the more traditional women's groups, with Labour and Liberals predominantly in the new women's groups. The types of group are quite different, although they do draw on a culture related to women, to which men are rarely exposed. Earlier, we noted the greater tendency for women to read 'women's' magazines and journals, drawing on a world of experience not shared by men. Given the influences of the New Women's Movement in Britain, in this respect, we may be moving closer to an explanation for differences in gender terms which we have found so striking in London's local politics.

It is not entirely clear quite how much can be claimed for such 'sub-cultural' differences, which address women *as* women, and as somehow 'different' to men. Yet there appears to be something in this, however diverse the literature and groups may otherwise be. These 'sub-cultural' differences in experience may be more important than is often acknowledged.

(f)   Concluding Remarks

The findings presented here challenge the conventional wisdom on women's position in local politics, which draws inspiration from two major sources. The first school of thought accords pre-eminence to political parties which express interests capable of being grouped largely within categories of social

165

class. Here, the women's movement is epiphenomenal, a product or consequence of the failure of political parties to hold on to their constituent groups.

Secondly, a Neo-Weberian variant of this approach, points to sectoral cleavages. In this conceptual framework, social movements have a life of their own, but are either superstructural phenomena which will ultimately reduce to their class-based differences, or are interest groups competing with other such groups in a curious pluralist environment.

The findings challenge both schools of thought, drawing on new social movement theory from a distinctly feminist perspective, seeing the New Women's Movement in Britain as having a pervasive influence on social life generally, effecting changes in taken for granted assumptions about gender. The women's movement is no mere epiphenomenon but a movement socially constructed by human players, often in the face of ideological resistances and material obstacles and barriers. Such a conclusion is strongly suggested in the findings from the Survey.

To begin with, we saw that London councillors, in common with councillors generally, are unrepresentative in statistical terms of the population they represent politically. Compared to their constituents, London councillors are younger (though Conservative female councillors are older), tend to own their housing, are more often married (though serial monogamy may be more common for Labour Councillors), often come from outside the Greater London area, and are more likely to be employed, full-time, than is generally the case.

But here similarities tend to cease, particularly if we consider the inter-relationships of party and gender. This approach enables us to cast doubt on received wisdom, which has hitherto considered councillors *either* by party *or* by gender. The analysis by McGrew and Bristow is a good case in point - here we can see how problematic it is to generalise from data based on party alone.

McGrew and Bristow argue that Conservatives are more oriented towards the community or the locality, whilst Labour councillors tend to give priority to party policy. Consideration of such issues cross-tabulated by party and gender, however, suggest that women are far more likely to be oriented to the locality, whilst males seek 'power'. McGrew and Bristow further find support for what I have called the embourgeoisement thesis of local politics - yet by analysing women councillors' position in the social class structure in comparison to men councillors where their better educational

166

qualifications are translated into lower socio-economic groupings, we find that only a weak (very weak) version of the thesis holds, refracted quite strongly by gender.

This is related more generally to women's perceptions of social class and ethnicity, which do *not* mirror male perceptions. For women, these identities are less clear when applied to themselves, with the implication that they experience their identity as women above all others. Further, their experience of participation in women's groups and campaigns prior to election casts doubt on the role of collective consumption in the mobilisation of urban movements.

These factors are clearly refracted by party, and generalisations about gender have been cautious. Perceptions of the women's movement as somehow radical, for example, *do* appear to translate along party lines: initiatives for Local Government Women's Committees have come from the left, and it is from the left that they find their greatest support. Yet women from other political parties have been prepared, more often than men, to reserve judgement before condemning. This is particularly interesting in that movement activists may be using the Labour Party to further their aims, suggested by the high incidence of highly educated Labour women councillors who were born outside London. Yet findings about these committees appear to cross over party political boundaries.

Once in local politics, of course, we have seen how the male 'brotherhood' of council officers and other councillors is thought to work against the specific interests of women; reflecting perhaps deeper biases about women held more generally in the population.

These biases are evident nowhere more clearly than in the process leading up to Council election. Despite ideas and beliefs about increased equality between the sexes it appears that men, whilst aware of the material barriers to women's increased participation, may do little to change their own behaviour, though for different reasons perhaps related to political party - Conservatives possibly seeing the inequality as biologically immutable, the others as a sad fact of life which could be changed. Aware that responsibilities for family and household stand in the way of women's participation, evidenced by there being few women councillors with children under five, dependent parents or disabled adults, male councillors appear to do little beyond acknowledgement, leaving a gap between ideology and reality; yet the level of ideology appears to be as real as the level of reality itself,[7] leaving the material barriers largely intact.

167

Despite this, women are becoming elected council members in increasing numbers. Though many councillors stood as candidates because they were *asked* to stand for election, the factors facilitating and hampering women's involvement stand out as a clear indictment of supposed equality of opportunity. Women are often there because the 'family had gone', their mothers or other female relatives had offered a role model, or they hoped to benefit the lot of women in some way.

It may well be that this orientation has a specific influence on women, drawing as they do on a distinct culture not shared by men. Their greater 'women's reading', involvement in women's groups, both new and traditional, and women's campaigns, suggests a place for *experience* in the politicisation of women that does not apply to men, and may well loosen the grip of party control on traditional political values.

Notes

1.   This proposition is statistically valid using a chi-squared test.

2.   These propositions are statistically valid using a chi-squared test.

3.   The issue of Local Government Women's Committees as well as Women's Units remains a live one. See Lines' (1990) report on the Conservative election pledge to scrap the London Borough of Ealing's Women's Unit.

4.   Whether or not constraints of housework and childcare have lessened was taken up in the interviews.

5.   Some councillors disagreed with the premise of the question.

6.   See Lowe (1986) for an interesting discussion of urban social movements and collective consumption.

7.   Geras, in his discussion of Marx, notes how levels of ideology are as 'real' as levels of reality or appearance (Geras 1972 p.292).

6 Women and local politics, and social movements and political parties

I'd like to control a Social Services or Women's Committee .... Your potential for effecting change and benefit to people's lives in an immediate sense is much greater than as an M.P.

(Labour Woman Councillor)

(a)   Introductory Remarks

The previous two chapters, which dealt with the London Survey of Local Authority Councillors, outlined a number of factors concerning women's involvement in local politics and the effect of the New Women's Movement in Britain on local political practice and ideas.

The major findings of the London Councillor Survey can now be summarised as follows:

(i)   there are different experiences for women and men in political socialisation and the route to participation in local politics. For all councillors the role of female relatives in politics is seen to

169

be prominent. For women, the reading of women's magazines and journals and involvement in women's groups and campaigns both prior to election and after is particularly salient. As a pre-political motivation on the road to participation women's experience in the women's movement is unparalleled, casting doubt on the role of collective consumption issues in the mobilisation of urban movements;

(ii)   there are different educational and socio-economic profiles for women and men, refracted by party, with women largely responsible for home and family and under-achieving, with educational qualifications translating into lower socio-economic occupations than men - thereby sounding a cautionary note for the embourgeoisement thesis of local politics;

(iii)   there are material and ideological barriers confronting women in their attempts to become elected members - a constellation of constraints and obstacles operating against women *as* women, notably lack of selection by political party, lack of confidence, style of politics and, particularly, responsibility for family and household;

(iv)   there is a belief that male councillors and male officers resist support for issues specifically affecting women;

(v)   activists within the New Women's Movement in Britain may have chosen to use existing channels of institutionalised party politics, in particular the Labour Party, at local levels to further their objectives; and

(vi)   political party and gender interact in a way which sometimes favours party issues and sometimes gender.

Of course, these findings are tentative and rest on a survey population restricted to London. As we saw when considering the problems of methodology, surveys suffer from a number of drawbacks, including spatial specificity and the respondents' interpretation of questions and issues as well as the researchers' interpretation of their answers and comments.

Nonetheless, the survey has drawn attention to issues of interest and concern to councillors themselves, thought worthy of further investigation and explored through a series of interviews which are reported in this chapter. Furthermore, the survey provided a wealth of background information, giving freedom to develop issues in depth - and whilst the average hour given to each councillor might seem a short time for an

170

interview, a great deal can be accomplished with people of their calibre who are used to analysing complex issues, getting to the point, summing up and explaining and arguing their views in an articulate way.

In what follows, attention has been paid to the councillors' own views, expressed freely and openly in anonymous interviews. Where possible the councillors' own words have been used, sometimes extensively, though where quotations are not used the discussion tries to express the experiences, views and intentions of councillors faithfully even if at times this appears conversational and journalistic. The findings are grouped under two headings: Women and Local Politics, and Social Movements and Political Parties.

(b)   Women and Local Politics

(b:i)   The 'Atypical Lot'
It soon became clear from talking to councillors that most of them had been invited to stand for office - and that many of them had regarded this as something of an honour.

But it also became clear that whilst most had been invited, women were likely to have been asked and to have accepted when they were either single, or had older children - usually over five years of age. A Labour woman councillor pointed out that women with young children, or females who were pregnant, were not selected. She cited Harriet Harman, Labour M.P. for Peckham, who was pregnant *when* she fought the 1983 General Election, *not before*. 'Women are simply not selected when pregnant' she said.

Some Labour female councillors had presented themselves and taken on the duties of Council office whilst looking after young children, though they were few in number and had suffered personal stress and marital strain as a result.

Most of the females interviewed, however, had entered political life when their children had started to grow up - usually from about five years of age upwards. This seemed to matter relatively little for the men, but for women it was crucial. One Conservative female councillor, for example, explained that she had been asked to stand in three different wards, but only when the children were older did she feel she could leave them. Why? Because 'I believe in bringing up your own children. I don't believe in one-parent families; if there is no money, you don't have children in the first place'.

A Conservative male councillor also saw child-care as the responsibility of women. If it meant them being out of local politics for ten to fifteen years this was a necessary sacrifice - nothing stopped them serving before and after having children. 'You can't balance it up', he said, 'people sometimes sacrifice families or marriages'; or, indeed, local politics.

These beliefs in women's role as primary carer responsible for child-care were echoed time and again, with the consequent effect on female representation acknowledged. Pondering her past experience, a Labour woman councillor reflected, 'I can remember thinking we are quite an atypical lot - we were either single, divorced, but certainly not in a conventional domestic arrangement where we had child care responsibilities'.

Other issues relating to the invitation to stand, or 'sponsorship' for office, were raised.

One Labour female councillor said she had been persuaded to stand 'against [her] better judgement', and had been frightened, and lacking in confidence; and another Labour female (though single) said she had been sought out by the Labour Party precisely because she was a women. No man mentioned issues related to gender either as reasons for standing, or as problems to be got around, and there were no men who referred to lack of confidence - if they lacked anything, it was experience.

(b:ii) A Constellation of Constraints
The London Survey had revealed a constellation of constraints operating against women *as* women in becoming councillors. These were: responsibility for home and family, lack of selection by political party, lack of confidence, and style of politics.

The interviewing programme confirmed these findings - in differing degrees - with one important exception: style of politics was felt not to be a factor. Indeed, wheeling and dealing and engaging in Machiavellian-style politics was considered a feature of political life generally and common to females and males alike, of all political parties.

A Conservative male councillor, for example, remarked 'The women on the Tory side could do deals with Alliance women'; and a Labour woman, 'we sometimes worked successfully with Tory women (not Tory men) - we could sometimes talk them round'. In referring to a recent local party incident one Conservative male councillor explained 'there was a contrived meeting of which Militant Tendency would have been proud - we point our finger at the Labour Party, but we've got our own things in the

172

Tory Party, it's just that normally they don't surface ... people in the Labour Party haven't got a thing on us when we get going!'

If there was any gender difference at all, it appeared that females were more able than males to negotiate and deal, leaving the men to their coups and putsches, whilst they got on with the business at hand. 'Style of politics', which it had been thought from the survey was a factor operating against womens' representation, was thought by those interviewed to be neither a barrier to their participation, nor a factor acting against them once involved.

On the other hand, lack of confidence, lack of selection by political party and responsibility for home and family *were* felt to operate quite strongly against women becoming councillors. Those who felt that lack of confidence militated against women argued that the denial of opportunities responsible for this situation could be reversed and that this need not be a long term problem.

In respect of party selection most councillors considered that things were beginning to change anyway with less prejudice in evidence now and that, at some time in the future, this factor would affect females less seriously - more will be said of selection later.

Responsibility for home and family, however, posed a problem of an altogether different kind. When asked to consider why this factor was considered to be the most important, councillors referred in particular to child-care. Men might contribute to housework but rarely to child-care. Women were invariably responsible for children, suffering guilt if they were not.

Responsibility for children and the onerous duties of Council office were not always compatible nor, necessarily, were child-care facilities such as creches the answer.[1] A Conservative woman councillor explained, 'provision of creches doesn't work very well. You see little children being brought out of the Council creche at 10 o' clock at night, babies asleep and toddlers tending to scream because they are half asleep. I mean I don't approve of it from the point of view of the children. In a sense that doesn't work, but getting babysitters works much better as a rule'.

But babysitters were not an answer where Council meetings went on through the night, as they increasingly did in some (though by no means all) cases. A Labour woman councillor asked me, 'Could you find a babysitter that would stay to 4 am?'

Reasons advanced to explain why women should bear this responsibility differed by gender and by party. Most women tended to see the responsibility as theirs alone, or as largely theirs. One Conservative woman remarked, 'I like my girls to be girls, my boys to be boys ... I like women to be ladies and I like men to be men; men are there to look after women - I don't even change an electric light bulb. I like men to be gentlemen, and open the door for ladies'. Two other Conservative women, younger than the one just quoted, did not see gender difference in quite these terms, but still saw women and men as having distinct responsibilities. One referred to the need to be 'One hundred per cent organised' in order to balance priorities and get things done.

Labour women, on the other hand, held males more responsible for this situation, one remarking, 'men don't want their wives out of the home - there's still male chauvinism'. Another commented, 'These ardent young men of the Left, they're so often there discussing feminism and how supportive they are of women's rights and you know that the "little wife" is at home keeping supper warm, and looking after the kids'.

So the female councillors felt that the responsibility for children was theirs and what is more felt guilt when not attending to child-care themselves.

The male councillors also saw the responsibility as resting squarely with women, though Conservative and Labour councillors differed as to why.

One male Conservative councillor explained that he played an active role in family life, but that 'Women would want to share, very directly, the first few years of their children's lives, due to biological reasons of bonding - something special between mother and child'. He was not the only Conservative male councillor to refer to 'bonding'.

Another Conservative male echoed these views, 'there are feminists that say a woman should be treated exactly the same as any male in any walk of life, and the fact that they produce [children] is quite irrelevant, or should be quite irrelevant, to their pursuing careers or interests along with any male. I would not go along with that. I would not see it, therefore, as being the state's responsibility, for example, to provide creches to enable women to participate in local government. It seems to me, if the woman wishes to participate, she has either to make her own arrangements for her own children, or not have children. It's no good beating the feminist drum and expecting other people to take the blame for a woman having made the choice to have her own children'.

Another Conservative man put the matter this way: 'Women have the ultimate responsibility, particularly when the children are growing up

174

because, after all, the majority of men are the salary earners, and as long as that's the case, 8 am to 6 pm, then perforce, the other partner will guard the nest'.

The idea that the man was the 'breadwinner' (See Barrett and MacIntosh 1980) was most often expressed by Labour male councillors, as justification for their working while the wife or partner took care of the children: after all, they argued, the money they brought home was for the family as a whole. Until male and female salaries were equalised, they saw themselves as primary wage earners.

Here, then, an example of the personal and political interacting in a way which blurs any clear boundary between the two: with personal beliefs and private practice concerning child-care reflecting strongly on the ability of women to participate in party political life. If lack of confidence and the reluctance of political parties to select women act as barriers to their participation, it is responsibility for young children above all else that affects their representation most decisively. As we saw from the London Survey, men are more likely to report seeing this as the principal determinant of exclusion, yet continue to justify their belief that women are primary child-carers. If women do not assume this role they suffer guilt, and if they do yet still present themselves for Council office, they suffer considerable personal stress and marital strain as a result, as we shall see.

(b:iii)   Men as Frustrators and Facilitators
Although it could be argued that women are, to some degree at least, co-conspirators in their own subordination, this argument which amounts to blaming the victim can not be pushed too far. Conscience, feelings of doubt, insecurity and personal responsibility derive from sources inside *and* outside oneself: people are both producers and products of their own societies and ideas do not float freely above social relationships - they are part of the constitutive element of social relations themselves.[2]

Ideas held by men that things are now somehow easier for women to become councillors conflict with beliefs about responsibility for child-care - and, if contradictory, tend to be justified.

A Labour male councillor reflected on these issues at length, 'I certainly don't think that the answer is the short term one. Society can provide all the sorts of supported infrastructures both for men and for women in terms of household, family, child-care responsibility. The deep-seated, deep-rooted issue as far as I am concerned is the inherent sort of male/female stereotypes with which we are brought up. We are still brought up with those stereotypes quite traditionally in some families where the division of responsibility over certain things is quite clear, is quite unequivocal. It is quite expected that women will stay at home and be the good loving subservient mother who cares for the home no matter what it is, from the bedsit to the house and the man will be the breadwinner. I am not saying that that is a dominant or prevailing family system but I do think that men have been jealous of their power and are extremely reluctant to relinquish or to think about changing the way that they are in society. But I think we learn from a very, very early age and that lots of things reinforce it during our lives. The place and the role of women in society and the place and the role of men. It's still difficult for women - inordinately difficult'.

The view that a woman's place is in the home, 'hearth and home' as some male Conservative councillors put it, is a strongly held one which sees men as the mediators between the two worlds of work and home. A Conservative man explained just how strongly held the view was by citing incidents at Selection Committees where single women had been asked why they were not married.

These beliefs and practices locate women within a social role - if not the help-mate of men, then at least dependent on them.

Not all men took this view. Some offered positive encouragement and material assistance taking care of children whilst the wife negotiated the public world. One Labour female councillor explained that her husband was 'co-operative', took care of the washing-up after she had cooked the evening meal for the family, and looked after their children while she attended Council meetings. A Conservative woman councillor - who also had an au-pair - said her husband would help out, 'providing nobody knew he was doing it, he's got a very chauvinistic attitude though he's very good around the house; but he wouldn't like anyone to know that'.

The assistance of male partners can clearly be crucial - though it should be noted that the men in the two cases just quoted were 'helping' - and the women either retained some responsibility, like cooking, themselves, or had female au-pair 'assistance'.

But even where help was more altruistically given - as it was in the case of one Liberal female councillor where her husband took on most of the family responsibilities including child-care - the woman concerned still suffered feelings of guilt. Having assumed Council office when her children were growing up, she felt she had 'missed a period of my children's life

176

because I wasn't around in the evenings'.

More often than not, however, men resisted their partners' transition into political office, or did little, if anything, to smooth the way.

For Conservatives this issue was rarely confronted - the young female councillor who had decided to make the move suffering from the Shirley Conran 'Superwoman' syndrome - having to live up to others' expectations of her 'superior' abilities. Labour women, on the other hand, tended to face up to this resistance much more often.

One Labour female councillor explained that her husband had 'positively objected' to her standing for election. 'My husband thought that I should have asked him first, because I'd be away from home and not have his meals ready ... he still gets distressed'.

Another Labour woman recounted the difficulties, leading up to her divorce, which started when she entered office. 'There was no way I was going to be at home at 7 o' clock at night when he came in, with a hot dinner on the table, like he'd had all his life. It was left in the oven, or on the top - but that didn't suit him'.

Of course, it could be argued that the tensions aroused in these cases simply put further stress on already strained relationships. One male Labour councillor explained, 'I have seen families split up over this, involving both male and female councillors. There are always two sorts of people who go into politics, those who go because they're interested in politics, and those who want to get out of the family. A lot of people will tell you that they do it for the good of the community, and all sorts of other things, but quite a large proportion actually do it because their home life is not tolerable, so one way of getting out of it is to spend all your time solving other people's intolerable lives by being a councillor. I did it because I wanted to do it'.

Nonetheless, the overwhelming evidence from the interviews leads to the conclusion that men resist, in a variety of ways, females' involvement in local politics. Some men offer positive encouragement and, more importantly, material aid, but women's increased representation would appear to be the consequence of their simply taking on more responsibility and confronting male resistance.

(b:iv) A Question of Priorities
Taking on political office carries very heavy obligations and a demanding work load. Where, before entering office, it had been possible for councillors to put things off, defer or delay, on assuming office their time was rarely, if

ever, their own as the pressing matters of office demanded ever-more of their attention.

Although refracted by Party - with Conservative males *appearing* to be less pressurised[3] than other councillors - it had become increasingly important for councillors to juggle and constantly re-order their priorities. The most interesting thing about this was how differently males and females coped.

Generally, *men tended to compartmentalise* the demands on their time, putting political duties and careers before the family, only adjusting those priorities when forced to. *Women, on the other hand, juggled and balanced* their priorities, ever-conscious of overlap and conflict, putting their families before all else in extreme situations. Any time off from paid employment was invariably used by the men to increase their political participation, and by women to care for the family.

One Liberal male councillor explained that when he considered standing for office he decided to draw 'strict parameters of time' around his various duties. A male Labour councillor put the matter this way: 'I would try to leave weekends free - it's the way you try to make it up to your family'. Another male Liberal councillor remarked in a similar vein, 'It's a question of degree, I get furiously involved (it's a gut reaction) in politics for a few days, then the family, then I pick up my politics again'. Paid work was also part of this frantic activity given attention, in turn, with the other undertakings.

But whilst priorities were struggled with and re-ordered, there was a sense of calling to political office for the men. A Labour male councillor put it thus: 'The family always came first, but there were things I felt I had to do. I've always felt that I've had to attend every committee that I'm on, unless I happen to be away, or at work, or something. So that's always been a priority, and it's a matter of juggling the rest of the priorities'.

Another Labour man explained,

'My wife was not critical enough of what she foresaw as the effect on our family and our family life of my taking this opportunity and thus additional responsibilities. It is something that she now recognises and regrets. She remembers clearly from the days when her father was a councillor, in another part of the country, the amount of time and work that he put in. It is quite clear now with hindsight, it didn't work and the pressures and the strains on the family, because once I had made a political commitment I wanted to sustain it, I wanted to see it through. Which I did with this and it has meant considerable sacrifice. It has certainly meant that my wife has supported me unequivocally through this period, unselfishly, and has done everything, and more for the family when I haven't been here to do it. It's meant that I have spent less time with my children, less time actually together as a family because although I might be here, the amount of reading and working is a lot. The amount of time away each evening, when I usually go straight from work to the Town Hall, we're talking at least four nights a week possibly five nights with a surgery once every few weeks, which will, in total, on top of an ordinary working week, now represent about 30 hours extra accumulated work. I think the strain has been quite inordinate. It's certainly meant that my relationship with my wife and children has suffered. I'm quite clear about saying that. It's been complicated .... and for at least 15 - 16 months my wife and I have been separated. That is not, obviously not, unconnected with politics, but it relates to the fact that what I gave up for politics meant that the quality of our relationship was sacrificed. So the personal toll has been really quite substantial in recent years. It's for that reason that I shan't be standing for election again.

I should also add that I have had virtually no social life at all. What spare time I have is either resting, sleeping or washing'.

This quote gives a flavour of the pressures, but also of the determination to carry through a political commitment, with the family to be somehow picked up later. Not all men followed this line. Two Conservatives, who described themselves as 'wets', told me that they had adjusted their political commitments when pressured by their wives.[4]

Women's reaction to the competing pressures was different. The Conservative 'Superwoman' already quoted taking more on board, being 'one hundred per cent organised', with au-pair and husband 'assistance'.

A Labour woman councillor said that when she had a young family, 'the Council arrangements had not been conducive'. With late night meetings, travel difficulties, no babysitting expenses (only an attendance allowance), and the claim on her time away from the family, she felt quite considerable pressures, resulting in her taking one of her youngsters with her to the Town Hall, a practice unheard of at the time.

179

A Liberal female, who worked part-time whilst serving as a councillor, was offered an opportunity to work full-time: 'I could have carried on being a councillor, but you can't make a career out of that, so I seriously took a decision that I needed to go out and start working for a career. We [the family] couldn't afford me working part-time'.

Women constantly balanced their priorities, like a juggler keeping the balls in the air, remaining aware of the process as a whole, whilst males compartmentalised their lives. As with Hegel's master and slave where only the slave remained aware of the totality of the process, so too female councillors, for whom the distinction between what was personal and what public and/or political, losing any meaning.[5]

(b:v) Civic Pride: The Local as a Major Political Aspiration

It became clear from the interviews that the duties of Council office were felt to be onerous; this may account for the two to three terms of office usually undertaken.[6]

Those councillors I interviewed who said they would not stand again often mentioned the time and energy-consuming nature of their duties and indicated that they intended to give more time to their families, or leisure pursuits, in the future.

It has to be said, however, that the responsibilities of office were also attractive to councillors - they carried on because they *enjoyed* being councillors and/or felt that their contribution mattered - many did not wish to pursue a career as an M.P., but wished to remain in *local* politics where they felt they had something to offer, and where they could make a difference to other peoples' lives.

This casts doubt on the belief or conventional wisdom - noted earlier - that local politics is seen as a major route to involvement in national politics, a kind of stepping-stone. Some of the councillors interviewed were considering moving in this direction, and two had put themselves forward as Prospective Parliamentary Candidates, but for most, their focus and their concern was the local. Some of the remarks made by councillors are worth considering.

First, it should be noted that many councillors were not attracted by national politics:

'Broadcasting was a big mistake - given the behaviour of some M.P.'s, you wonder why we elected them ... they're like animals - they

180

wouldn't be allowed to behave like that in the Council Chamber. If there was that level of noise and interruption, we would clear the Chamber - it's absolute bedlam!' (Conservative man);

'A number of my friends are in the House of Commons, and I hear things about marriages breaking up, and relationships with their secretaries .... The thing about Cecil Parkinson wasn't the fact that he was caught out, but that he was the only *one* who was caught out!' A seat taken out in the country, 'puts an enormous strain on marriages and of course the husband's down in town still seeing all his old mates' (Conservative man); and

'I just don't want to join that elitist male club' (Labour woman).

But that, secondly, local politics was itself attractive, and viewed positively:

'Historically, the Liberal Party has put a great deal of emphasis on its local councillors and really does see them as being on a par, and in many cases perhaps even more influential, within the Party than Prospective Parliamentary Candidates' (Liberal woman);

'I get a kick out of being in local politics, promoting changes and seeing transformed communities' (he had helped initiate various Tenant's Associations, with women in charge of them) (Labour man); and

'I'd like to control a Social Services or Women's Committee .... Your potential for effecting change and benefit to people's lives in an immediate sense is much greater than as an M.P. (Labour woman).

There is a very real sense in the quotations that local politics matters and has been chosen for its own sake, for the opportunities it provides to effect change about things that are seen to matter, and for people above all else.

This sense of altruism pervaded the interviews, and the fact that it was women more often than men, and Labour and Liberal councillors (a little more frequently) than Conservatives who cited their desire to achieve and use power for the benefit of others, casts doubt on the conventional wisdom[7] that the Conservatives generally are more oriented to the community. Other councillors are *at least* as oriented and committed to their communities as Conservatives, if not more so.

(c)   Social Movements and Political Parties

(c:i)   Opportunities and Resistances

We have seen that New Social Movement theorists argue that the social movements of the 1960s owe their existence to the failure of Western Social Democratic and Eastern Communist Parties to keep in touch with their constituent base. On this argument, social movements are an 'unintended effect' of existing political practice and thereby epiphenomenal.

The position taken here is contrary. It is argued that rather than being derivative of some external force or pressure, social movements are created or made by individuals and groups who take advantage of opportunities presented through changes in the social structure. For the New Women's Movement in Britain this has meant taking advantage of opportunities provided by such things as increasing educational qualifications and career openings, to push for change in the face of ideological and material resistance.

The London Councillor Survey and interviews with councillors now enable us to consider the argument - to explore contemporary history through the lived experience of local authority councillors.

An important question in all this is the degree to which opportunities are taken in the face of obstacles, barriers and outright resistance.

In the London Councillor Survey it was noted that 65% of men and 56% of women thought it was now easier for women to become councillors, than compared to about fifteen years ago - more men than women (Chapter 5). But that other factors - such as responsibility for home and family - were thought to act as an obstacle to women's involvement. In the interviews councillors were asked whether they thought it *was* now easier for women to become councillors. Only four councillors replied that it was *not* now easier and seven hedged their bets, saying yes *and* no; the remaining fourteen said they thought it *was* now easier. However, nearly all the responses were qualified. 'Not easy but easier', 'Maybe a bit easier now that women are a fashionable topic', 'On balance, only just', 'Not easier, but less difficult - to do with attitudes', 'But people generally feel women's place is in the home'.

All of these quotes came from councillors who had answered that it was now easier for women to become councillors.

A male Labour councillor explained: 'It's about the same, because people talk about it more, and it's the flavour of the month, it's a popular issue .... But not much has changed'.

A female Liberal councillor summed up the general feeling when she said why most councillors had replied that it was now easier for women to get elected: 'because it's more accepted, though I don't think their life is any easier, and I don't think it's any easier for them to get elected. I still think there's a slight bias in the general public, that they don't think it's a woman's role'.

Councillors referred time and time again to the public perception that a woman's place was 'in the home', despite the increased numbers of women in local politics and their increasing share of responsible positions for example chairing Local Authority committees and leading Councils. It seemed that councillors could see women in increasing numbers, assuming ever-greater responsibilities, but that they remained mindful that women still had responsibility for 'hearth and home'.

It would seem that ideas about equality for women are somewhat in advance of social and political practice.

A Liberal female councillor put the point most concisely: 'Consciousness has changed, but not the political help to enable women to participate in local politics'.

A gap between ideology and the reality of women's experience, particularly marked for the woman in question, whose own consciousness she explained had been raised when she gave birth to a child between returning a completed questionnaire and the interview: 'I've realised it, particularly since my child was born, that it was incredibly difficult fighting a campaign with a young baby, and it's also quite difficult to get people to babysit so that you can sit on umpteen committees and sub-committees and play a full role as a councillor. If I were a man, I don't think there would be quite the same pressures on me, because I think it's still seen - I'm sure my husband would deny this - as my role to make sure that the baby is looked after if I've got things to do on the Council. I think, particularly for women with young children, things haven't really changed that much'.

Women have, quite simply, taken on more responsibility in assuming political office, and if ideas are changing about women's role, social practice is lagging behind. Indeed, it could even be argued that the belief that things

183

are now easier for women operates against them since the men who believe this to be even partially true may see little point in changing 'already facilitative' social and political arrangements. The barriers are likely, therefore, to remain erect and women forced to realise their aspirations for local political office in the face of both ideological and material obstacles. The consequence, as we have already noted, is personal stress and marital strain.

(c:ii) There is Nothing New About the New Women's Movement in Britain

'There's always been a women's movement'
(Male Labour Councillor)

Most councillors had difficulty describing the women's movement - they often referred to its aims or objectives rather than say what they thought it was. This had been expected there are no clearly agreed definitions of what social movements are, no card-carrying members to identify (Barry 1990 and 1991). Nonetheless, the councillors interviewed invariably accepted that there was such a thing as a women's movement.

It was possible to discern from their responses that the movement had recently gone through two phases: the first during the late 1960s, and the second from the end of the 1970s to the early 1980s. This is worth developing since the surveys quoted in Chapter 4 on representation gave details of female councillor representation just before and after these phases:-

1964	1976	1985
(Maud Report)	(Robinson Report)	(Widdicombe Report)
12%	17%	19%

There was an appreciation of a long tradition of feminist and women's movement activity - notably among Conservative males, one referring to the Suffragettes and the mobilisation of female workers in the First and Second World Wars, as well as events in America in the 1960s. A Conservative woman commented, 'I think there is opening up as regards women altogether ... I think late sixties were glimmering a bit ... right through the 70s, more things were opening up to women all over the place. Not solely politics, not particularly politics'.

It also became clear that opportunities for 'new blood' coming into local politics in the late 1960s had increased as wide electoral swings were experienced in London.

In London in 1967 and 1968, as we saw in Chapter 3, the Tories enjoyed a massive landslide, to be reversed some four years later at the next local elections. Given the 100% membership election of London Boroughs paralleled by only the English and Welsh Shire Metropolitan Counties and Scottish Authorities (see Widdicombe 1986, Research Volume I p.48), the massive swings caused upheavals of a major kind: indeed, some of the councillors I interviewed who had become elected at this time talked of the events in dramatic terms.

Not only did many established councillors lose their seats, but many young fresh-faced young candidates standing for hitherto unwinnable seats found themselves catapulted into political office to assume responsibilities for which they had clearly not been prepared. 'Who would have thought that Islington would go Tory?', reflected one. Another had only been a party member for three years when he stood and was elected, another just twenty one years of age when he took office as a Tory councillor and witnessed a displaced Labour councillor with 'tears running down his face'.

This is the period when increasing numbers of women became elected as councillors - as we have seen, their representation in this period went up from 12% to 17%.

The second period occurred in the late 1970s and early 1980s. By this time as we have seen, the Labour Party had lifted its ban on proscribed organisations and elements of what came to be known as the 'New Urban Left' (Gyford 1985 p.17) began to filter into local socialist politics.

By the early 1980s some of the changes concerning women were beginning to be felt. One Labour woman councillor who had taken a decision to stand down at the 1986 local election in favour of a younger woman referred to a slow process which had accelerated over the last five to six years as females increasingly put themselves forward, especially women with young children.

A male Labour councillor remarked, 'Women in the Labour Party are now younger and better educated; the women we used to have in the old Labour Party were more the "housewife type"; they were much more conventional'. The change in the educational profile of female councillors was also noted by a Labour woman who drew attention to the benefits extending to working class women: 'Some working class feminists with

185

university qualifications go into marriage with the idea that they'll lead their own lives, whereas it took me a long time ...'. She continued, 'I didn't appreciate how the other half lives - they are unblinkered'.

But why were women coming forward at this time? A single Labour woman explained that in the 1960s women in the women's movement were working outside party political structures, which were seen as 'white and male dominated'. At the end of the 1970s and early 1980s, however, many of these women, herself included, decided to work within established structures and moved over to the Labour Party; though she felt this was peculiar to London, the North being less sensitive to such influences, being still a 'male bastion'.

Selection procedures in the Labour Party were changing - one female Labour councillor referred to moves within her party during 1982 and 1986 to put at least one black person and one woman forward for selection.

A male Labour councillor even went so far as to say that they would now 'go out of [their] way to select a woman in some cases, and on some of the shortlistings there are usually at least two women included out of five or six'.

Shortlisting is, nonetheless, no guarantee of selection. The process itself, which might discriminate against women, has to be experienced, the gatekeepers have to be passed. A Conservative male councillor commented: 'they might be put on a shortlist because they're a woman, but not selected because they're a woman'. Echoes of this may lie behind the remark of a male Liberal councillor that it was now easier for older women in his party to become councillors - where responsibilities for child-care had lessened.

But moves to promote women were also in evidence in the Liberal Party, one male Liberal councillor explaining that, 'sometimes women were chosen for marginal seats, but this is now changing in the Liberal Party where we are pushing women'. It seemed that not only were more women being selected, but that in order to ensure they were being put forward for winnable seats, women were increasingly represented on the Liberals' 'Candidates Approval Selection Procedure'. He went on: 'We insist that on a panel of three people one has to be a woman'.

Conservatives referred to women rising increasingly to political office 'on their merits', though as one male Tory noted, this might well have had something to do with the 'influence of the women's movement', which gave females a higher profile than had hitherto been the case.

Interestingly, one male Labour councillor referred to the positive

186

vetting procedures instituted by his party as having some 'negative consequences'. A Labour Party member and councillor for many long years, he had not been reselected at a recent election. 'I'm out because of positive discrimination, a coloured person was chosen - I'm very, very unhappy about it as I don't believe in positive discrimination ... what does a woman or a black person offer that's different to a white male? We're all as good as anyone else'. He went on, 'being removed as a councillor was shattering and I never did anything to stop it ... I've usually been in a position of people begging me to do it; it came as quite a blow and it's taken me some time to get over it'. The situation was seen as particularly hurtful as the councillor in question had been receiving an extremely high percentage of the local vote, although he had seen the tide of opinion turning in favour of more 'positive' selection procedures and believed that to fight it would have been swimming against the tide, a futile gesture which would have got him nowhere.

It is difficult to know how far this is representative of practice within the Liberal and Labour Parties. Clearly, if someone new is selected for a seat when the total number of seats remains the same, someone else loses out[8] - and there may not always be sufficient members ready, or prepared, to stand down to make way for 'new blood'. This is an interesting example of male resistance though it has to be said that the councillor in question assumed equality between the sexes as axiomatic, and in some respects could be viewed as ahead of his time. In respect of child-care, for example, he said, 'I sometimes looked after our children more than my wife, but so what!'

Here, then, a casualty of Party policy, a man who could be said to have been practicing some of the very things the policy was designed to bring about. He was, nonetheless, somewhat atypical of the men generally.

(c:iii) The Women's Movement, Social Democratic Parties and the Media

Evidence of changes in Labour and Liberal Party selection procedures coinciding with moves into Labour politics by women's movement activists lends support to the argument that the women's movement and social democratic politics have something in common.

For one Conservative female, the women's movement, 'evolved, it became very orientated towards lesbianism. I don't care about sexual identities, but it [the women's movement] lost credibility - the right wingers shunned it ... then there was a left wing orientation as the Left took it over'. She continued, 'You had to wear fatigues and have your hair cut short, you had to join the gay liberation front, and grow your nails out here ... I became very anti-...'. She was annoyed: 'Why can't I be a member of the women's movement?'

It was more common for Conservatives to see the women's movement as only recently identified with 'the Left'. It was seen as having originated outside party politics and as still having some autonomy. Labour councillors also argued that whilst their party might for the moment be a convenient vehicle for the women's movement, its roots and continuing strength lay outside the party - one Labour male citing Greenham Common in evidence.

So what was it that Conservatives generally were reacting to when, in the London Councillor Survey, they said they were not supporters of the women's movement - the social movement itself, or specifically 'the Left'? The answer was, overwhelmingly, 'the Left'.

Referring to selection procedures which positively encouraged the representation of women, a Conservative male councillor reflected, reminiscent of Hayek and his notion of a 'spontaneous order' (Hayek 1975 p.57), 'I don't accept the philosophy behind it, that the composition should reflect the make-ups of society, because that is artificial, it's contrived ... it should happen naturally and spontaneously, but if it doesn't, well you just have to wait for it to happen, it shouldn't be forced because that's artificial. It's the quota, and I don't like quotas'.

Other councillors referred to the action taken by members from the London Borough of Camden to support the English Collective of Prostitutes in their occupation of the Church of the Holy Cross in London's King's Cross.[9] This issue had received wide and sensational media coverage.

The question of media coverage and the amplification of issues into areas of public concern was a factor mentioned by a number of councillors - one Conservative woman arguing that it was the media that was largely responsible for the public identification of the Left with CND, gay rights and lesbianism: 'The media have got the women's movement down as left wing orientated, peace movement involved, almost all run by lesbians. It doesn't matter if you are, or if you're not, you're labelled'.

The following remark from a Conservative male councillor is worth quoting at length. He was referring to the Women's Committee of a neighbouring Borough who had been pointed out to him: 'A group of heavies entered the bar, and they looked intimidating; they were actually female heavies, not male heavies, and I wouldn't want to mix with those by any stretch of the imagination. They're pretty frightening people I reckon.

They have got this new consciousness, this new feminist, women's movement, consciousness and identity and, as such, they're a determined group of people and much as I disagree with their ideas - never would agree with their ideas - one can't ignore them; but at the same time they're not trying to persuade people, they're trying to bully and tell people what they want done'.

It transpired that the 'heavies' were, 'all younger women, part of the Shirley Williams generation ... pupils who've been educated beyond their intellect or have not been educated enough. Either way, a little knowledge can be a dangerous thing'.

The idea that the Left tended to produce dangerous women was linked to lesbianism: 'they are women of the Left, or those left pressure groups, who have a women's group connotation as well. I've got a lot of prejudice against them, because they tend to be unattractive, they tend to be vicious, and generally unpleasant. They're frequently lesbian and this is partly one of the banners that they fly. To be a member you've got to be a lesbian, which seems to me to be absurd'.

So it was that Conservatives tended to react to the Left and to sensationalised images of feminist 'heavies' deriving largely from the media.

There was something of a reaction to women *as* women in all this. Another Conservative male councillor explained, 'I've never yet seen a pretty feminist, most of them are pretty much, on a physical basis, a disaster area; I wonder if they have a chip on their shoulder ... they're not going to be Miss World, so it's a vent to their frustrations'.

Even so, councillors saw the women's movement itself as being both outside as well as inside party politics. One Conservative female councillor said, 'We have a strong women's movement in the Conservative Party - *all* women's opinions are asked, even the tea lady's at Tory Women's gatherings'.

A strong sense of feminist consciousness pervaded the thinking of a number of Conservative female councillors. The Conservatives, I was advised, had always taken account of women's views through Women's Advisory Committees, Women's Branches and Women's Conferences.

One Conservative male councillor remarked: 'the Conservative Party has quite seriously wooed the opinion forming women in a series of conferences where several hundred have been present. Some saw Norman Tebbitt as very patronising'.

A Conservative female councillor maintained that she was 'a feminist'.

'Well I never accepted when I was a child that I wasn't the equal of my cousins, who were all boys. I never would accept it and I reckoned that it didn't make any difference whether you were a boy or a girl what sort of education you wanted, and should get if you could'.

A female Labour councillor summed it all up this way: 'One of the strengths of the women's movement is that it can incorporate woolly-minded individuals like myself alongside radical lesbian feminists at the other end of the spectrum ... whereas political parties get too hung up on theory - they miss the reality of life, of starting from where people are'.

(c:iv) Social Movements and Political Parties: the Potential for Change

We have just noted changes in female representation in local politics, from 12% in 1964, to 17% in 1976, and 19% in 1985, and that these increases were in line with women's movement influence in the late 1960s and social democratic party selection procedure changes in the early 1980s.

Over the first period women's representation increased by approximately 42%, in the second around 12%.

On the face of it, this would seem to suggest, quite strongly, that the late 1960s wave of women's movement activity and consciousness raising was more effective in securing increased female representation in local politics than the procedural changes introduced by social democratic parties; three and a half times more effective.

Social movements are difficult to define. They are clearly not organised groups although organised groups may be involved - and they are not political parties with hierarchies, leaders and party-lines, although movement activists may become members. But in dealing with established parties, organisational factors can work for or against social movements. This is not to suggest that the party-line in any of the parties in local authorities is necessarily rigid or inflexible.

First, whilst the 'traditions of good personal relationships between leading party figures of the different parties' noted by Widdicombe (Widdicombe 1986 Research Volume I p.35) may be less a feature of London's political life, most councillors respected their opposite numbers - one male Conservative, for example, said he regarded the local Liberals as simply wrong in their views, they were 'not evil people'. Secondly, local politics produces strong-minded, able councillors, 'we're not a dragooned body of frightened people' as one Conservative man put it. Thirdly, whilst around one half of all the councillors interviewed said that the party-line *was*

190

strong in local politics, they invariably saw this as a feature of their opponents' party structures, rather than their own.

The party-line can, nonetheless, be strong on occasion, when pressure is brought to bear. If the cost of provision for such things as creches, for example, is felt to be too high, I was informed by some Conservative councillors that proposals would be vetoed by the Party. It also transpired that some Conservative men put Conservative women 'in their place' if they overstepped the party-line during their service on a Local Government Women's Committee. Another Conservative male took the decision not to stand for re-election since he had become, 'fed up with putting my hand up for things I didn't believe in'.

Such cases were the exception rather than the rule, however, and whilst the party line seemed stronger in the Conservative Party, some Conservative women *and* men supported the principle of creche provision above cost, even if they remained mindful of the need for good 'value-for-money' provision. Some Conservative men and even more Conservative women were also less than dismissive of Local Government Women's Committees.

Clearly, there are gains to be made for social movement objectives through local political negotiation. As a Conservative male councillor explained, nursery provision may result from cross-party agreement, though for different reasons: for the Conservatives, it provides a good start in life for the children, whilst for the Labour Party, it enables the mother to work.

Nor is there *necessarily* any kind of 'traditional' male resistance to initiatives for women, or if there is, it is not necessarily obstructive.

A Conservative male councillor suggested that male Trade Unionists were far more dangerous to the aims of the women's movement than male Tory councillors, even when pushing the 'hearth and home line'. 'These guys tend to be written off as "old buffers"', he said, 'they're seen as dinosaurs. They *were* mainstream but they're now washed up, and sometimes laughed at'.

Social movement influence can, it seems, operate through local politics, crossing-over party boundaries.

One Conservative woman objected to Women's Refuges on the grounds that they resulted in institutionalised depression for the women concerned. She had, accordingly, pushed for flats for women who had been subjected to male violence. 'I could quite easily have broken with my Party if necessary over these flats for women'. We also find a male Conservative councillor opposing the provision of a late night taxi service for women, but adding, 'I have little sympathy as I'm not a woman experiencing this [potential danger of attack]. If I were, I might feel differently'.

The role of experience is thus important, though it is by no means crucial. A male Labour councillor said he had been pushing women's issues for years. He explained, 'I've always had these views - back in the early 1970s, we looked at areas with tenancies where wives had been given a raw deal. Where marital breakdown, we gave tenancy to the person who had custody of the kids (usually women). If there were arrears we'd stuff the husband for them'. He went on, 'Council policy then was that if there was an unmarried woman with a baby, she would get one bedroom. Another councillor and I helped to change that in favour of separate bedrooms'. He had also been involved in the setting up of Tenant's Associations, where women took leading roles.

Here, then, a sense of permeation of ideas about women, a diffusion of consciousness deriving from the women's movement. A Labour woman councillor offered an interesting metaphor for this permeation of ideas: 'The women's movement is to do with women breaking out of the straitjacketing and stereotyping together and attempting to shift the parameters within which they operate, and different groups of women have worked in different areas to do this. The initial excitement of the pioneering feminists led to a lot of women examining what they were doing, and a lot of structures - schools, Local Authorities - looking at what they were doing with a view to ensuring it was not discriminating, but encouraging to women. The women's movement is such an amorphous mass that has achieved an enormous amount, and potentially even more - *it's like a mass of jelly*, as it gets pushed in one area, it squeezes through and moves on' (my emphasis).

A mass of jelly, or nitro-glycerine?

(c:v) The Languages of Gender and the Vocabularies of Local Politics
For Stedman Jones, 'Social alliances do not simply happen, they are brought into being and re-created by the construction and periodic reconstruction of a common political discourse' (Stedman Jones 1983 p.253).

Discourse concerns language as well as, for authors such as Foucault (1977a and 1979) social practice and social relations, and Stedman Jones relates these very directly in this quotation to notions of social action and social change, to social *movement* itself. But there is more in this quotation,

192

concerning the nature of politics, since social alliances can occur outside institutionalised party politics - indeed for radical feminists the personal is political and power a constituent part of all social relationships (Redstockings 1969).

The language of gender is, in this sense, becoming a part of the vocabulary of local politics. The acceptance by some Conservative women of Local Government Women's Committees, with others more likely to suspend judgement than their male party colleagues is evidence of this.

There is also a sense that women have achieved and are set to achieve more for women in local government than hitherto.

When councillors were asked what had been achieved, if anything, by the increased involvement of women in local politics, the silences on the tapes were deafening. Only after taking thought did councillors offer their responses.

Broadly, councillors fell into two groups in their reactions to this question.

First, a group consisting of predominantly Conservative males with some Labour men and Conservative women, suggested that little or nothing had been achieved beyond a few limited gains for women. For this group, change was slow, painfully slow. A male Conservative councillor remarked,

'Whilst the Ladies can well debate on the desirability, once you've started talking and decide on how we are going to structure this administratively, functionally, organisationally, they're lost! What we need is more people who've been through a business life, then had their children, or the other way round, but have got that experience to draw on, rather than come in and to spend maybe two cycles learning the hard way'.

A Conservative female councillor added, 'In my age, we didn't have the opportunities; the professional business woman is a very recent - the last few years - invention'. She had previously referred to the 'under fortyish group in the Conservative Association, who are now coming along - I'm sure they'll have a terrific impact'.

The second group, composed largely of Labour and Liberal women with some Conservative females and Labour men, felt that a great deal had been achieved. They tended to focus, quite specifically, on changes in consciousness, or awareness, of women's issues which had affected all concerned. The role of *experience* in all this was clear, with many references to women's greater understanding of, and sensitivity to, housing, social services, and family issues. Many more references were made to issues where women could be said to have been *proactive*, rather than *reactive*: innovations in respect of Local Government Women's Committees, the highlighting of violence done to women in terms of mugging and rape, the funding of women's groups and association with women's groups thereby maintaining links with grass roots bodies and the effects on the selection policies of the Labour and Liberal Parties.

Women, I was told, had also made Local Authorities more responsive, they had helped Councils to pioneer contract-compliance equal opportunities packages, and had influenced many committees in respect of 'the woman's angle'. There was some disagreement over whether such things as planning involved women, though some councillors clearly thought it did and that other councillors ought to recognise this, even if they said they did not. Two Labour women councillors even made quite spontaneous references to the role of female officers in local authorities (apart from women's units) who, it was suggested, brought a greater sensitivity to the bureaucracy in its dealing with local people - one woman Housing Officer was quoted as being more sympathetic over sheltered housing than her male colleagues.

The use of females in leading positions as role models and encouragement to other women was cited: women were leading councils and chairing committees, though one Labour man thought this might be peculiar to London. Yet the role of women, it was argued, should not be underestimated. As one Liberal woman explained, 'I find a lot of women, particularly older women, will come to see me *because* I am a woman ... my constituents say, "we feel we can talk to you *because* you are a woman"'.

Perhaps the most significant thing in all this was the initial silence. As we saw in Chapter 3, when following the insight of Foucault, the silences in the literature on local politics say a great deal about attitudes to women. So too in the interviews.

Nearly all the councillors were silent for a while before answering. One Labour woman started to talk about the two party system and whether it proved helpful to women, when she stopped and said '... it's very interesting that, I've never thought of it that way'. A Liberal woman began to recount an instance where someone had given her a lift home in a car, and realised as she was talking that there had been attacks on women locally '...isn't it peculiar - until you said that ... that had never entered my head. No one said it's unsafe for women - for *children* home from school, yes'.

The kinds of issues raised were many and varied, including laundries, violence against women, toilets and baby-changing facilities in town centres, the Youth Service, entry 'phones on housing estates, planning and women's centres. Social services, education, housing and transport were often mentioned, and health and safety on the streets involving street lighting and walkways were frequently referred to. 'An incredible number of issues', a female Liberal councillor remarked.

It may be that these issues concerning women were deep in the consciousness of the councillors concerned, unarticulated by many until the moment they crystallised their thoughts. Perhaps this is an example of changes being wrought in the consciousness of councillors by the New Women's Movement in Britain. *History* has not yet happened but it is in the process of happening, of being *made*.

As one Liberal woman councillor put it, 'I'm a great one for saying to a friend who is sitting at home and wants to go out and work, that despite what your husband says, you tell him it's what you want to do. So I suppose you could say I'm a part of the women's movement'.

(d)   Concluding Remarks

It is not easy to reach general conclusions about the interviewing programme. The practice of politics and the permeation and diffusion of ideas about the women's movement is complex.

Nonetheless, it is possible to offer a few tentative conclusions.

a: That most councillors are asked to stand for office, though for women, offers are usually made, and acceptances more likely, when single or where children are over five;

b: That a constellation of constraints operates against women as women - notably lack of selection by political party, lack of confidence and, most importantly, responsibility primarily for child-care and secondly, for domestic labour - style of politics is not a factor;

c: That male partners can facilitate women's transition into political life by offering encouragement and, more importantly, assuming responsibility (even equally shared) for child-care and housework, but that men invariably frustrate women's political aspirations;

d: That women are less conscious of the boundaries around their various responsibilities, putting their families first in extreme situations, whereas men tend to compartmentalise their lives and prioritise highly their political activities;

e: That for councillors generally, and women councillors in particular, the local is the major political aspiration;

f: That social change over the past twenty years or so has been painfully slow, with educational, career and contraceptive opportunities coinciding with changes in attitude about women's role in society, and that social structure and ideology are in a dialectical relationship with ideas about equality for women sometimes acting as barriers to their achievement of representation in local politics;

g: That there is nothing new about the New Women's Movement in Britain, which has recently gone through two phases: the first in the late 1960s affecting changes in consciousness generally, the second in the late 1970s and early 1980s when women's movement activists took the decision to move into social democratic party politics - principally the Labour Party;

h: That it is the new women's movement's more recent association with social democratic party politics together with sensational media representation of the women's movement and the 'left', which accounts for Conservative councillors' hostility - their concern being focused against the 'left' and alarming images of strident activism, rather than the women's movement itself;

i: That the language of gender is becoming part of the vocabulary of local politics, due to the influence of the New Women's Movement in Britain; and

j: That social movements have considerable potential for effecting change, having had greater effect in securing female representation in local politics than through the selection procedures of social democratic party politics, but that women's involvement in local politics has produced considerable gains for women, and that further research is needed before any more can be claimed for social movement activity.

<u>Notes</u>

1. One Labour female referred to the prohibitive cost for poor working class women, who were prevented from political participation by the cost of child-care.

2. This comment can be justified in theoretical terms. The interested reader is referred to Godelier (1983) and Foucault (1979 pp.92-8).

3. This is, perhaps, not too surprising given that there are more wives of Conservative councillors at home as was noted in the London Councillor Survey.
   Barron et al note that women county councillors suffer more stress related to the family than men (Barron et al 1987 p.66), and that women councillors and Labour councillors suffer stress more generally than Conservatives and men (*op. cit.*pp.70-71). This may be related to lighter casework loading (*op. cit.*pp.74-75).

4. In both cases the wives' political views were privately different to their husbands', though this was not publicly known. Both were 'Alliance' supporters - and traditionally Liberal.
   A couple sharing political beliefs is termed the 'political household' by Barron et al (1987 p.153). In their study of county councillors, 'none of the families ... that we identify as approaching the "political household" model is Conservative'.

5. This analogy is drawn by Dorothy E. Smith (1979) between women and men.

6. A characteristic noted in the London Councillor Survey.

7. As argued by McGrew and Bristow (1984), and discussed in Chapter 4.

8. This may not be a general 'problem', given that so many councillors are asked to stand for election.

9. See James (1983) 'Hookers in the House of the Lord'.

7 Conclusion

This book has considered the relationship between the New Women's Movement in Britain and local politics in London, in an attempt to explore the influence of a social movement on one area of political life.

Because of the dearth of available material on London councillors, a review of Government Reports on Local Government councillors and a survey of all female councillors together with a sample of male councillors in the Greater London area has been presented, along with a report of the subsequent in-depth interviewing programme.

What conclusions have been reached?

This chapter presents the main findings[1] under three headings: (a) The Limits of Conventional Wisdom; (b) Women and Local Politics; and (c) Social Movements and Political Parties.

(a)   The Limits of Conventional Wisdom

The review of Government Reports on Local Government Councillors, the London Survey and the interviewing programme presented here, supply detailed information on London councillors and provide the social, political and economic background necessary to a consideration of London's local politics. In the process two findings, which challenge received wisdom, are worthy of special note.

First, a cautionary note for the 'embourgeoisement thesis' of local politics. If this thesis has any explanatory power, it has so only for men. The experience of women, whose educational qualifications translate into lower socio-economic groupings casts doubt on the validity of the thesis. The 'embourgeoisement thesis' is highly conditioned by gender.

Second, conventional wisdom tends to see Conservatives as oriented to the community, with Labour as the vehicle for the transmission of party objectives. This conclusion is so highly refracted by gender as to be largely meaningless, since it appears to be women who are more strongly oriented to the locality than men. But even this is somewhat overstated, since *all* councillors, of whatever party or gender, exhibit strong expressions of civic pride and an almost over-riding concern for their local communities.

(b)   Women and Local Politics

The London Councillor Survey and interviewing programme took the questioning of certain elements of conventional wisdom a step further.

First, women's route into local politics was explored. Here, the majority of councillors, female and male alike, expressed the view that it was now easier for women to become councillors, compared to about fifteen years ago. Yet when pressed on this point, they qualified their responses. It became clear that whilst 'equal opportunities' had opened up new possibilities for women, the belief that things were now easier might actually operate against them. In this sense, the social structure and ideology can be said to be in something of a dialectical relationship, in that barriers and obstacles thought to have been overcome might well remain intact. It is clear from the interviews that men can both facilitate women's progress into political life, or severely limit it - the 'male brotherhood' usually acting to frustrate women's aspirations.

Interestingly, it was only men who saw women as their own worst enemies.

The second major issue which was explored and is related to this, concerned the precise nature of the barriers confronting women's involvement. It transpired that the style of politics was not a problem for women, but that selection by political party, lack of confidence and responsibility for domestic labour and child-care were. The most important of these factors was responsibility for children as well as other dependents. Most councillors had been asked to stand when single, childless, or their children were growing up, or dependents gone.

Two issues stand out in all this. First, the awareness of male councillors of the precise nature of this material barrier to women's greater participation. The persistence of beliefs about women's place and male bread-winners suggests that it will be some time before this barrier is removed. Secondly, that women's delayed involvement in local politics, their deferred 'sponsorship' to use Turner's terminology, might lead to only partial assimilation into the gamut of party political values associated with local politics.

The third finding worthy of note concerns the juggling of priorities of family, work and political activity which is highly conditioned by gender. Male councillors, it appears, compartmentalise their lives, giving priority to political objectives in the last instance. Women, on the other hand, are far less likely to acknowledge the boundaries of compartmentalisation retaining, like Hegel's slave, a perception of the totality. In the last instance, of course, it has been women who have sacrificed their political lives or their jobs for their families and children - and men who have sacrificed their families and children for their politics or their jobs.

The fourth finding worth mentioning here has to do with the role of experience and is one of the *major* findings to emerge from the empirical research.

To begin with, it is worth recalling the Conservative male councillor who said that he would not be prepared to support the funding of a late night taxi service for women, but adding, 'I have little sympathy as I'm not a woman experiencing this [potential danger of attack]. If I were, I might feel differently'. Secondly, we noted the world of experiences and assumptions in women's reading of newspapers, magazines and journals aimed primarily at them as women - a world rarely accessed by men. Thirdly, we acknowledged the crucial role played by politically active mothers and other female relatives in councillors' lives - more than could have been anticipated from a reading of the literature on local politics.

Finally, we saw that some 50% of all female councillors had either belonged to a women's group or had experience of a campaign over women's issues before being active in party politics. As a pre-political motivator on the road to participation, women's experience in the Women's Movement is unparalleled.

(c)   Social Movements and Political Parties

One of the major sub-themes of this book has concerned the relationship between social movements and political parties; and one of the most important questions addressed has concerned their respective efficacy in changing consciousness.

We have seen that activists from the New Women's Movement in Britain in the 1980s chose to work 'in and against' the local state, to use institutionalised mechanisms of social democratic party political machinery. Yet the movement itself has remained alive both within *and* outside these structures. The relationship is clearly a difficult one, with the ghost of Michels (1911) stalking the Council Chambers, an ever-present reminder of the dangers of organisation and oligarchy. The relationship has thus remained tentative and ever-changing, with social democratic parties using aspects of local government machinery to institute change for the benefit of women.

One of these innovations has been Local Government Women's Committees, a feature of local government life originating in the 1980s - and starting of course in London itself, a reminder of the dangers of the 'London Effect', and over-generalisation.

Yet it is precisely here, in the heartland of social-democratic feminism, that we find ideas about Women's Committees firmly established for whilst some of these committees have been scrapped, others have been created, with Women's Committees and Units spreading to other parts of the country. Interestingly, Conservative women are more inclined to reserve judgement on these committees than their male counterparts.

The language of gender, it would seem, is becoming an integral part of the vocabulary of local politics. Not only has the New Women's Movement in Britain succeeded in increasing female representation in local politics in greater numbers than social democratic party selection procedures, but more and more issues are now seen to affect women as women, and more women are prepared to cross the party line for issues affecting women as their experience shows.

But these insights do not yet come easily to councillors, whose consciousness, judging from initial silences concerning women's achievements, is only now slowly changing. History is, perhaps, not yet made but in the process of construction.

(d)   Final Remarks

Researchers into social movements face considerable problems. The call for
a historically informed political sociology poses particular methodological
difficulties.

Attempts to ground theory, to interrogate theoretical preconception,
always risk the charge of empiricism. Yet it is precisely the attempt to relate
the theoretical and the empirical which is historical sociology's strength.

Witness Flandrin's (1979) scholarly account of families in former
times in France and England, where he moves from a consideration of
catechisms and the great dictionaries of the seventeenth and eighteenth
centuries, to a reconceptualisation of Laslett's statistical data on a Kent
village in order to question the significance of the nuclear family form in the
development of industrial capitalism.

Witness too Ginzburg's (1980) painstaking reconstruction of
Menocchio's heretical sixteenth century cosmology from the archival records
of Pope Paul III's Roman Inquisition as an attempt to uncover a remote oral
tradition of 'village atheism' otherwise lost to history.

This book rests squarely within that tradition. It is neither 'Grand
Theory' nor 'Abstracted Empiricism', but an attempt to connect the two
through engagement with 'substantive' issues (Wright Mills 1959 p.86).

This book is a venture which addresses the crucial issue of
consciousness, an issue about which the literature on new social movements
makes assumption through example, allusion and assertion. This book is an
exploration of that issue, an attempt to capture the explanatory grasp of
consciousness, that elusive breath of history.

Notes

1.   Only the main findings are presented here - the final section of each
      chapter summarises the findings in some detail; Chapter 6 opens with
      a summary of Chapters 4 and 5.

Appendix I
Expert informants consulted

Expert Informants Consulted (where consulted because of their
position in an organisation, I have indicated the organisation at
the time the interview was given)

Allen, Kate	Councillor, London Borough of Camden
Barron, Jackie	Bristol Polytechnic
Bouchier, David	University of Essex
Campbell, Beatrix	Journalist and author of *The Iron Ladies*
Dean, Rosalind	Local Government Operational Research Unit
Game, Chris	INLOGOV, University of Birmingham
Goss, Sue	Chair of Southwark Women's Committee
Goudie, Mary	Hansard Society
Gyford, John	University College, London
Harding, Vanessa	Historian, Birkbeck College, University of London
Hills, Jill	University of Manchester
Husbands, Chris	London School of Economics and Political Science, University of London
Hollis, Patricia	Leader of Norwich City Council and author of *Ladies Elect*

Lovenduski, Joni	Loughborough University
McIntosh, Mary	University of Essex
Martlew, Clive	The Planning Exchange, Glasgow
Rendell, Margherita	Institute of Education, University of London
Saunders Vosper, Sue	Birkbeck College, University of London
Stone, Isabella	Equal Opportunities Commission and Sheffield Polytechnic
Stradling, Robert	The Hansard Society
Surety, Graham	Councillor, London Borough of Camden
Thornton, Glynnis	Chair, London Labour Party
Tongue, Carol	MEP, London East European Constituency
Webster, Barbara	INLOGOV, University of Birmingham
Wilkinson, Anne	Labour Party Headquarters
Williams, Geoff	GLC Planning Office
Williams, Margaret	Chairman of the Greater London Area Women's Committee, Conservative Central Office
Wise, Valerie	Chair of GLC Women's Committee
Young, Ken	Research Advisor to the Widdicombe Committee, Policy Studies Institute
Zeitlin, Jonathan	Historian, Birkbeck College, University of London

Appendix II
Organisations consulted

<u>Organisations Consulted</u>

The organisations consulted included:
Association of London Authorities
Association of Metropolitan Authorities
Chatham House (Royal Institute of International
        Affairs)
Commission of the European Communities
Conservative Party
Economic and Social Research Council (ESRC)
ESRC Data Archive
Equal Opportunities Commission
European Consortium for Political Research
Feminist Library (formerly the Women's Research and
        Resources Centre)
Greater London Council (GLC)[1]
International Union of Local Authorities (British
        Section)

Labour Party
London Boroughs Association
Local Government Information Unit
Market and Opinion Research International Ltd (MORI)
National and Local Government Officers' Association
National Council for Civil Liberties - Women's Rights
     Unit
Royal Institute of Public Administration
School for Advanced Urban Studies - University of
     Bristol
Social Surveys (Gallup Poll Ltd)
Standing Conference of Local Government Women's
     Committees (later to be known as the National
     Association of Local Government Women's Committees)
The 300 Group
Women's National Commission
Workers' Educational Association

Note

1.   Contact was later made with the Women's Equality Group of the London Strategic Policy Unit which was formed in March 1986 to carry out research and information work into several areas, including 'women's equality'.

BIRKBECK COLLEGE UNIVERSITY OF LONDON
SURVEY OF LONDON COUNCILLORS
Section 1: Political participation

1. What is your current party political membership?:

    (a) Conservative   ( )
    (b) Labour   ( )
    (c) Liberal   ( )
    (d) SDP   ( )
    (e) Other (please specify) _____ ( )

    _____

2. How long have you been a member of this party?: _____ (years)

3. How long have you been a Councillor?: _____ (years)

4. Why did you decide to stand for election as a Councillor?: _____

   _____

   _____

5. Before you made this decision had you been active in any other local organisation or campaign?:

    Yes ( )
    No ( )

    If yes, please name _____

    _____

6. For women respondents only —

    (a) Were you an active member of any women's group or organisation before you became active in party politics?:

       Yes ( )
       No ( )

       If yes, please name: _____

       _____

       If no, were you involved in any campaigns over women's issues?:

          Yes ( ) — please name: _____

          No ( )   _____

    (b) Are you now a member of any women's group or organisation?:

       Yes ( )
       No ( )

       If yes, please name: _____

       _____

7. Have any members of your family   If yes, who?:
   ever been involved in politics?:

                                         (a) Mother ( )
                                         (b) Father ( )
      (a) Yes ( )   (c) Other (please specify)_____
      (b) No ( )   and in what way: _____

                                             _____

Section 2: Opinions on women's involvement in local politics

8. Compared with about fifteen years ago, it is now:

    (a) Easier for women to become Councillors   ( ) Please
    (b) Harder for women to become Councillors   ( ) tick
    (c) About the same   ( ) one

9. Would you regard yourself as a supporter of the women's movement?:

    (a) Yes (   )
    (b) No (   )

    If no, how would you describe your attitude?:

    (a) Sympathetic   (   )
    (b) No particular view   (   )
    (c) Not sympathetic   (   )   Please tick one
    (d) Other (please specify)   (   )

    _____

    _____

10. Which of the following do you think best describes the women's movement (please tick only one)?:

    (a) It concentrates on women's legal rights and equal opportunities   (   )

    (b) It attempts to work with other groups in attacking fundamental
    social inequalities, of which women's exploitation is a part   (   )

    (c) It pushes for a radical change away from a male-dominated society   (   )

    (d) It attempts to deal with all matters of concern to women (from equal
    opportunities to patriarchy)   (   )

    (e) Other (please specify)_____   (   )

    _____

    _____

11. Compared to other key issues, what sort of priority would you say <u>other Councillors</u> give to issues specifically affecting women (please tick one box for men Councillors, and one for women Councillors)?:

	Men Councillors	Women Councillors
(a) Relatively high	( )	( )
(b) Relatively low	( )	( )
(c) Sometimes high, sometimes low	( )	( )

12. What sort of priority do <u>you</u> think should be given to issues specifically affecting women?:

    (a) A higher priority than at present   (   )
    (b) A lower priority than at present   (   )   Please tick
    (c) Leave things as they are   (   )   one

13. What sort of priority do <u>Council officers</u> in your Authority give to issues specifically affecting women?:

    (a) Relatively high   (   )
    (b) Relatively low   (   )   Please tick
    (c) Sometimes high, sometimes low   (   )   one

208

14. Which of the following do you think best describes Local Government Women's Committees?:

    (a) They have been a successful innovation   ( ) Please

    (b) Too early to pass judgement   ( ) choose

    (c) They have been largely unsuccessful   ( ) one

    (d) Other (please specify) _____( )

    _____

    Please give reasons for your choice: _____

    _____

    _____

15. Which one of the following best explains why relatively few women become elected members (please tick only one)?:

    (a) Women are less likely to be selected by their political party   ( )

    (b) Women see the 'style' of politics as being inappropriate for them   ( )

    (c) Women lack confidence   ( )

    (d) Responsibility for household and family takes priority   ( )

    (e) Other (please specify) _____

    _____ ( )

    Please give reasons for your choice: _____

    _____

    _____

Section 3:

Now I should be grateful if you would please answer a few questions about yourself.
Please tick or enter your answer where appropriate.

16. Which newspaper(s) and journal(s) do you read on a regular basis?: _____

    _____

17. Which social class would you say you belong to, if any?: _____

    _____

18. Which ethnic group would you say you belong to, if any?: _____

    _____

19. Sex:

    (a) Male   ( )

    (b) Female   ( )

21. Marital status:

    (a) Single   ( )

    (b) Married   ( )

    (c) Divorced or separated ( )

    (d) Widowed   ( )

20. Age:

    (a) 21-30   ( )

    (b) 31-40   ( )

    (c) 41-50   ( )

    (d) 51-60   ( )

    (e) 61-70   ( )

    (f) Over 70   ( )

22. Place of birth:

    (a) Town _____

    (b) Country _____

23. How long have you lived in London?:

_____ (years)

25. Do you have any children?:

    (a) Yes   ( )
    (b) No   ( )
    If yes: (a) How many?_____

            (b) What are their ages?_____

            (c) How many live with you?____

24. What sort of accommodation do you live in?:

    (a) Private rented   ( )
    (b) Council rented   ( )
    (c) Owner-occupied   ( )
    (d) Other (please specify) _____ ( )

_____

26. Do you provide care for anyone else in your household (other than children) e.g. elderly parent(s), disabled adult?:

    (a) Yes   ( )
    (b) No   ( )

27. Please enter your current occupational status, and if married, that of your spouse:

	Yourself	Your Spouse
(a) Present employment	_____	_____
(b) Full-time	Yes ( ) No ( )	Yes ( ) No ( )
(c) Part-time	Yes ( ) No ( )	Yes ( ) No ( )
(d) If part-time, number of hours per week	_____(hours)	_____(hours)

28. Please indicate your participation in education:

    (a) Did you attend?:
        (i) State secondary school   ( )
        (ii) Independent/private school   ( )
        (iii) Other (please specify) _____ ( )

    (b) Age you completed full-time education:_____

    (c) Please enter highest educational qualification obtained: _____

29. If you have any comments, please feel free to add them in the space below.

THANK YOU FOR COMPLETING THIS QUESTIONNAIRE.

Bibliography

Government Publications and Research Indices Consulted

Report from the Select Committee on Violence in Marriage: Together with The Proceedings of the Committee (Session 1974-75). Vol. 2. Report, *Minutes of Evidence and Appendices* (HC 553-II), HMSO, London

Committee on the Management of Local Government (1967) - Vol.1 *Report of the Committee.* Vol.2 *The Local Government Councillor* (MOSS L. and PARKER S.R.), HMSO, London

Committee of Inquiry into the System of Remuneration of Members of Local Authorities (1977) - Vol.I *Report* Cmnd. 7010. Vol.II *The surveys of Councillors and local authorities*, HMSO, London

Committee of Inquiry into the Conduct of Local Authority Business (1986) - *The Conduct of Local Authority Business: Report of the Committee of Inquiry into the Conduct of Local Authority Business.* Cmnd. 9797. *The Conduct of Local Authority Business: Research Volume II: The Local Government Councillor.* Cmnd. 9799, HMSO, London *The Conduct of Local Authority Business: The Government*

Response to the Report of the Widdicombe Committee of Inquiry (July 1988) Cmnd. 433, HMSO, London

Aslib (Index to Theses with Abstracts) (various editions), Aslib, London

CENSUS 1981: DEFINITIONS (1981) Reference CEN81 DEF, HMSO, London

CENSUS 1981: Key Statistics for local authorities: Great Britain General - Register Office for Scotland (1984) (Ref. CEN81 KSLA), HMSO, London

Current Research in Britain: Social Sciences, Dissertation Abstracts International, Series A. (The Humanities and Social Sciences) - formerly *Dissertation Abstracts* (various editions) University Microfilms Inc., Michigan

ECONOMIC STATISTICS FROM THE 1981 CENSUS, STATISTICAL SERIES NO. 31 (1984), GLC, London

Historical Research for Higher Degrees in the United Kingdom, University of London, Institute of Historical Research, Theses in Progress and Theses Presented (various editions) Institute of Historical Research, University of London

MUNICIPAL YEAR BOOK (various editions) Municipal Journals Ltd., London

NEW EARNINGS SURVEY part f (1985) 'Hours, Earnings of Part-time women employees, types of collective agreement', HMSO, London

OPCS Census Newsletter (various editions), OPCS, London

OPCS Classification of Occupations, 1980 (1980), HMSO, London

OPCS County Monitor (1982) Reference, CEN81 CM 56, OPCS, London

OPCS General Household Survey (1980), HMSO, London

Other Publications

ABRAMS P. (1982) *Historical Sociology*, Open Books, Somerset

AGONITO R. (1977) *History of Ideas on Woman: A Source Book*, Paragon Books, New York

AMORY M. (1987) 'If you stop learning you stop achieving', *Labour Party News*, No.1, Jan/Feb, p.13

ANDERSON P. (1983) *In the Tracks of Historical Materialism*, Verso, London

ANDREWS G. (1986) 'Council Staff face election ban' and '"Abuse of political power" puts pressure on Town Halls' in *Guardian*, 20th June

212

ASCHER K. (1987) *The Politics of Privatisation: Contracting Out Public Services*, Macmillan, Basingstoke

ASHTON F. (1987) 'Feminism in the 80s: Fact or Fiction?' in ASHTON F. and WHITTING G. (eds.) *Feminist Theory and Practical Policies: Shifting the Agenda in the 1980s*, School for Advanced Urban Studies, Bristol, pp 117-130

ASHTON F. (1988) 'Feminism and the New Right', *New Socialist*, No.54, March/April, p.27

ATKINSON J. (1984) 'Manpower Strategies for Flexible Organisations', *Personnel Management*, August, pp 28-31

BACHRACH P. and BARATZ M.S. (1962) 'Two Faces of Power', *American Political Science Review*, 56, pp 947-952

BANKS J. (1972) *The Sociology of Social Movements*, Macmillan, London

BANKS J. A. and BANKS O. (1976) 'Feminism and Social Change - A Case Study of a Social Movement' in ZOLLSCHAN G.K. and HIRSCH W. (eds.) *Social Change: Explorations, Diagnoses and Conjectures*, Schenkman, Wiley, New York, pp 680-702

BANKS O. (1981) *Faces of Feminism*, Martin Robertson, Oxford

BARRATT BROWN M. (1972) *From Labourism to Socialism: The Political Economy of Labour in the 1970s*, Spokesman Books, Nottingham

BARRETT M. (1980 and 1988) *Women's Oppression Today*, Verso, London

BARRETT M. and McINTOSH M. (1980) 'The "Family Wage": Some Problems for Socialists and Feminists', *Capital and Class*, No.11, pp 51-72: Reprinted in WHITELEGG E. *et al* (eds.) *The Changing Experience of Women*, Martin Robertson, Oxford, pp 71-87

BARRETT M. and McINTOSH M. (1982) *The Anti-Social Family*, Verso, London

BARRON J., CRAWLEY G. and WOOD T. (1987) *Married to the Council? The Private Costs of Public Service*, Bristol Polytechnic, Bristol

BARRON R.D. and NORRIS G.M. (1976) 'Sexual Divisions and the Dual Labour Market' in BARKER D.L. and ALLEN S. (eds.) *Dependence and Exploitation in Work and Marriage* Longman, London, pp 47-69

BARRY J. (1990) *Local Government Councillors in London: The Influence of the New Women's Movement* (Unpublished Ph.D. Thesis) Birkbeck College, University of London

BARRY J. (1991) *The New Women's Movement in Britain: Critical Reflections* (Polytechnic of East London Occasional Papers on Business, Economy and Society, Occasional Paper No.1)

BATLEY R. and STOKER G. (eds.) (1991) *Local Government in Europe: Trends and Development*, Macmillan, London

BATSTONE E. (1988) *The Reform of Workplace Industrial Relations: Theory, Myth and Evidence*, Oxford University Press, Oxford

BEALE J. (1982) *Getting It Together: Women as Trade Unionists*, Pluto Press, London

BEAUVOIR S. De (1949) *The Second Sex*, Penguin (1972), Harmondsworth

BEBEL A. (1879) *Woman Under Socialism*, Schocken Books (1971), New York

BEECHEY V. (1979) 'On Patriarchy', *Feminist Review*, No.3, pp 66-82

BEETHAM D. (1977) 'From Socialism to Fascism: The Relation Between Theory and Practice in the Work or Robert Michels', *Political Studies*, Vol.XXV, pp.3-24

BELL C. and NEWBY H. (eds.) (1977) *Doing Sociological Research*, George Allen and Unwin, London

BELL C. and ROBERTS H. (eds.) (1984) *Social Researching: Politics, Problems, Practice*, Routlege Kegan and Paul, London

BELL D. (1962) *The End of Ideology: On The Exhaustion of Political Ideas in the Fifties*, The Free Press, New York

BELL D. (1976) *The Coming of Post-Industrial Society: A Venture in Social Forecasting*, Penguin, Harmondsworth

BERGER P. (1963) *Invitation to Sociology*, Penguin (1966), Harmondsworth

BERNSTEIN E. (1899) *Evolutionary Socialism*, Schocken Books (1961), New York

BOUCHIER D. (1983) *The Feminist Challenge*, Macmillan, London

BOURQUE S.C. and GROSSHOLTZ J. (1973) 'Politics an Unnatural Practice: Political Science Looks at Female Participation', *Politics and Society*, Vol.4, No.1, Fall, pp 225-266

BOWEN E.S. (1964) *Return to Laughter*, Anchor, Doubleday, New York (Elenore Smith Bowen is the *nom de plume* of Laura Bohannan)

BRISTOW S. (1980 a) 'Women councillors - a massive measure of equality', *Municipal Journal*, 15 August, p 1019

BRISTOW S. (1980 b) 'Women councillors - An Explanation of the Under-representation of Women in Local Government', *Local Government Studies*, Vol. 6, no. 3, pp 73-90

BRISTOW S. (1982) 'More women in county government', *County Councils Gazette*, Vol. 74(II), February, pp 372-373

BRISTOW S., KERMODE D. and MANNIN M. (1984) (eds.) *The Redundant Counties?: Participation and Electoral Choice in England's Metropolitan Counties*, G.W.A. Hesketh, Ormskirk

BURKE E. (1790) *Reflections on the Revolution in France*, Penguin (1969), Harmondsworth

BURKE P. (ed.) (1973) *A New Kind of History from the writings of Lucien Lebvre*, Routlege Kegan and Paul, London

BUTTON S. (1984) *Women's Committees: A study of gender and local government policy formulation*, Working Paper 45, School for Advanced Urban Studies, Bristol

BYRNE T. (1986) *Local Government in Britain*, Penguin (4th Ed.), London

CAMPBELL B. (1987) *The Iron Ladies: Why do Women Vote Tory?*, Virago, London

CARTER A. (1988) *The Politics of Women's Rights*, Longman, Harlow

CARTER F. (1986) 'Spend, spend, spent?', *Trouble and Strife*, No.8, Spring, pp 51-56

CASTELLS M. (1977) *The Urban Question*, Edward Arnold, Leeds

CASTELLS M. (1978) *City, Class and Power*, Macmillan, London

CASTELLS M. (1983) *The City and the Grassroots*, Edward Arnold, Leeds

CLARKE J., COCHRANE A. and SMART A. (1987) *Ideologies of Welfare: From Dreams to Disillusion*, Hutchinson, London

CLAYTON H. (1986) '"Rule of law" Call in Council reforms', *The Times*, 20 June

CLEGG S. (1975) 'Feminist Methodology - Fact or Fiction', *Quality and Quantity*, 19, pp 83-97

COBBETT W. (1830) *Rural Rides*, Penguin (1967), Harmondsworth

COCHRANE A. (1985) 'The attack on local government: what it is and what it isn't', *Critical Social Policy*, 12, Spring, pp 44-62

COCKBURN C. (1977) *The Local State: Management of Cities and People*, Pluto Press, London

COHEN J.L. (1985) 'Strategy or Identity: New Theoretical Paradigms and Contemporary Social Movements', *Social Research*, Vol.52, No.4, Winter, pp 663-716

COLE G.D.H. and POSTGATE R. (1956) *The Common People*, Methuen, London

COLLINS C.A. (1978) 'Considerations on the Social Background and Motivation of Councillors', *Policy and Politics*, 6, pp 425-447

CONRAD J. (1902) *Heart of Darkness*, Penguin (1973), Harmondsworth

COOTE A. and CAMPBELL B. (1982 and 1987) *Sweet Freedom: The Struggle for Women's Liberation*, Blackwell (2nd Edition), Oxford

CRICK B. (1982) *In Defence of Politics*, Penguin (2nd Ed.) Harmondsworth

DAHL R.A. (1961) *Who Governs? Democracy and Power in an American City*, Yale University Press, New Haven

DAHLERUP D. (ed.) (1986) *The New Women's Movement*, Sage, London

DALLA COSTA M. and JAMES S. (1972) *The Power of Women and the Subversion of the Community*, Falling Wall Press (1975), Bristol

DAVIES H.J. (1988) 'Local Government Under Siege', *Public Administration*, Vol.66, No.1, Spring, pp 91-101

DEAKIN N. (1986) 'Introduction' to COHEN G. *et al The New Right: image and reality*, The Runnymede Trust, London

DEARLOVE J. (1979) *The Reorganisation of British Local Government: Old Orthodoxies and a Political Perspective*, Cambridge University Press, Cambridge

DEX S. (1985) *The Sexual Division of Work*, Wheatsheaf, Brighton

DOBB M. (1946) *Studies in the Development of Capitalism*, Routledge and Kegan Paul, London

DUNLEAVY P. (1980) *Urban Political Analysis*, Macmillan, London

DUNLEAVY P. (1981) *The Politics of Mass Housing in Britain, 1945-1975*, Clarendon, Oxford

DUVERGER M. (1964) *The Idea of Politics: The Uses of Power in Society*, Methuen (1966), London

EDWARDS J. (1988/89) 'Local Government Women's Committees', *Critical Social Policy*, 24, Winter, pp 50-64

ELIAS N. (1939) *The Civilising Process*, Blackwell (1978), Oxford

EOC FACTSHEET (1987) *The Fact about Women Is...*, Equal
Opportunities Commission Statistics Unit, Manchester

ETTORRE E.M. (1978) 'Women, urban social movements and the lesbian
ghetto', *International Journal of Urban and Regional Research*, Vol.
2, No. 3, pp 499 - 520

EVANS J. *et al* (1986) *Feminism and Political Theory*, Sage, London

EVANS R.J. (1977) *The Feminists*, Croom Helm, London

EVANS R.J. (1986) 'The Concept of Feminism: Notes for Practicing
Historians', in JOERES R.E. and MAYNES M.J. (eds.) *German
Women in the Eighteenth and Nineteenth Centuries*, Indiana University
Press, U.S.A., pp 247-258

EVERSLEY D.C. (1975) 'Searching for London's Lost Soul, or How not
to get from the There and Then to the Here and Now', *The London
Journal*, Vol.1, No.1, May, pp 103-117

FEBVRE L. (1973) 'History and Psychology', 'Sensibility and history:
how to reconstitute the emotional life of the past' and 'A new kind of
History' in BURKE P. *op. cit.* pp 1-43

FITZGERALD M. (1984) *Political Parties and Black People:
participation, representation and exploitation*, The Runnymede Trust,
Nottingham

FLANDRIN J.L. (1979) *Families in Former Times*, Cambridge University
Press, Cambridge

FLANNERY K. and ROELOFS S. (1983) 'Local Government Women's
Committees', in HOLLAND J. (ed.) *Feminist Action No. 1*, Battle Axe
Books Ltd, London, pp 69-91

FORRESTER C. (1984) *From Activism to Office: Women and Local
Government in Edinburgh*, Occasional Paper No. 13, Planning
Exchange, Glasgow

FOUCAULT M. (1977 a) *Discipline and Punish*, Peregrine, Penguin,
Harmondsworth

FOUCAULT M. (1977 b) 'Power and Sex: An Interview with Michel
Foucault', *Telos*, 32, pp 152-161

FOUCAULT M. (1979) *The History of Sexuality - Volume 1: An
Introduction*, Pelican, Harmondsworth

FOUCAULT M. (1982) 'The Subject and Power', Afterword to
DREYFUS H. and RABINOW P. (eds.), *op. cit.* pp 208-226

FRANKEL B. (1987) *The Post-Industrial Utopians*, Polity Press,
Cambridge

FREEMAN J. (1970) 'The Tyranny of Structurelessness' in *Untying the Knot: Feminism, Anarchism and Organisation*, Dark Star Press and Rebel Press, (1984) London

FREEMAN J. (1975) *The Politics of Women's Liberation*, Longman, London

FREEMAN J. (ed.) (1983) *Social Movements of the Sixties and Seventies*, Longman, London

FRIEDMAN M. (1962) *Capitalism and Freedom*, University of Chicago Press, Chicago

GELB J. (1986) 'Feminism in Britain: Politics without power?', in DAHLERUP D. (1986) *op. cit.*, pp 103-121

GERAS N. (1972) 'Marx and the Critique of Political Economy', in BLACKBURN R. (ed.) (1972) *Ideology in Social Science*, Fontana, London

GINZBURG C. (1980) *The Cheese and the Worms*, Routledge and Kegan Paul, London

GLASER B.G. and STRAUSS A.L. (1967) *The Discovery of Grounded Theory: Strategies for qualitative research*, Aldine, Hawthorne, New York

GODELIER M. (1983) 'The ideal in the real', in SAMUEL R. and STEDMAN JONES G. (eds.), *Culture, Ideology and Politics*, Routledge and Kegan Paul, London, pp 12-38

GOLDTHORPE J.H. (1967) 'Social Stratification in Industrial Society' in THOMPSON K. and TUNSTALL J. (eds.) (1971) *op. cit.*, pp 331-347: Originally published in BENDIX R. and LIPSET S.M. (eds.) (1967) *Class, Status and Power*, Routledge and Kegan Paul, London

GOLDTHORPE J.H. (1971) 'Theories of Industrial Society: Reflections on the Recrudescence of Historicism and the Future of Futurology', *European Journal of Sociology*, Vol.XII, No.2, pp 263-288

GOLDTHORPE J.H. (1983) 'Women and Class Analysis: In Defence of the Conventional View', *Sociology*, Vol.17, No.4, November, pp 465-488

GOLDTHORPE J.H. (1984) 'Women and Class Analysis: A Reply to the Replies', *Sociology*, Vol.18, No.4, November, pp 491-499

GOSS S. (1984) 'Women's Initiatives in Local Government', in BODDY M. and FUDGE C. (eds.), *Local Socialism?* Macmillan, London, pp109-132

218

GOUGH I. (1979) *The Political Economy of the Welfare State*, Macmillan, London

GOULDNER A.W. (1973) 'Anti-Minotaur: The Myth of a Value-Free Sociology' in GOULDNER A.W. *For Sociology: Renewal and Critique in Sociology Today*, Penguin (1975), Harmondsworth, pp 3-26

GRAMSCI A. (1971) *Selections from Prison Notebooks* (Edited and translated by HOARE Q. and SMITH G.N.), Lawrence and Wishart, London

GREER G. (1970) *The Female Eunuch*, Granada (1971), St Albans, Herts

GRIFFIN J.H. (1962) *Black Like Me*, Panther, Granada (1964), London

GUARDIAN (1986) 'Council Staff face election ban' and '"Abuse of political power" puts pressure on Town Halls' by ANDREWS G., 20th June

GUNN S. (1986) 'Reforms call aimed at influence of party politics within councils', *The Times*, 20 June

GYFORD J. (1983) 'The new urban left: a local road to socialism?', *New Society*, 21 April, pp 91-93

GYFORD J. (1984) *Local Politics in Britain* (2nd Edition), Croom Helm, Beckenham, Kent

GYFORD J. (1985) *The Politics of Local Socialism*, George Allen and Unwin, London

GYFORD J., LEACH S. and GAME C. (1989) *The Changing Politics of Local Government*, Unwin Hyman, London

HADDON R. (1973) 'Foreword' in KERR C., DUNLOP J.T., HABISON F. and MYERS C.A. *Industrialism and Industrial Man*, Penguin Harmondsworth, pp 1-27

HALFORD S. (1988) 'Women's initiatives in Local Government ... where do they come from and where are they going?', *Policy and Politics*, Vol.16, No.4, pp 251-259

HALL S. (1977) 'The Hinterland of Science: Ideology and the "Sociology of Knowledge"'in CENTRE FOR CONTEMPORARY CULTURAL STUDIES, *On Ideology*, Hutchinson, London, pp 9-32

HALL S. (1983) 'The Problem of Ideology - Marxism Without Guarantees' in MATTHEWS B. (ed.) *op. cit.*, pp 57 - 85

HALL S. (1987) 'Gramsci And Us', *Marxism Today*, June, pp 16-21

HAMILTON P. (1974) *Knowledge and Social Structure*, Routledge and Kegan Paul, London

HAMPTON W. (1987) *Local Governmment and Urban Politics*,
   Longman, Harlow

HANMER J. (1977) 'Community action, Women's Aid and the Women's
   Liberation Movement', in MAYO M. (ed.), *Women in the Community*,
   Routledge and Kegan Paul, London, pp 91-108

HANSON A.H. and WALLES M. (1970) *Governing Britain*,
   Fontana/Collins, London

HARALAMBOS M. (ed.) (1986) *Sociology: a new approach*, Causeway
   Press, Ormskirk, Lancashire. (Also 3rd edition, 1990, Unwin Hyman,
   London)

HARDING S. (1987) 'Introduction: Is There a Feminist Method?' in
   HARDING S. (ed.) *Feminism and Methodology*, Indiana University
   Press, Bloomington, Indiana and Open University Press, Milton
   Keynes, pp 1-14

HARTMANN H. (1979) 'The Unhappy Marriage of Marxism and
   Feminism: Towards a More Progressive Union', *Capital and Class*,
   No.8, Summer, pp 1-33: Reprinted in SARGENT L. (ed.) *Women and
   Revolution*, Southend Press (1981), Boston: and *The Unhappy
   Marriage of Marxism and Feminism: A Debate on Class and
   Patriarchy*, Pluto Press (1986), London, pp 1-41

HARTMANN H. (1981) 'The Family and the Locus of Gender, Class,
   and Political Struggle: The Example of Housework', *Signs*, Spring,
   Vol.6, No.3, pp 366-394

HAYEK S.A. (1975) 'The Principles of a Liberal Social Order', in
   CRESPIGNY A. De and CRONIN J. *Ideologies of Politics*, Oxford
   University Press, Oxford, pp 55-75

HEDLUND-RUTH G. (1984) *The Impact of the Women's Liberation
   Movement on Local Politics - experiences from Norway and Sweden*,
   IPSA Research Committee on Sex Roles and Politics, Round Table,
   Sofia

HILLS J. (1982) 'Women Local Councillors - A Reply to Bristow', *Local
   Government Studies*, Vol. 8, no. 1, pp 61-71

HILLS J. (1986) 'Introduction', in EVANS J. et. al., *Feminism and
   Political Theory*, Sage, London, pp vi-x

HILTON R. (1978) *The Transition from Feudalism to Capitalism*, Verso,
   London

HOLLAND P. (1988) 'Still Revolting?' in SEBESTYEN A. (ed.) *'68, '78, '88: From Women's Liberation to Feminism*, Prism Press, Bridport, Dorset, pp 134-140

HOLLIS P. (1987) *Ladies Elect: Women in English Local Government 1865-1914*, Oxford University Press, Oxford

HOWE E. (1984) 'Towards More Choice for Women', *New Society*, 24 May, pp312-314

HOWE S. (1988) 'Gender Agenda', *New Society*, 25 November, p.6

HUNTER F. (1953) *Community Power Structure: A Study of Decision Makers*, University of North Carolina Press, Chapel Hill

HUWS U. (1984) 'The New Homeworkers', *New Society*, 22 March, pp 454-455

ILERSIC A.R. (1959) *Statistics*, (Thirteenth Ed. 1964), HFL Publishers Ltd, London

JACKSON P.W. (1967) *Local Government*, Butterworths (1970), London

JAMES S. (1983) 'Hookers in the House of the Lord' in HOLLAND J. (ed.) *op. cit.*, pp 180-203

JOSHI H. (1988) 'Changing Roles of Women in the British Labour Market and the Family', Paper presented at the 1988 meeting of the *British Association (Section F)*, September, pp 1-37

KEANE J. (1988) *Democracy and Civil Society*, Verso, London

KEITH-LUCAS B. and RICHARDS P.G. (1978) *A History of Local Government in the Twentieth Century*, George Allen and Unwin, London

KERR C., DUNLOP J.T., HARBISON F. and MYERS C.A. (1960) *Industrialism and Industrial Man*, Penguin (1973), Harmondsworth

KETTLEBOROUGH H. (1988) 'Consulting women in the community about local government services', *Critical Social Policy*, 21, Spring, pp 56-67

KUHN T. (1970) *The Structure of Scientific Revolutions*, University of Chicago Press, 2nd Edition, Chicago

KUMAR K. (ed.) (1971) *Revolution: the Theory and Practice of a European Idea*, Weidenfeld and Nicolson, London

LABOV W. (1982) 'The Logic of Nonstandard English' in GIGLIOLI P.P. (ed.) *Language and Social Context* Penguin/Harmandsworth, pp.179-215

LACLAU E. and MOUFFE C. (1981) 'Social Strategy: Where Next?',
    Marxism Today, Jan, pp 17-22
LACLAU E. and MOUFFE C. (1985) *Hegemony and Socialist Strategy:*
    Towards a Radical Democratic Politics, Verso, London
LARRAIN J. (1979) *The Concept of Ideology*, Hutchinson, London
LAWS S. (1989) ''68, '78, '88', *Trouble and Strife*, No.16, Summer, pp
    30-35
LE GRAND J. and ROBINSON R. (eds.) (1984) *Privitisation and the*
    Welfare State, George Allen and Unwin, London
LICHTHEIM G. (1967) *The Concept of Ideology and Other Essays*,
    Vintage Books, New York
LINES K. (1990) 'Will Women's Units Survive?', *Guardian*, 5th June
LOACH L. (1985) 'The Pains of Women in Labour', *Spare Rib*, No. 159,
    October, pp 18-20
LOACH L. (1986 a) 'Is There a Life After the GLC?', *Spare Rib*,
    No.164, March, pp 10-11
LOACH L. (1986 b) 'Daughters of the Fighting Couple', *Spare Rib*,
    No.171, October, pp 10-11
LOACH L. (1986 c) 'Labour's New Women', *Spare Rib*, No.171,
    October, pp 36-39
LONDON EDINBURGH WEEKEND RETURN GROUP (1979) *In and*
    Against the State, Pluto Press, London
LOVENDUSKI J. (1986) *Women and European Politics*, Wheatsheaf,
    Brighton
LOVENDUSKI J. and HILLS J. (eds.) (1981) *The Politics of the Second*
    Electorate: Women and Public Participation, Routledge and Kegan
    Paul, London
LOW PAY UNIT (undated) *Part-Time Workers: Your Wages - Your*
    Rights, Low Pay Unit, London
LOWE S. (1986) *Urban Social Movements: The City after Castells*,
    Macmillan, Houndmills, Hampshire
LUKES S. (1974) *Power: A Radical View*, Macmillan, London
LUKES S. (ed.) (1986) *Power*, Blackwell, London
LUXEMBURG R. (1899) 'Social Reform or Revolution' in HOWARD
    D. (ed.) *Selected Political Writings: Rosa Luxemburg*, Monthly
    Review Press, London, pp 52-134
MACGREGOR S. (1981) *The Politics of Poverty*, Longman, Harlow

MACGREGOR S. (1988) *The Poll Tax and the Enterprise Culture: The implications of recent local government legislation for democracy and the welfare state*, Centre for Local Economic Strategies, Manchester

MACINTYRE A. (1973) 'The essential contestability of some social concepts', *Ethics*, Vol. 84, pp 1-9

MACPHERSON C.B. (1962) *The Political Theory of Possessive Individualism: Hobbes to Locke*, Oxford University Press, Oxford

MCGREW A. and BRISTOW S. (1984) 'Candidate to Councillor: A Study of Local Political Recruitment' in BRISTOW S., KERMODE D. and MANNIN M. (1984) *op. cit.* pp 69-99

MCINTOSH M. (1979) 'The Welfare State and the Needs of the Dependent Family' in BURMAN S. (ed.) *Fit Work for Women*, Croom Helm, London, pp 153-172

MACHIAVELLI N. (1961) *The Prince*, (translated by G. BULL) Penguin (1975), Harmondsworth

MARTIN R. (1977) *The Sociology of Power*, Routledge and Kegan Paul, London

MARTLEW C., FORRESTER C. and BUCHANAN G., (1985) 'Activism and Office: Women and Local Government in Scotland', *Local Government Studies*, Vol. 11, no. 2, pp 47-65

MARX K. (1844) 'Economic and Philosophical Manuscripts' in *Early Writings*, Penguin (1975), Harmondsworth, pp 279-400

MARX K. (1852) *The Eighteenth Brumaire of Louis Bonaparte*, Progress Publishers (1934), Moscow

MARX K. (1859) 'Preface to A Contribution to the Critique of Political Economy' in MARX K. *Preface and Introduction to A Contribution to The Critique of Political Economy*, Foreign Languages Press (1976), Peking

MARX K. (1867) *Capital Volume 1*, Penguin (1976), Harmondsworth

MARX K. (1875) 'Critique of the Gotha Programme' in FEUER L.S. (ed.) (1959) *Marx and Engels: Basic Writings on Politics and Philosophy*, Fontana (1969), London, pp 153-173

MARX K. and ENGELS F. (1848) *The Communist Manifesto*, Penguin (1967), Harmondsworth

MAYO M. (ed.) (1977) *Women in the Community*, Routledge and Kegan Paul, London

MELUCCI A. (1985) 'The Symbolic Challenge of Contemporary Movements', *Social Research*, Vol.52, No.4, Winter, pp 789-816

MELUCCI A. (1988) 'Social Movements and the Democratization of
Everyday Life' in KEANE J. (ed.) *Civil Society and the State: New
European Perspectives*, Verso, London, pp 245-260

MELUCCI A. (1989) *Nomands of the Present: Social Movements and
Individual Needs in Contemporary Society* (eds.) KEANE J. and MIER
P.) Radius, Hutchinson, London

MERQUIOR J.G. (1979) *The Veil and the Mask: Essays on Culture and
Ideology*, Routledge and Kegan Paul, London

MICHELS R. (1911) *Political Parties*, Free Press (1968), New York

MILIBAND R. (1982) *Capitalist Democracy in Britain*, Oxford
University Press, Oxford

MILL J.S. (1869) *The Subjection of Women* in *Mary Wollstonecraft A
Vindication of the Rights of Women, John Stuart Mill, The Subjection
of Women*, Dent (1929), London

MOSCA G. (1939) *The Ruling Class: Elementi di Scienza Politica* (Edited
and Revised by A. LIVINGSTON, Translated by H.D. KAHN)
McGraw-Hill, New York

MOSSUZ-LAVAU J. and SINEAU M. (1984) *The Situation of Women
in the Political Process in Europe, Part II, Women in the political
world in Europe*, (Preliminary Report submitted to the Council of
Europe in December 1982. Up-dated in June 1984), Directorate of
Human Rights, Council of Europe, Strasbourg

NORRIS P. (1986) 'Women in Congress: A Policy Difference?', *Politics*,
Vol.6, No.1, pp 34-40

NORRIS P. (1987) *Politics and Sexuality: The Comparative Position of
Women in Western Democracies*, Wheatsheaf Books, Brighton

OFFE C. (1984) *Contradictions of the Welfare State* (Edited by KEANE
J.), Hutchinson, London

OFFE C. (1985) 'New Social Movements: Challenging the Boundaries of
Institutional Politics', *Social Research*, Vol.52, No.4, Winter, pp 817-
868

PARETO V. (1976) *Sociological Writings* (Selected and Introduced by
S.E. FINER, translated by D. MIRFIN), Basil Blackwell, Oxford

POLLERT A. (1987) *The 'Flexible Firm': A Model in Search of a Reality
(Or a Policy in Search of a Practice)?*, Warwick Papers in Industrial
Relations, No.19, December, University of Warwick, Coventry

POLLERT A. (1988) 'The "Flexible Firm": Fixation or Fact?', *Work,
Employment and Society*, Vol.2, No.3, September, pp 281-316

RAHMAN N. (1986) 'Sweeping Aside Women's Employment Rights', *Low Pay Review*, 27, Autumn, pp 8-13

RANDALL V. (1982 and 1987) *Women and Politics*, Macmillan, London

REDSTOCKINGS (1969) 'Redstockings Manifesto' in TANNER L.B. (Compiler and editor) *Voices from Women's Liberation*, Mentor, New American Library, New York, pp 109-111

REGAN D. (1987) *The Local Left and its National Pretensions*, Centre for Policy Studies, London

RENDEL M. (1982) 'A worldwide panorama of research and teaching related to women', *Cultures*, Vol.111 (3), pp 102-120

RICHARDS P.G. (1983) *The Local Government System*, George Allen and Unwin, London

ROWBOTHAM S. (1972) 'The Beginnings of Women's Liberation in Britain' in WANDOR M. (Compiler) *op. cit.*, pp 91-102

ROWBOTHAM S. (1973) *Woman's Consciousness, Man's World*, Penguin, Harmondsworth

ROWBOTHAM S. (1983) *Dreams and Dilemmas*, Virago, London

ROWBOTHAM S. (1988) 'Rainbow Politics', *New Statesman and Society*, 2 September, p.23

ROWBOTHAM S. (1989) *The Past Is Before Us*, Pandora, London

ROWBOTHAM S., SEGAL L. and WAINWRIGHT H. (1979) *Beyond the Fragments*, Merlin Press, London

SANDERS C. (1989) 'Society: Double trouble', *New Statesman and Society*, 10th February, p.28

SAUNDERS P. (1979) *Urban Politics: A Sociological Interpretation*, Hutchinson (1983), London

SCHATTSCHNEIDER E.E. (1960) *The Semisovereign People: A Realist's View of Democracy in America*, Holt, Rinehart and Winston, New York

SCHUMPETER J.A. (1943) *Capitalism, Socialism and Democracy*, George Allen and Unwin (1976), London

SCHUTTE A. (1976) 'Carlo Ginzburg', *Journal of Modern History*, Vol. 48, pp 296-315

SCHWARTZ B. (1982) '"The People" in history: the Communist Party Historians' Group, 1946-56', in JOHNSON R., McLENNAN G., SCHWARTZ B. and SUTTON D. (eds.) *Making Histories: Studies in history-writing and politics*, Centre for Contemporary Cultural Studies, Hutchinson, London, pp 44-95

SCOTT J. (1990) *Ideology and the New Social movements*, Unwin Hyman, London

SEABROOK J. (1984) *The Idea of Neighbourhood*, Pluto Press, London

SEGAL L. (1979) 'A Local Experience', in ROWBOTHAM S. *et al Beyond The Fragments*, Merlin Press, London pp.157-209

SHARPE L.J. (1962) *A Metropolis Votes*, Greater London Group, LSE, London

SHAUL M. (1982) 'The Status of Women in Local Governments: An International Assessment', *Public Administration Review*, No. 6, pp 491-500

SHOWSTACK SASSOON A. (ed.) (1987) *Women and the State: The shifting boundaries of public and private*, Hutchinson, London

SMITH D.E. (1974) 'Women's Perspective as a Radical Critique of Sociology', *Sociological Inquiry*, 44 (1), pp 7-13

SMITH D.E. (1979) 'A Sociology for Women' in SHERMAN J.A. and BECK E.T. (eds.) *The Prism of Sex*, University of Wisconsin Press, Madison, Wisconsin, pp 135-187

SOFER A. (1984) 'Women's Witch Hunt', *New Society*, 13 September, pp 285-286

SOFER A. (1986) 'Local Symptoms', *New Society*, 21 November, pp18 19

SPENDER D. (1980) *Man Made Language*, Routledge and Kegan Paul, London

SPENDER D. (ed.) (1981) *Men's Studies Modified: The Impact of Feminism on the Academic Disciplines*, Pergamon Press, Oxford

SPENDER D. (1983) *There's Always Been a Women's Movement This Century*, Pandora Press, Routledge and Kegan Paul, London

SPENDER D. (1986) 'What is Feminism? A Personal Answer', in OAKLEY A. and MITCHELL J. (eds.) (1986) *op. cit.*, pp 208-218

STACEY J. and THORNE B. (1985) 'The Missing Feminist Revolution in Sociology', *Social Problems*, Vol.32, No.4, April, pp 301-316

STACEY M. (1969) *Methods of Social Research*, Pergamon Press, Oxford

STACEY M. (1981) 'The Division of Labour Revisited or Overcoming the Two Adams' in ABRAMS P., DEEM R., FINCH J. and ROCK P. (eds.) *Practice and Progress: British Sociology 1950-1980*, George Allen and Unwin, London, pp 172-190

STACEY M. and PRICE M. (1981) *Women, Power and Politics*, Tavistock, London

STANWORTH M. (1984) 'Women and Class Analysis: A Reply to
Goldthorpe', *Sociology*, Vol.18, No.2, May, pp 159-170
STEDMAN JONES G. (1983) *Languages of class in studies in English
working class history 1832 - 1982*, Cambridge University Press,
Cambridge
STEPHENSON J. (1988) 'Ineffective Tribunals?', *New Society*, 29 April,
pp24-25
STOKER G. and WILSON D. (1986) 'Intra-organisational politics in local
authorities: towards a new approach', *Public Administration*, Vol. 64,
No. 3, pp 285-302
SUSSER B. (1974) 'The Behavioural Ideology: A Review and a
Retrospect', *Political Studies*, Vol. XXII, pp 271-288
THOMSON P. (1987) 'When Sisters fall out', *New Society*, 30
January, pp 31-32
THE TIMES (1986) '"Rule of law" Call in Council reforms' by
CLAYTON H. and 'Reforms call aimed at influence of party politics
within councils' by GUNN S., 20 June
TOCQUEVILLE A. de (1949) *L'Ancien Regime* (Translated by
PATTERSON M.W.), Basil Blackwell, Oxford
TOCQUEVILLE A. de (1956) *Democracy in America*, Mentor, New
American Library, New York
TOURAINE A. (1981) *The voice and the eye: An analysis of social
movements* (Translated by A. DUFF), Cambridge University Press,
Cambridge
TOURAINE A. (1985) 'An Introduction to the Study of Social
Movements', *Social Research*, Vol.52, No.4, Winter, pp 749-787
TOYNBEE P. (1987) 'Lambeth's walk on the wild side', *Guardian*, 11
May
TURNER R.H. (1960) 'Modes of Social Ascent through Education:
Sponsored and Contest Mobility' in HALSEY A.H., FLOUD J. and
ARNOLD ANDERSON C. (eds.) *Education, Economy and Society*,
Free Press (1961), New York, pp 121-139: Previously appeared in
American Sociological Review, Vol.xxv, (1960), No.5
WALKER A. (ed.) (1982) *Community Care: The Family, The State and
Social Policy*, Martin Robertson, Oxford
WEBER M. (1930) *The Protestant Ethic and the Spirit of Capitalism*,
George Allen and Unwin (1976), London

WEBER M. (1947) *The Theory of Social and Economic Organisation*, The Free Press, New York

WEBER M. (1968) *Economy and Society: Vol.2*, University of California Press, Berkeley

WEBER M. (1984) 'Some Data on Women's Political Culture in Europe', printed as the Appendix in WEBER M., ODORISIO G.C. and ZINCONE G. *The Situation of Women in the Political Process in Europe*, Vol.1, Part 1 , Directorate of Human Rights, Council of Europe, Strasbourg, pp 53-74

WEBSTER B. (1983) 'Women's Committees', *Local Government Policy Making*, November, pp 27-34

WEIR A. (1977) 'Battered Women: some perspectives and problems', in MAYO M. (1977) *op. cit.*

WHEEN F. (1985) *The Battle for London*, Pluto Press, London

WILLIAMS M. (1985) *Participation in Public Life and Local Level*, British Federation of University Women, London

WILLIAMS R. (1985) *The Country and the City*, Hogarth Press, London

WILSON E. (1977) *Women and the Welfare State*, Tavistock, London

WILSON E. (1982) 'Women, the "Community" and the "Family"' in WALKER A. (ed.) (1982) *op. cit.*, pp 40-55

WITHERSPOON S. (1985) 'Sex Roles and Gender Issues' in JOWELL R. and WITHERSPOON S. (eds.) *British Social Attitudes: the 1985 Report*, Gower, Aldershot, Hants, pp 55-94

WOLLSTONECRAFT M. (1792) *A Vindication of the Rights of Woman*, in *Mary Wollstonecraft A Vindication of the Rights of Woman, John Stuart Mill, The Subjection of Women*, Dent (1929), London

WOMEN MATTER, BIRMINGHAM (1987) 'Birmingham Women's Committee Scrapped', *Spare Rib*, No.180, July, pp 12-13

WRIGHT MILLS C. (1956) *The Power Elite*, Oxford University Press, Oxford

WRIGHT MILLS C. (1959) *The Sociological Imagination*, Penguin (1970), Harmondsworth

Index

300 GROUP 138, 162, 165

ABBOTT D. M.P. 66
ABOLITIONIST MOVEMENT,
    AMERICAN 2
ABRAMS P. 5, 6, 9, 27
AGONITO R. 61
ALLIANCE 29
AMORY M. 40, 53
ANNALES 8, 27
ASCHER K. 51, 63, 131
ASHTON F. 58
ATKINSON J. 114

BACHRACH P. 35
BAINS 62
BARATZ M.S. 35
BARRATT BROWN M. 58

BARRETT M. 5, 59, 123, 175
BARRON J. 75, 81, 100, 130,
    197
BARRON R.D. 114
BARRY J. 2, 3, 5, 9, 61
BATLEY R. 4
BATSTONE E. 114
BEAUVOIR S. De 62
BELLOS L. 40
BERGER P. 7
BEVERIDGE 58
BLOCH M. 8
BOUCHIER D. 3, 5
BOURQUE S.C. 36, 37, 43
BRISTOW S. 13, 38, 71, 78,
    80, 81, 83, 103, 106, 117,
    151, 166, 197

BRITISH SOCIAL ATTITUDES
SURVEY 66, 99, 100
"BROTHERHOOD" 146, 199
BURKE E. 32
BURKE P. 27
BUTTON S. 38
BUTTSKELLISM 51
BYRNE T. 28, 32, 38, 43,
     46, 52, 129

CALLAGHAN J. 45
CAMPBELL B. 3, 4, 5, 31,
     33, 59, 69
CARTER A. 38
CARTER F. 40
CASTELLS M. 9, 38, 57, 60,
     157
CITY OF LONDON 11, 28
CLARKE J. 58
CLAY CROSS 40
COBBETT W. 2, 4
COCHRANE A. 58
COCKBURN C. 38, 43, 57
COHEN J. 5
COLE G.D.H. 8
COLLECTIVE CONSUMPTION
     157, 170
COLLINS C.A. 38
COMMISSION FOR RACIAL
     EQUALITY 92
COMMUNITY-CARE 59,
     100-101
COMMUNITY POWER
     STUDIES 35-37
CONSERVATIVE PARTY 5,
     40, 51, 53, 63, 69, 71, 75,
     88, 140, 175, 185, 186,
     189, 191, 193

COOTE A. 3, 5, 31, 59
COSMOPOLITAN 83

DAHL R.A. 35, 36
DAHLERUP D. 5, 17, 31, 133,
     138
DAVIES H.J. 59
DEAKIN N. 58
DEARLOVE J. 37, 38, 61
DEMOCRACY 31, 41, 49, 51,
     52, 55-60
DESCARTES R. 7
DEX S. 123
DICKENS C. 11
DUNLEAVY P. 57, 157
DUVERGER M. 34, 62

ELIAS N. 27
EMBOURGEOISEMENT 123,
     125, 166, 170, 199
ENGLISH COLLECTIVE OF
     PROSTITUTES 188
EQUAL OPPORTUNITIES
     COMMISSION (EOC) 54,
     100
ETTORRE B. 58
EVANS J. 33, 38
EVERSLEY D.C. 11

FABIANISM 58
FEBVRE L. 8
FITZGERALD M. 94
FLANDRIN J.L. 8, 28, 202
FLANNERY K. 10, 38
FORRESTER C. 38
FOUCAULT M. 30, 36, 192,
     194, 197
FOWLER REVIEW 58

FREEMAN J. 5, 31
FRIEDMAN M. 34

GELB J. 5
GERAS N. 168
GERMAN SDP 10
GINZBURG C. 8, 9, 202
GODELIER M. 197
GOLDTHORPE J. 123
GOSS S. 10, 38
GOULDNER A. 61
GRAMSCI A. 58
GRANT B. 53
GREATER LONDON COUNCIL
    (GLC) 10, 11, 16, 21, 28,
    33, 40, 46, 51, 53, 63, 71,
    73
GREENHAM COMMON 188
GROSSHOLTZ J. 36, 37, 43
GYFORD J. 27, 37, 41, 46, 47,
    52, 57, 62, 64, 185

HADDON R. 125
HALL S. 8
HAMILTON P. 8
HAMPTON W. 38, 41, 43
HANMER J. 58, 59
HANSON A.H. 34
HARALAMBOS M. 88
HARMAN H. M.P. 171
HARTMANN H. 123
HATTON D. 53
HAYEK F.A. 58, 188
HEDLUND-RUTH G. 17, 59,
    138
HEIDELBERG 8
HEGEL F. 180, 200
HERBERT COMMISSION 11

HESELTINE M. M.P. 92
HILLS J. 38, 39, 111
HOBBES T. 7
HOLLIS P. 38
HUMAN FIGURATION 7
HUNTER F. 35, 36, 37

IDEOLOGY 7, 40, 51, 62, 166,
    170, 183, 184, 196, 199
INNER LONDON EDUCATION
    AUTHORITY (ILEA) 11,
    16, 28, 51
INTERNATIONAL
    MONETARY FUND
    (IMF) CRISIS 51

JACKSON P.W. 34, 35
JAMES S. 197
JOSEPH Sir K. M.P. 42
JOSHI H. 100, 131, 132

KEANE J. 2, 5
KEITH-LUCAS B. 10, 11, 38,
    40
KERMODE D. 38
KERR C. 125
KETTLEBOROUGH H. 59
KUHN T. 61

LABOUR PARTY 4, 40, 47, 51,
    53, 71, 88, 138, 140, 141,
    170, 172, 173, 185, 186,
    187, 192, 196
LABOUR WEEKLY 63
LABOV W. 25
LACLAU E. 59
LASLETT P. 28, 202
LAWS S. 83

LAYFIELD 41
LIBERAL PARTY 29, 71, 186, 187, 194
LICHTHEIM G. 5
LINES K. 168
LOACH L. 40
LOCAL GOVERNMENT WOMEN'S COMMITTEES 10, 39, 40, 53, 63, 138-142, 159, 162, 165, 167, 169, 191, 193, 194, 201
LOCKE J. 58
LONDON 9, 10, 11, 16, 28, 46, 68-202
LONDON COUNTY COUNCIL (LCC) 10
LONDON EDINBURGH WEEKEND RETURN GROUP 58
LOVENDUSKI J. 38
LOW PAY UNIT 110
LOWE S. 168
LUKES S. 36

MACGREGOR S. viii, 59
MACPHERSON C.B. 58
MCGREW A. 13, 38, 71, 78, 80, 81, 83, 103, 106, 117, 151, 166, 197
MCINTOSH M. 59, 123, 175
MACHIAVELLI N. 172
MALLABY 35, 43
MANNIN M. 38
MARBURG 8
MARTIN R. 35, 36
MARTLEW C. 38, 69, 75, 81, 151, 157

MARX K. 7, 114, 168
MAUD 4, 30, 32, 35, 41-50, 56, 57, 61, 62, 71, 103, 184
MAYO M. 61
MELUCCI A. 5, 6
MERQUIOR J.G. 62
MICHELS R. 10, 201
MILIBAND R. 10, 37
MILITANT 51, 172
MILL J.S. 32, 34
MOSGA G. 77
MOSS L. 42
MOUFFE C. 59

NALGO 61
NATIONAL AND LOCAL GOVERNMENT ADVISORY COMMITTEE 51
NEW RIGHT 33, 58
NEW URBAN LEFT 47, 60, 185
NIETZSCHE F. 34
NORRIS G.M. 114
NORRIS P. 38, 62

OFFE C. 5
OFFICERS, COUNCIL 146-9, 170, 194
OUTWRITE 83

PARETO V. 77
PARKER S.R. 42
PARKINSON C. M.P. 181
PLATO 34
POLITICAL FAMILIES 83-85
POLLERT A. 114
POPLAR 40

POSSESSIVE INDIVIDUALISM
58
POSTGATE R. 8
POULSON AFFAIR 46
PRESTHUS R. 36
PRICE M. 66, 83, 130

RANDALL V. viii, 5, 38
REDSTOCKINGS 193
REGAN D. 32, 41, 51, 52, 59
RICHARDS P.G. 11, 38, 40, 62
RIDLEY N. M.P. 53, 54
ROBINSON 4, 30, 42, 45-51,
56, 57, 62, 63, 123, 132,
184
ROELOFFS S. 10, 38
ROMAN INQUISITION, POPE
PAUL III 202
ROWBOTHAM S. 28, 59

SANDERS C. 65
SAUNDERS P. 57, 60, 146, 157
SCHATTSCHNEIDER E.E. 36
SCHUTTE A. 8, 9
SCHUMPETER J. 32
SCOTT A. 2, 5
SEGAL L. 59
SHARPE L.J. 62
SHAUL M. 38, 151
SHOWSTACK-SASSOON A.
58
SMITH Adam 58
SMITH D.E. 197
SOCIAL AND COMMUNITY
PLANNING RESEARCH
56
SDP 29
SOCIAL POLICY 57-60

SOFER A. 38, 40, 63, 64
SPARE RIB 33, 40
SPENDER D. 34
SPONSORSHIP 77
STACEY J. 34
STACEY M. 66, 83, 130
STANWORTH M. 123
STEDMAN JONES G. 8, 192
STEWART J. 61
STOKER G. 4
SUFFRAGETTES 184
SUPERWOMAN (Shirley
Conran) 177, 179
SUSSER B. 34

THORNE B. 34
TOCQUEVILLE A. De 32
TOURAINE A. 5, 6
TOYNBEE P. 40
TROUBLE AND STRIFE 33, 40
TURNER R. 77, 103, 200
TWIN-TRACKING 53, 64

URBAN SOCIAL
MOVEMENTS 32, 60,
170

VALUE-FREEDOM 8, 9, 61

WAINWRIGHT H. 33
WALKER A. 59, 100
WALLES M. 34
WEBER M. 7, 8, 36, 61
WEBSTER B. 38
WEIR A. 59
WHEATLEY 46, 47
WHEEN F. 11

WIDDICOMBE 4, 13, 15, 16,
    19, 30, 42, 50-57, 63-6 5,
    66-132, 185, 190
WILLIAMS M. 38
WILLIAMS R. 11
WILLIAMS S.M. M.P. 189
WILSON E. 58, 59
WITHERSPOON S. 66, 154
WOMAN'S OWN 83
WOMEN'S AID 59, 191
WOMEN'S COMMITTEES - see
    LOCAL GOVERNMENT
    WOMEN'S
    COMMITTEES
WRIGHT MILLS C. 1, 7, 61,
    62, 202

ZUBAIDA S. viii